Rudolf H. Moos

Evaluating Educational Environments

Jossey-Bass Publishers

San Francisco • Washington • London • 1979

EVALUATING EDUCATIONAL ENVIRONMENTS
Procedures, Measures, Findings, and Policy Implications
by Rudolf H. Moos

Copyright © 1979 by: Jossey-Bass, Inc., Publishers
433 California Street
San Francisco, California 94104
&
Jossey-Bass Limited
28 Banner Street
London EC1Y 8QE

Library of Congress Catalogue Card Number LC 79-83568

International Standard Book Number ISBN 0-87589-401-1

Manufactured in the United States of America

JACKET DESIGN BY WILLI BAUM

FIRST EDITION

Code 7904

A Joint Publication in the
Jossey-Bass Higher Education
& Social and Behavioral Science Series

Preface

For the past fifteen years I have been trying to understand how environments function. My concern began with psychiatric treatment settings. In *Evaluating Treatment Environments: A Social Ecological Approach* (Moos, 1974a), I presented methods by which the social environments, or treatment atmospheres, of such settings could be evaluated and changed to better suit their purposes. I reported conceptually similar work on correctional and community settings in a subsequent volume (Moos, 1975). In that work I focused primarily on the social climate, or, as I called it (and was criticized for calling it), the personality of the environment. While conducting the research, I realized that to understand the social climate of an environment fully one must focus on the physical and architectural setting, the types of people present (the human aggregate), and the organizational structure within which they function. This realization led me to summarize much of the knowledge about environmental impact on human behavior in *The Human Context: Environmental Determinants of Behavior* (Moos, 1976c).

The work presented here extends my earlier research to educational settings. It presents a more inclusive and coherent conceptualization of domains of social-environmental dimensions and of the determinants and impacts of these domains. The conceptual framework is applied to two educational settings: university student living groups and junior high school and high school classrooms. I chose these settings because I wanted to focus on the educational experiences that are most salient to students in their highly formative adolescent and young adult years. Since the vast majority of secondary school students live at home, the classroom is the most important educational environment they participate in. During college years, however, many students feel that their most significant experiences occur in living groups. My purpose was to identify similarities in the underlying social-environmental patterns and impacts of the two settings and to attempt to develop general principles that apply to both.

The work also discusses the development of two new scales for evaluating the social environments of these settings, and it examines a broad range of student outcome indexes, including styles of coping with college life, personal interests and values, drinking patterns, indexes of health and physical functioning, absenteeism, and satisfaction with learning. Data were collected from national samples of over 10,000 college students from 225 living groups and over 10,000 junior and senior high school students from more than 500 classrooms.

The book discusses fundamental issues in educational evaluation and thus will be useful to the growing number of professionals involved in conducting and evaluating educational programs. The material on facilitating and evaluating social change will be of interest to people working in student housing offices, counseling centers, school personnel and guidance departments, and to people performing overall community evaluations. The book will be useful to psychometrically oriented evaluation researchers as well as to practically oriented educational innovators. It is relevant to professionals involved in many human service settings, since the conceptual and theoretical approaches are applicable to a wide range of human environments.

Chapter One provides a conceptual overview and develops a social-ecological framework by which to evaluate and change educational settings. The rest of the book is divided into three parts. Part One focuses on student living groups. Chapter Two presents the development of the University Residence Environment Scale (URES). The use of this scale to compare living groups is discussed in Chapter Three, which also provides descriptions of six types of student living units. A conceptual framework and empirical results concerning the determinants of these six types of social climates are presented in Chapter Four. Chapters Five and Six investigate the impact of the six types of living groups on a range of outcome criteria.

Part Two focuses on junior and senior high school classrooms. The descriptive and psychometric work on the Classroom Environment Scale (CES) is presented in Chapter Seven, along with an empirical formulation of six types of classroom social environments. Chapter Eight discusses the determinants of these six types, with special emphasis on the kind of school and the class subject matter. Chapter Nine delineates the effects of the six classroom types and reviews recent work on the impact of classroom learning environments. Chapter Ten describes cross-cultural research on the character and impact of classroom settings in developing countries.

Part Three integrates the foregoing material. Chapter Eleven emphasizes practical applications for changing educational settings, and Chapter Twelve provides an overview of the results and a discussion of important methodological and conceptual issues.

The work summarized here was developed over a twelve-year period, and over fifty journal articles and manuscripts on the URES and the CES have been published. Since most of the psychometric and statistical details are covered in these articles,

I have elected to minimize discussion of these technical aspects of the research, referring the reader to primary sources. This allows me to present a more coherent summary and conceptual overview of the research program. The primary source manuscripts are available in published journals or can be obtained from the Social Ecology Laboratory, Department of Psychiatry and Behavioral Sciences, Stanford University, Stanford, California 94305. The additional questionnaires used (the Residence Hall Information Form [RHIF] and the College Experience Questionnaire [CEQ] can also be obtained from the Social Ecology Laboratory. The URES and the CES, including their manuals and scoring stencils, are available from Consulting Psychologists Press, 577 College Avenue, Palo Alto, California 94306.

Although I am primarily responsible for formulating and writing this book, many people assisted and collaborated with me in various phases of the research program. When referring to specific projects, I name the person involved in the work; when I discuss projects or ideas that developed over several years, I refer to "my colleagues and I."

Evaluating Educational Environments represents my continuing effort to describe and measure the environment and to understand how people create and are influenced by it. My colleagues and I have succeeded in constructing new measurement techniques for evaluating living group and classroom settings, for providing conceptual frameworks to help understand the determinants and impacts of such settings, and for developing practical procedures to improve educational settings. Although I believe these are important accomplishments, there is still much to be done. People and environments reciprocally influence each other, and I have presented a conceptual framework that reflects this knowledge. But the empirical work itself reflects the more usual idea that educational settings influence students or "cause" varied outcomes. Architectural, organizational, and social climate characteristics can also reciprocally influence each other, but I have only constructed a unidirectional model that describes how architectural and organizational characteristics cause social climate. These unresolved issues remain to be addressed in future work.

Acknowledgements

This work was generously supported by Grant MH16026 from the Center for Epidemiologic Studies of the National Institute of Mental Health, Grant AA02863 from the National Institute on Alcohol Abuse and Alcoholism, and Veterans Administration Research Project MRIS 5817-01. The classroom project was also supported in part by the Center for the Study of Education, Institution for Social and Policy Studies, Yale University.

The work on the development of the URES was conducted in collaboration with Marvin Gerst. The data on student living groups and their impacts were collected by Alan DeYoung, James Kulik, Jean Otto, and Penny Smail, all of whom also participated in various projects on the description, evaluation, and effects of these living groups (see Chapters Four, Five, and Six). Bernice Van Dort was responsible for coding and organizing the data files and for all the statistical analyses involved in these projects, as well as in other projects in which she was a full collaborator (see Chapters Three and Five). James Hearn and Dean Nielsen were responsible for the later phases of the data collection and organization. Amnon Igra provided invaluable support in organizing the final data files and developing statistical and computer procedures, and he also carried out some of the analyses presented in Chapters Four and Six. During the last two years of the college project, Elisabeth Lee was responsible for solving the myriad day-to-day problems in coding and computer analysis, and she conducted what must have seemed like a never-ending series of statistical procedures.

The data on classrooms were gathered over several years in an ongoing collaboration with Edison Trickett, who is now a professor in the Department of Psychology at the University of Maryland. Marilyn Cohen, Jean Otto, Paul Schaffner, and Penny Smail provided valuable assistance in collecting the data, and Robert Shelton and Bernice Van Dort were instrumental in facilitating the statistical analyses. Michael Paige carried out the cross-cultural work in Indonesia while he was a graduate student at Stanford University; he is now an assistant professor in the Department of Education and an acting assistant director of the

International Student Adviser's Office at the University of Minnesota.

As the book progressed, I was fortunate to have several critical reviewers. Though I did not always welcome their comments, they helped me improve the final product more than they realize. James Hearn and Kevin Marjoribanks provided comments on the first draft, and John Finney, Amnon Igra, and Sonne Lemke gave me comments on the second. I sometimes thought that no one could criticize the chapters once these readers considered them acceptable, but I doubt that this will prove true.

Louise Doherty and Susanne Flynn typed the many drafts of each chapter. I was happy when the book was finished, but they were positively elated. During these final stages of manuscript preparation, Darrow Chan competently organized the extensive bibliography, and Jane Clayton provided very useful help in proofreading, copy editing, and indexing.

Bernice Moos worked on various phases of the project, from inception to completion. She helped compile and analyze much of the data and collaborated in the work on alcohol consumption in living groups and absenteeism in classrooms. Although she would have been happier had I never written this book, I dedicate it to her: for adapting to all the other books, for selecting the right educational setting for Karen and Kevin, and for unusual persistence in coping with an absent husband.

Stanford, California   Rudolf H. Moos
January 1979

Contents

xiii

The Author

Rudolf H. Moos is professor of psychiatry and behavioral sciences at Stanford University and chief of research for the Psychiatry Service at the Palo Alto Veterans Administration Medical Center, where he directs the Social Ecology Laboratory.

Moos was born in Berlin in 1934; he was awarded both the B.A. degree with honors (1956) and the Ph.D. degree (1960) in psychology from the University of California, Berkeley. After work as a postdoctoral fellow in the Interdisciplinary Training Program at the University of California School of Medicine, San Francisco, he moved to Stanford University and the Veterans Administration Medical Center in Palo Alto, where he has been since 1962. During 1969-70 he was a visiting professor at the Institute of Psychiatry and at Maudsley and Royal Bethlam Hospital in London.

Among the books that he has authored or coauthored are *Evaluating Treatment Environments: A Social Ecological Approach* (winner of the 1975 Hofheimer Award for outstanding research from the American Psychiatric Association); *Evaluating Correctional and Community Settings* (1975); *The Human Context: Environmental Determinants of Behavior* (1976); and *Environment and Utopia: A Synthesis* (with R. Brownstein, 1977). Moos has also developed a set of widely used scales that measure the characteristics of social environments, has served on the editorial boards of several professional journals, and has contributed extensively to the literature on the measurement and impacts of an array of different types of social settings.

Currently engaged in studies focusing on the outcome of treatment for alcoholism and on the role of environmental resources in posttreatment functioning, Moos has just completed work on the development of a Multiphasic Environmental Assessment Procedure, which comprehensively evaluates the physical and social environments of sheltered care settings.

Moos lives with his wife, Bernice, and his children, Karen and Kevin, in Los Altos Hills, California.

Evaluating Educational Environments

Procedures, Measures, Findings, and Policy Implications

1

Framework for Evaluating Environments

A principal develops an alternative open school to help students who cannot adjust to traditional classes. Shocked at the lack of emphasis on reading, writing, and arithmetic in the public schools, parents wait in line to ensure their children's enrollment in a back-to-basics program. A teacher suggests that a conceptually mature child be placed in a class with more advanced students. A counselor recommends that a shy, introverted child be transferred to a class in which students are friendly, the teacher is supportive, and there is little competition. A school nurse notes that a hyperactive child might function better in a more structured classroom setting. A high school senior, puzzled over which college or university to attend, gathers information on a range of possibilities.

All of these people are responding to the belief that the social environment has important effects on satisfaction, learning, and personal growth. Their search for information and their decision making reflect the assumptions that one can distinguish different types, or dimensions, of social environments, that these dimensions can have distinct influences, and that such influences may differ from one person to another. I believe these assumptions are valid. In this book I present a social-ecological framework to evaluate educational settings, and I describe the development of scales that measure the social environments of university student living groups and junior and senior high school classes. I discuss research on the determinants and impacts of these social environments and note the conceptual and practical implications of the foregoing material.

My attempt to evaluate the social environments of educational settings was influenced by three converging lines of evidence (Moos, 1976a). First, personality and other individual difference variables (traits) only partially account for variance in behavior. One of the oldest examples of this type of work is the Character Education Inquiry, conducted by Hartshorne and May (1928). Young children were exposed to several different situations in which they might exhibit such dishonest behaviors as lying, cheating, and stealing. The correlations among these behaviors were too low to provide evidence for a unified character trait of honesty. This result was controversial, and alternative conclusions emerged from later analyses of the original data, but the fact remains that only about 25 percent of the variance in such "traits" as honesty can be accounted for by consistent individual differences (see Endler and Magnusson, 1976, for a recent review). Furthermore, when the same people are observed in different settings, they usually show considerable variation in their behavior (Levinson, 1978; Tars and Appleby, 1973). These studies show that the environment in which behavior takes place must be considered in order to predict individual functioning more accurately.

Second, stable long-term settings, especially child-care

settings, can have a powerful impact. Children's values change differentially according to the expectations of particular group care settings. The more intensive, committed, cohesive, and socially integrated the setting, the greater its impact (Shouval and others, 1975; Wolins, 1974). Placing institutionalized children in supportive adoptive homes can make a remarkable difference in their later intellectual functioning, occupational achievement, and marital and family status (Scarr and Weinberg, 1976; Skeels, 1966). The environment can exert a potent influence on the extent and kind of change that occurs in human characteristics.

Third, popular and professional writers have illustrated the varied impacts of educational settings in case studies. In *Death at an Early Age*, Jonathan Kozol (1967) vividly described the destructive impact of the physical and social environments of the Boston public schools on the hearts and minds of black children (see Jackson, 1968, for rich naturalistic descriptions of classrooms, and Grant and Riesman, 1978, for case studies of reform-oriented colleges). Educators, sociologists, anthropologists, and popular novelists have described educational settings in exhaustive detail. Conclusions about the influence of different environments vary, but all authors agree that the social-ecological setting in which students function can affect their attitudes and moods, their behavior and performance, and their self-concept and general sense of well-being.

An Integrative Conceptual Framework

This book focuses on the importance of environmental influences on stability and change in student behavior and attitudes. Since a comprehensive model is needed to help organize this task, I turn now to a conceptual framework that illustrates the relevance of four domains of environmental variables to the evaluation of educational settings. The framework synthesizes the major sets of indexes involved in creating a social-ecological perspective on educational development. This type of perspective is becoming prominent in developmental psychology (Bronfenbrenner, 1977), clinical and community psychology (Holahan, 1978), gerontology (Lawton and Nahemow, 1973), and psychosomatic medicine and health psychology (Moos, 1979). I call this framework *social-ecological* to emphasize the inclusion of social-environmental (for example, social climate) and physical-environmental (that is, ecological) variables, which must be considered together (Moos, 1976c, chap. 1).

In brief, the model shown in Figure 1 notes the existence of both environmental and personal systems, which influence each other through selection factors. Most environments admit new members selectively, and most people select the environments they wish to enter. The personal and environmental systems also affect each other through mediating processes of cognitive appraisal and activation or arousal (motivation). These mediating factors are influenced both by personal characteristics (a highly talented student is more likely to experience a lack of challenge in a classroom; some students are more easily motivated than others) and environmental characteristics (challenging classrooms tend to be seen as competitive; some environments are more likely to motivate students than others).

The next step in the model involves the student's efforts to adapt to the environment by using a preferred set of coping skills. These skills are determined in part by the personal system (people have varied coping repertoires; for example, some are more prone to join organizations than others) and the environmental system (some settings reward organizational activities more than others). A student's use of a coping skill may also change both systems. A student who joins an organization may change his or her attitudes (a change in the personal system) and/or help to create a new social group (a change in the environmental system).

Efforts at adaptation ultimately affect such outcome indexes as personal interests and values, self-concept and health, and aspiration and achievement levels. These criteria are also affected directly by the personal system (students with higher aspiration levels on entrance to college usually have higher aspiration levels at the end of their freshman year) and the environmental system (smaller colleges tend to have students with higher morale). Changes in these indexes can in turn influence

Figure 1. A Model of the Relationship Between Environmental and Personal Variables and Student Stability and Change

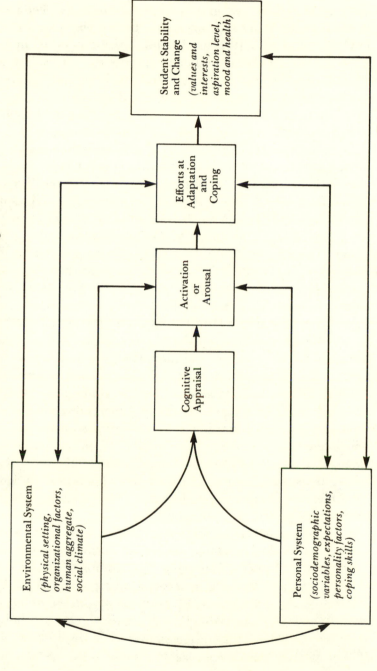

both systems (changes in a student's values may become integrated into his or her self-concept; a student with high aspiration levels may make a setting more competitive). As noted in Figure 1, these personal and environmental processes may result in either stability or change. For example, a college setting oriented toward traditional religious values and academic accomplishment may help students to maintain their religious beliefs and to increase their aspiration and achievement levels.

Cognitive appraisal and activation are mediating variables involved in the *process* of person-environment interaction, and they influence efforts to adapt (coping) and the results of such efforts (outcome). This is the case even though variables in the latter two domains can be directly predicted from characteristics of either the environmental or (more usually) the personal system. We do not need information about appraisal or activation to predict students' college grades from their high school grades, but these mediating processes are involved in the dynamics of adapting to college. I will now briefly discuss each set of variables shown in Figure 1 to illustrate the model.

The Environmental System. Although there are an infinite number of environmental variables, they are conceptualized here in four major domains: the physical setting, organizational factors, the human aggregate, and social climate. Each of these domains can influence educational outcomes directly, as well as indirectly through the other sets. My focus is on the extent to which the social climate is determined by and mediates the influence of the other three domains. For example, the influence of the physical environment (open plan classes) on student development may be mediated through its effect on the social environment (increased cohesion).

Physical Setting. Architecture and physical design can influence psychological states and social behavior. For example, Myrick and Marx (1968) noted that school designs could be categorized as either cohesive or isolating. They studied two schools having only one or two main classroom buildings (cohesive design) and one school having several separate buildings (isolated design). Students and teachers at the isolated design school spent more time traveling to and from rooms and had less time to interact informally before and after class. The cohesive layout facilitated the formation of larger student groups, which promoted student conversations that were less in keeping with the goals of the school administration. Myrick and Marx concluded that a cohesive design encourages interaction through its compact layout and the provision of central areas where students can gather. An isolated design discourages interaction because of its extended layout, lengthy corridors, and alternate routes for getting from one place to another.

Getzels (1974) focused on the idea that varied architectural arrangements of classrooms imply varied images of the student. The rectangular classroom in which pupils' chairs are bolted to the floor in straight rows and the teacher's desk is front and center fits the image of the "empty organism" that learns only from the teacher. The square classroom in which pupils' chairs are movable and the teacher's desk is in a corner fits the image of the "active organism" participating in the learning process. The classroom without a teacher's desk, in which the pupils' desks are trapezoidal (to make a circle when placed next to one another), fits the image of the "social organism" learning primarily from peers. The open classroom, featuring several activity and resource centers and no desks at all, fits the image of the "stimulus-seeking organism" searching for novel, challenging experiences by which learning takes place. Thus, the physical organization of the classroom is shaped by particular values about the learning process and in turn, shapes how students learn.

Organizational Factors. Educational institutions are often assessed on such dimensions as size, faculty-student ratio, average salary level, and affluence or wealth; these dimensions are then related to student behavior or achievement. For example, Astin (1977) found that students at large institutions are less involved in campus government, are less likely to interact with faculty and to achieve in such areas as leadership and athletics, and are less satisfied with faculty and classroom instruction. Organizational factors such as size probably exert their effect primarily through the type of social environment they help to create. In this respect, Pace (1969) reported that large institutions have less sense of community (cohesion and support) and propriety (considerate and "proper" behavior), whereas those with better libraries have more emphasis on awareness (personal growth through self-understanding) and scholarship (academic achievement and scholarly interest).

Another example was provided by Barker and Gump (1964), who found that students in small schools were involved in a wider range of settings than were students in large schools. Students from large schools experienced vicarious satisfactions associated with being part of an imposing institution, whereas those from small schools cooperated more closely with fellow students, met more challenges, and developed greater self-confidence. Barker and Gump explained these findings by positing that large-school settings are likely to be overpopulated (that is, to have more students than are needed for activities, such as when fifty students try out for a school play having only ten parts), whereas settings in small schools are likely to be underpopulated (not enough students are available to fill the ten parts). One effect of these differences is the creation of more cohesive and demanding social environments in small schools. These studies show that an organizational factor (size) can affect the social environment (cohesion and demand), which in turn can affect students' functioning and sense of competence.

The Human Aggregate. The aggregate characteristics of students in a setting, such as age, ability level, socioeconomic background, and educational attainment, are situational variables in that they define relevant characteristics of the environment. This idea is based on the notion that most of the social and cultural environment is transmitted through other people. It implies that the character of an environment depends in part on the typical characteristics of its members. Holland's (1973) theory of vocational types and the characteristic social environments formed by people in different occupations stems from this formulation, as does the suggestion that school context or selectivity (for example, average ability level, socioeconomic status, and ethnic composition) affects aspiration and achievement levels (Alwin and Otto, 1977; McDill and Rigsby, 1973).

The impact of school composition variables is mediated

largely by the social climate they help to create. For example, Brookover and others (1978) found that school climate variables (in particular, a sense of academic futility) mediated almost all of the influence of school differences in socioeconomic and racial composition on achievement. They concluded that the sense of futility characteristic of a school can "explain" much of the between-school differences in achievement that are usually attributed to racial and socioeconomic composition variables; they further state that "favorable climate rather than specific composition is . . . the necessary condition for high achievement" (p. 317).

The human aggregate approach is illustrated by Astin's (1968) Inventory of College Activities (ICA), which provides information about the aggregate characteristics of students in a college in terms of their activities (such as dating, going to church, drinking beer, and voting in a student election), the median number of hours spent per week in different pursuits (such as attending class, studying, and reading for pleasure), and the kinds of organizations to which they belong. Astin found remarkable diversity among the environments of 246 colleges and universities; the proportion of students who engaged in an activity often varied from no students in some institutions to nearly all students in others. This diversity suggests that students on different campuses will encounter quite varied settings and that such settings will influence their experience and behavior.

To illustrate this point, Astin discussed an example in which a new student enrolls in an institution with high academic standards. The following social-environmental stimuli occur relatively frequently in this school: classroom examinations, discussions among students about grades, studying, intellectual arguments among students, and debates between faculty and students. Exposed to these and related stimuli, the new student might feel more competitive, inferior, anxious about possible academic failure, and hostile toward fellow students (changes in immediate subjective experience). Presumably, the student would be affected differently if he or she attended a different college. In terms of short-term behavioral effects, this student may devote more time to studying, spend less time in social activities, and perhaps increase his or her intellectual aggression; as a result, the student may have greater feelings of loneliness and isolation. Alterations in self-concept and changes in behavior that could persist beyond college, such as devoting a great deal of time to the job or competing constantly with others, could also result from this student's experiences.

Social Climate. I have illustrated how educational settings can be evaluated by three major domains of environmental variables. Each of these domains can affect the other two, and each can affect the social climate. As I see it, the social climate is both a fourth domain of environmental variables and the major mediator of the influences of the other three.

Pace (1962) illustrated the importance of the social climate of a college or university. He pointed out that only certain information about a college is commonly available. It is easy to determine its size, whether it is coeducational or not, its location, when it was founded, what degrees it offers, whether it is public or private, whether it is religious or nonsectarian, what it costs, and so forth. However, Pace believes that having learned the answers to all these questions one still knows little of what is important about a college.

> Suppose one asked the same kinds of questions about a prospective college student: What is his height and weight, sex, residence, age, vocational goal, religious affiliation, and his family income. Knowing all these things one is still left in ignorance about what kind of a person the prospective student really is. The important knowledge concerns his aptitudes and interests, his motivations, and emotional and social maturity. In short the crucial knowledge concerns his personality. So, too, with a college the crucial knowledge concerns its overall atmosphere or characteristics, the kinds of things that are rewarded, encouraged, emphasized, the style of life which is valued in the community and is most visibly expressed and felt [Pace, 1962, p. 45].

The social climate perspective is based on descriptions of environmental "press" obtained from an inferred continuity and consistency in otherwise discrete events. For example, if students in a university are assigned seats in classrooms, if attendance records are kept, if the faculty see students outside of class only by appointment, if there is a prescribed form for all term papers, and if neatness counts, then the press at the school most likely emphasizes orderly responses from the students. These conditions establish the climate, or atmosphere, of a setting.

The Personal System. Varied sets of individual characteristics can help to explain people's responses to environmental contexts. Background and personal indexes include age, sex, ability level, interests and values, ego strength and self-esteem, and preferences for such coping styles as active engagement in the environment, tension reduction, and exploration. As shown in Figure 1, these factors help to determine what an environment means to an individual and what psychological and intellectual resources are available to adapt to the setting. Variables such as intelligence and the level of cognitive development influence a student's abilities to seek or use information and to counteract uncertainty or a sense of powerlessness.

Other categories of personal factors include attitudes and expectations, and roles and role concomitants. For example, an individual's role can affect how an environment is perceived. People who have more responsible organizational roles (such as administrators, professors, and teachers, as compared with high school and college students) tend to perceive educational settings more positively. Expectations of new environments can influence both an individual's choice and later perception of an environment. How people see the various components of the environment, their adaptive responses, and the degree of stability or change they show in various outcome criteria are partially defined by personal factors, such as the degree to which people believe that ability and skill (rather than luck and chance) affect the outcome of their efforts.

Mediating Factors: Appraisal and Activation. Personal and environmental factors influence each other, creating a process of *cognitive appraisal*. Cognitive appraisal is the individual's perception of the environment as being either potentially harmful, beneficial, or irrelevant (primary appraisal) and his or her perception of the range of available coping alternatives (secondary appraisal). One usually cannot relate an "objective" environmental variable directly to a "dependent" outcome variable. Although both the environmental system (students in high-rise buildings are more likely to use elevators) and the personal system (a physically handicapped student may not be able to join an athletic team) can affect behavior directly, cognitive appraisal is an essential mediating factor in most issues related to student functioning (see Lazarus and Cohen, 1977). Activation or arousal usually occurs when the environment is appraised as necessitating a response. This prompts efforts at adaptation, or coping, which may change the environmental system (students decide to use a recreation room as a library or study hall) or the personal system (students seek and obtain information that changes their attitudes or expectations).

Coping and Adaptation. The situations chosen for studying coping and adaptation often involve major life changes, such as the death of a close relative, financial disaster, or serious illness. However, more common transitions, such as going to school for the first time and the move from high school to college, present adaptive tasks requiring the use of coping skills (see Moos, 1976b, for background material). Everyday situations can also demand coping responses.

> Even in the smoothest and easiest of times behavior will not be adequate in a purely mechanical or habitual way. Every day raises its little problems: what clothes to put on, how to plan a time-saving and step-saving series of errands, how to schedule the hours to get through the day's work, how to manage the cranky child, appease the short-tempered tradesman, and bring the long-winded acquaintance to the end of his communication. It is not advisable to tell a group of college students that they have no problems, nothing to cope with during the happy and uneventful junior year. They will quickly tell you what it takes to get through that golden year, and as you listen to the frustrations, bewilderments, and sorrows, as well as the triumphs and joys, you will have a hard time conceptualizing it all as well adapted reflexes or smoothly

running habits. Life is tough, they will tell you, in case you have forgotten; life is a never ending challenge. Every step of the way demands the solution of problems and every step must therefore be novel and creative, even the putting together of words and sentences to make you understand what it is like to cope with being a college junior [White, 1974, p. 49].

High school and college experiences are a major set of influences in the transition from adolescence to adulthood. Entering college significantly taxes students' skills in a number of areas—emotional, social, and intellectual. Competent high school seniors use several coping skills to prepare themselves mentally for the anticipated challenges of college. Some students remind themselves of analogous past experiences that they managed well (like moving to a new neighborhood and making new friends), while others rehearse their expected new roles, identify themselves with a group having a record for doing well (such as graduates from their high school), or lower their levels of aspiration (recognizing they may not be at the top of their class in college, for instance). It should be noted that the placement of variables in either the coping or outcome blocks in the model is arbitrary, since coping skills may mediate outcomes or be outcome criteria, depending on the interest and conceptual framework of the investigator.

Underlying Patterns of Social Environments

Since the focus here is primarily on social climate, I turn now to a description of three domains of social-environmental variables. These domains help to organize and comprehend existing research and to formulate strategies for further conceptual and practical advances. During the past fifteen years, my colleagues and I have completed work in ten types of social settings. Two of these are educational settings (student living groups and high school classes), three are the primary settings in which most people function (families, work settings, and social and task-oriented groups), three are treatment-oriented settings (hospital-based and community-based psychiatric treatment programs and sheltered-care settings), and two are total institutions (correctional institutions and military basic training companies).

We have developed scales to measure the social environments of each of these settings. The dimensions (subscales) on these scales have been derived empirically from independent data obtained from respondents in the relevant setting. These vastly different settings can be described by common or similar sets of dimensions, which I have conceptualized in three broad domains: relationship dimensions, personal growth or goal orientation dimensions, and system maintenance and change dimensions. The specific dimensions included in the relationship and system maintenance and change domains are similar in most settings, although some environments impose unique variations. The goal orientation dimensions measure the underlying aims of the environment and consequently vary much more from setting to setting.

Relationship dimensions assess the extent to which people are involved in the setting, the extent to which they support and help one another, and the extent to which they express themselves freely and openly (see Table 1 for examples). Each setting has an involvement or cohesion dimension. Involvement in a student living group reflects students' commitment to the house and to its residents and the degree of social interaction and friendship. Involvement in a classroom refers to the attentiveness of students to class activities and their participation in discussions. Cohesion in a family reflects the degree to which family members participate and are emotionally involved with each other. Involvement in a work setting measures employees' concern about and commitment to their jobs and the enthusiasm and constructiveness they display.

The degree of support present in a setting is especially important. Emotional support in a student living group reflects concern for others in the group, efforts to aid one another with academic and personal problems, and the emphasis on open, honest communication. Affiliation in classrooms measures the extent to which students work with and come to know each other in class, and teacher support assesses the personal interest and friendliness the teacher displays toward students. Peer cohe-

Table 1. Three Domains of Social Climate Dimensions

| | Domain | | |
| | | | System Mainte- |
Type of Setting	Relationship	Personal Growth	nance and Change
Educational Setting			
University student living group	Involvement Emotional support	Independence Traditional social orientation Competition Academic achievement Intellectuality	Order and organization Student influence Innovation
Junior or senior high school classroom	Involvement Affiliation Teacher support	Task orientation Competition	Order and organization Rule clarity Teacher control Innovation
Primary Setting			
Family	Cohesion Expressiveness Conflict	Independence Achievement orientation Intellectual-cultural orientation Recreational orientation. Moral-religious emphasis	Organization Control
Work milieu	Involvement Peer cohesion Staff support	Autonomy Task orientation Work pressure	Clarity Control Innovation Physical comfort
Treatment Setting	Involvement Support Spontaneity Conflict	Autonomy Practical orientation Personal problem orientation Anger and aggression	Order and organization Clarity Control (resident influence) Physical comfort

sion and supervisor support in work settings assess friendship and open communication among employees and between supervisors and employees. Support in treatment programs measures how helpful residents are toward one another and how concerned and helpful staff are toward residents.

Personal growth, or goal orientation, dimensions measure

the basic goals of the setting, that is, the areas in which personal development and self-enhancement tend to occur. The nature of these dimensions varies among settings according to their underlying purposes. For example, in student living groups these dimensions include independence (diversity of behavior and lack of social sanctions), academic achievement (the importance of classroom and academic accomplishments and concerns), and intellectuality (the emphasis on cultural, artistic, and scholarly activities). In high school classrooms these dimensions are task orientation (the emphasis on accomplishing specific academic objectives) and competition (the stress on students' competing with each other for recognition and grades). Families, work milieus, and psychiatric treatment settings have related but different personal growth goals, as shown in Table 1.

System maintenance and change dimensions measure the extent to which the environment is orderly and clear in its expectations, maintains control, and responds to change. The basic dimensions are order and organization, clarity of expectations, control (or, conversely, resident or student influence), and innovation. For example, clarity in a work setting indicates how well employees know their daily routine and how explicitly rules and policies are communicated. The relevant dimensions in classroom settings and in student living groups are listed in Table 1 (see Moos, 1974a, 1974b, 1975, 1976c, for further discussion and more complete lists of dimensions in the three domains).

The dimensions identified in other measures of educational settings can be conceptualized in terms of these three social-environmental domains, as shown in Table 2. For example, the College and University Environment Scale (CUES) is composed of seven subscales (Pace, 1969). A sense of community, high campus morale, and good faculty-student interactions describe a friendly, cohesive, group-oriented setting and are relationship dimensions. In the personal growth domain, awareness measures the emphasis on personal and political meaning and on self-understanding and reflectiveness, whereas scholarship measures the emphasis on intellectuality, scholastic discipline, and academic achievement. Two dimensions can be listed in the

Table 2. Dimensions of Organizational Climate Scales

	Domain		
Instrument	*Relationship*	*Personal Growth*	*System Maintenance and Change*
College and university environment scale	Community Campus morale Faculty-student relationships	Awareness Scholarship	Practicality Propriety
Institutional functioning inventory	Institutional esprit	Intellectual-esthetic extracurriculum Societal improvement Undergraduate learning Knowledge advancement Meeting of local needs	Freedom Democratic governance Self study and planning Concern for innovation Human diversity
Learning environment inventory	Cohesiveness Friction Cliqueness Apathy Favoritism	Difficulty Speed Competition Goal direction	Formality Democratic governance Disorganization Diversity Environment
Individualized classroom environment questionnaire	Personalization Participation	Independence Investigation	Differentiation
Organizational climate index	Closeness Group life	Intellectual climate Personal dignity Achievement standards	Orderliness Impulse control (constraint)

system maintenance and change domain. Orderly supervision in the administration and in class work is a central aspect of practicality, which falls into the system maintenance domain. Propriety describes a polite, considerate, proper, and conventional environment in which group standards of decorum are important. This dimension mainly assesses organization and clarity (system maintenance), but it also relates to conventional and traditional aspects of the environment.

The Institutional Functioning Inventory (IFI; Peterson and others, 1970) consists of eleven dimensions, which appear in Table 2 categorized into the appropriate domains. Institutional esprit is a relationship dimension. Five dimensions of the IFI belong in the personal growth domain: intellectual-esthetic extracurriculum (availability of activities and opportunities for intellectual and esthetic stimulation outside the classroom), concern for improving society, concern for undergraduate learning, concern for advancing knowledge, and concern for meeting local needs (emphasis on providing educational and cultural opportunities for adults in the surrounding area). And freedom (lack of restraint on academic or personal life), democratic governance (opportunity for participation in decision making), self-study and planning (emphasis on long-range planning for the institution), concern for innovation (commitment to experimentation in educational practice), and human diversity (heterogeneity of faculty and student body) are system maintenance and change dimensions. Table 2 also categorizes the dimensions identified in two other scales, the Learning Environment Inventory (Anderson and Walberg, 1974) and the Individualized Classroom Environment Questionnaire (Rentoul and Fraser, in press).

Stern (1970, pp. 68-70) has identified seven factor dimensions based on extensive research with the Organizational Climate Index (OCI) in educational and industrial settings. The first two dimensions, closeness and group life, reflect the relationship domain. Three of Stern's dimensions fall into the personal growth domain; these are labeled intellectual climate, personal dignity, and achievement standards. Stern's last two dimensions, orderliness and impulse control (or constraint), are system maintenance factors. Stern's conceptualization is similar to the one provided here, but he does not distinguish between the relationship and personal growth domains or include the concept of system change in his control, or system-oriented, press.

The present work indicates that the three domains can characterize the social environments of varied settings. Other investigators have described conceptually similar sets of social-environmental variables, suggesting that these domains are of general utility (Bales, 1970; Epstein and McPartland, 1976; Walberg, 1976). At the minimum, we can conclude that all three domains must be evaluated to obtain a reasonably complete picture of the social environment of a setting. The formulation of three broad categories of social-environmental dimensions can help investigators to construct new measurement techniques for other settings. It also provides a convenient framework for describing and integrating the research to be described in this book.

Implementation of the Framework

The conceptual framework provides a general model of the process of person-environment interaction, only a portion of which is operationalized here. The primary focus is on the environmental system, particularly with regard to social climate, although variables relevant to the physical setting, organizational factors, and the human aggregate are considered. Three central issues are addressed pertaining to social climate: (1) the construction of reliable measurement instruments, (2) the extent to which the physical setting, organizational factors, and the human aggregate determine social climate, and (3) the extent to which social climate mediates the effects of these three sets of variables and has additional independent effects on outcome. In terms of the paths shown in Figure 1, I focus primarily on how the environmental and personal systems influence efforts at adaptation and outcome, although the relation of certain coping skills to such criteria as physical symptoms and alcohol consumption is also considered. Some evidence is presented on the relationship between the personal system and cognitive appraisal, but this is limited to appraisal as measured by perceptions of individual students on the Social Climate scales, which represent only one portion of this domain.

The model shown in Figure 1 notes that people and settings mutually affect each other with respect to stability and change. However, the data presented deal with the influence of personal and environmental characteristics on outcome, and not with the reciprocal influence of outcome on these characteristics. Some examples of how people can create and change the settings they occupy are given in Chapters Four and Eleven, and the thorny issue of the extent to which environments have impacts on people is raised in Chapter Twelve.

In our empirical work on these issues, my colleagues and I used various statistical procedures, including multiple-regression techniques. The relationships between personal and environmental variables (that is, the problem of multicollinearity) led us to focus either on simple correlations or on a partitioning of explained variance into unique and shared components (Mood, 1971). There is no wholly satisfactory solution to the multicollinearity problem, but the above two approaches are relatively straightforward. Together they help to clarify the independent and shared relationships among different sets of variables. The results reported here are all statistically significant at conventional levels ($p < 0.05$), but exact significance levels are noted only in a few instances. Given the relatively large sample sizes, it seemed most useful to focus on the meaningfulness and coherence of the results and on the proportions of explained variance in different criteria.

Five Guiding Principles

Five principles helped to guide our work. 1. Environmental assessment is important in its own right. Many investigators focus on impact and evaluate only those aspects of educational settings they believe to be related to the outcome they wish to explain. This approach can lead to the omission of factors that affect outcome and to superficial understanding of the environment and the processes by which it functions. The educational setting must first be adequately conceptualized before its impact on students' attitudes and behavior is evaluated.

2. The development of environmental assessment procedures should be guided by a flexible conceptual orientation. The notion of environmental press helped us to formulate and select items that identify characteristics of living group and classroom settings. The framework of three domains of environ-

mental functioning guided the organization of the dimensions to be evaluated. Previous work in this area lacked a theoretical or conceptual framework and so produced isolated empirical findings that are difficult to organize into a coherent body of knowledge.

3. Students' perceptions provide an important perspective on educational settings. Information about living groups and classrooms can be obtained by outside observers, who may be more "objective," but it is difficult for such people to know what the setting is like without actually participating in it. Students conversely have time to form accurate, durable impressions of an educational setting's social milieu.

4. Special attention should be given to the microsettings in which students actually spend most of their time, such as classrooms and living groups. These settings are meaningful and important to students, are relatively homogeneous and cohesive, and are likely to have strong impacts. Students also tend to be in control of these settings, which are more flexible and changeable than the larger environments of which they are a part.

5. Environmental assessment procedures should be useful to people in educational settings. From a practical point of view, my colleagues and I want to provide students and staff in classrooms and living groups with a simple way to evaluate their social environments. Our hope is that the resulting information will enhance staff and program evaluation as well as ongoing efforts to change and improve students' living and learning settings.

2

Social Environments of Student Living Groups

Many people praise the virtues of on-campus living groups, but others have raised serious questions about their long-term effects. Compared with commuters, students who live in residence halls encounter more diverse experiences and people, participate in more cultural and extracurricular activities, develop greater personal and social competence, and are more satisfied with college life. Students who live at home fall short of the learning and personal development typically desired by the institutions they attend. Entering freshmen who commute are less competent and less experienced, have fewer achievements to their credit, and operate in a more limited environment than residents, missing many of the varied opportunities offered by a wider participation in college life (Astin, 1975; Chickering, 1974). However, students who stay in dormitories for all four undergraduate years change less during college, are more likely to avoid offbeat places and people, and are more socially and interpersonally isolated. Students who move off campus are more critical, verbally skilled, energetic, impulsive, and interested in intellectual matters (Katz and Associates, 1968). These contrasting results suggest that the value of residence hall experiences tapers off after the student's first or second year. Residence halls may simply provide intermediate housing that eases the transition from the relative control of living at home to the relative freedom of living in an independent, off-campus setting.

Brothers and Hatch (1971) sounded a more discordant note when they questioned the extent to which residence halls enhance individual development or facilitate a liberal education. They pointed out that many residence halls have formal policies which considerably restrain and regulate individual freedom, and that the close loyalties and informal norms developed in more cohesive halls can be more restrictive than a set of formal rules. Residence groups can help the student to adjust to the institution, enhance the opportunity for informal exchanges, and encourage intellectual and cultural pursuits and a sense of common purpose and identity. But residence groups can also become narrow and superficial communities that circumscribe students' horizons and restrict their opportunities for growth.

A more radical view was advanced by Kamens (1977), who argued that colleges need to create and validate certain myths concerning the college experience. These myths include the notions that colleges are selective, that smaller colleges have a stronger influence on socialization, that the demographic structure and geographic location of a college make a difference, and that a collegiate residential structure fosters student development. Kamens believed that residential structures symbolically validate the authority of colleges. They remove students physically and socially from other groups and thereby reaffirm identification with the college. In this view, the dimensions on which residential structures vary (such as the presence of rules, the number of students living in the unit, and the proportion of faculty or nonstudent staff) reflect different degrees of intensity of socialization rituals.

Thus, although most people agree that residence halls influence students, whether these influences are "for better or for worse" remains a debatable issue. Residence halls can be used to house students, to control student behavior, or to attain educational objectives that otherwise might not be realized. They can also be used as prestige symbols or as a focus for high educational aspirations. The student cultures that develop in residence halls differ according to these varied purposes. Some promote traditional norms and values, some promote academic achievement and competition, some promote intellectual and cultural interests, while others do not create a distinctive milieu or set of values but rather amplify the wider campus culture.

These contrasting living group cultures can affect student stability and change. For example, at least two related social processes, accentuation of interests and progressive conformity, can influence college students. Students entering college with certain personal orientations get involved in activities consistent with those orientations, develop relationships with faculty and other students as a result of the orientations, and change personally and socially in areas where they have concentrated their attention. The qualities students bring to college usually persist and become accentuated during their stay. Living in a residence hall can enhance the accentuation process, since students often become more like (that is, they progressively conform to) the other students with whom they associate (Astin and Panos, 1969; Vreeland and Bidwell, 1965).

For example, Brown (1968) arranged freshman room assignments so that the ratio of science students to humanities students was four to one on two floors and one to four on two other floors. He found a progressive conformity effect, in that a number of the students in the "minority" groups changed their majors to fields related to those of the majority groups on their residence hall floor. He also found that more of the minority group expressed dissatisfaction with residence hall life. DeCoster (1966, 1968) placed high-ability students in certain residence halls so that they formed either 50 or 100 percent of the population. Control groups of students were randomly assigned to other residence halls. High-ability students living together did better academically, felt that their living units were more conducive to study, and considered their fellow residents to be more considerate and respectful of others. However, the less talented students living with the 50 percent concentration of high-ability students did more poorly academically (as shown by lower grade point averages and higher dropout rates).

Homogeneous assignment and self-selection enhance the interests and values of some students but can result in dissatisfaction and stress for deviant students, especially in highly cohesive settings. Scott (1965) found that the most satisfied members of fraternities and sororities were those whose values were compatible with the dominant group, that members who liked one another were more likely to hold similar values, that students who held deviant values were more likely to become alienated and drop out, and that attrition among students who held deviant values was most pronounced in more cohesive units.

These findings show that college living groups may have long-term consequences (for example, change of major), that they may enhance or retard student growth, and that there can be stressful effects on deviant students. The fact that entering students are usually open to change and amenable to the influence of the campus environment underscores the need to analyze student residential arrangements. In this respect, students report that the most significant experiences they have in college arise from their associations with the other people in their living units (Feldman and Newcomb, 1969). Although some investigators have written naturalistic descriptions of living groups, very few methods have been constructed to quantify the socioenvironmental characteristics. The existing instruments measure only a limited number of dimensions, include little or no information about psychometric and other statistical properties, and generally have been used on only one or two campuses (see Brown, 1973, for a brief review).

The University Residence Environment Scale

Marvin Gerst and I (Gerst and Moos, 1972; Moos and Gerst, 1974) set out to develop a way to measure the social environments of student living groups and to obtain information about the usual patterns of behavior that occur within them. From a research perspective, we wanted to construct a method for assessing living groups and relating their characteristics to differential impacts on students. From a practical point of view, we wanted to provide housing office administrators and staff with a simple way to evaluate a living unit's social climate. To accomplish these goals, we thought it desirable that each student and staff resident have an opportunity to present their perceptions of the living group, since the perceptions of the people who function in a setting constitute an important perspective on the "reality" of that setting.

Accordingly, we developed the University Residence Environment Scale (URES) to measure the social environments of campus living groups, such as dormitories, fraternities, and sororities. There are three basic forms of the URES: (1) a 100-item Form R (real form) to assess the actual living unit, (2) a 100-item Form I (ideal form) to assess conceptions of an ideal living unit, and (3) a 100-item Form E (expectations form) to assess incoming students' or staff members' expectations of a living group. The URES focuses on student-student and student-staff relationships, on various aspects of personal and intellectual development, and on the organizational structure of the living group. The rationale for the construction of the scale is derived from the theoretical contributions of Henry Murray (1938) and his concept of environmental press. The underlying idea is that the consensus among individuals characterizing their environment defines the social, or normative, climate, which exerts a powerful influence on students' attitudes and behaviors.

Item Selection and Development of the Initial Form. We employed several methods to obtain a pool of items and to gain a naturalistic understanding of living group climates. We arranged meetings with residents to discuss both their perceptions of their houses and their likes, dislikes, and general observations of residence hall life. We studied various social-environmental scales to generate relevant items and searched published material for descriptions of varied residential arrangements and for dimensions along which living groups might vary. Observations by university housing personnel were solicited and formulated into items. These sources generated a pool of items, which two raters independently sorted into categories. The categories were developed from a rough grouping of the items themselves, from lists of environmental press drawn from Murray (1938) and Stern (1970), and from our previous work (Moos, 1974a).

The selection of items for the initial form of the URES was guided by the initial set of dimensions and by the general concept of environmental press. Each item had to identify characteristics of a setting that could exert a press toward involvement, toward academic achievement, toward innovation, or toward some other area. A press toward involvement is inferred from the following items: "People in the house often do something together on weekends," and "There is a feeling of unity and cohesion here." A press toward academic achievement is inferred from such items as "People around here tend to study long hours at a stretch," and "In the evening many people here begin to study right after dinner." A press for innovation is inferred from items like these: "In this house, people often do unusual things," and "Around here there is a minimum of planning and a maximum of action."

We gave the resulting 274-item version of the URES to students and staff in thirteen living groups at a private university. These units included men's, women's, and coed houses, large and small groups, and houses composed of only freshmen, only upperclassmen, or all four undergraduate classes combined. Criteria used to select items for a revised form included the following: (1) Items should significantly discriminate among the houses tested; (2) items should have overall true-false splits less than 80 to 20 percent; and (3) to control for social desirability and halo effects, item responses should not be significantly correlated with the respondent's score on the Marlowe-Crowne Social Desirability Scale (Crowne and Marlowe, 1964). Application of these criteria resulted in a 140-item revised form of the URES, composed of fourteen subscales, each of which included ten items (five scored true and five scored false to control for an acquiescence response set). Of these items, 95 percent discriminated among the thirteen living groups (one-way analysis of variance), and only 6 percent were correlated with the Marlowe-Crowne scale.

Development and Description of the Final Form. We employed several new criteria to select items and subscales for the final 100-item Form R of the URES. A random sample of 505 students was chosen from a representative group of seventy-four residence halls. The selection was made to insure proportional sex and class representation within each floor of each residence. Item intercorrelations, subscale intercorrelations, and item-to-subscale correlations were calculated for three successive trials, with item deletion and subscale recomposition after each trial. We reorganized the subscales using criteria of high item-to-subscale correlations, low to moderate correlations among subscales, and maximum item discrimination among living groups. The application of these criteria resulted in the 100-item URES Form R (four items are unscored), grouped into ten subscales (Gerst and Moos, 1972). Table 3 lists the ten subscales and their definitions. The full 100-item scale and scoring key are given in Appendix A.

The involvement and emotional support subscales are relationship dimensions, assessing the extent to which students and staff support and help each other and the degree to which they are involved in the house and its activities. The second group of subscales, which are personal growth dimensions, assess personal and intellectual maturational processes. Independence and traditional social orientation measure the emphasis on personal and social maturation, while competition, academic achievement, and intellectuality measure the priority given to different aspects of academic growth. The order and organization, student influence, and innovation subscales are system maintenance and change dimensions, which tap information about the organizational structure of the house and about the processes and potential for change in its functioning.

Table 3. Brief URES Subscale Descriptions

Subscale	Description
Relationship Dimensions	
1. Involvement	Degree of commitment to the house and residents; amount of interaction and feeling of friendship in the house.
2. Emotional support	Extent of manifest concern for others in the house; efforts to aid one another with academic and personal problems; emphasis on open and honest communication.
Personal Growth, or Goal Orientation, Dimensions	
3. Independence	Degree of emphasis on freedom and self-reliance versus socially proper and conformist behavior.
4. Traditional social orientation	Stress on dating, going to parties, and other traditional heterosexual interactions.
5. Competition	Degree to which a wide variety of activities, such as dating and grades, are cast into a competitive framework.
6. Academic achievement	Prominence of strictly classroom and academic accomplishments and concerns.
7. Intellectuality	Emphasis on cultural, artistic, and other intellectual activities, as distinguished from strictly classroom achievements.
System Maintenance and Change Dimensions	
8. Order and organization	Amount of formal structure, neatness, and organization (rules, schedules, established procedures).
9. Student influence	Extent to which student residents formulate and enforce rules and control use of the money, selection of staff, roommates, and the like.
10. Innovation	Organizational and individual spontaneity of behaviors and ideas; number and variety of new activities.

URES Form R Test Statistics

Subscale Internal Consistencies and Intercorrelations. The internal consistencies for the ten Form R subscales were calculated using Kuder-Richardson Formula 20 and average within-living-group variances for the items, as suggested by Stern (1970). The internal consistencies are all acceptable, ranging from 0.88 for involvement to 0.77 for competition and innovation. The mean of the subscale intercorrelations is 0.18, indicating that the subscales measure diverse aspects of the environment and have a common variance that is small enough to tap the unique components of living group climates (see Moos and Gerst, 1974, for the internal consistencies and intercorrelations).

A factor analysis (varimax rotation) was performed to identify item clusters by a method other than combining the conceptual and empirical procedures that were employed in constructing the subscales. In general, the factors that emerged closely paralleled the Form R subscales. The main exceptions were that one factor was a combination of several involvement and emotional support items, another combined some support and competition items, and a third merged some intellectuality and innovation items. These results raised the possibility of a seven- or eight-subscale solution, but we kept the original ten subscales since they measured conceptually distinct dimensions, related to different impacts on students, and had different practical implications.

Test-Retest Reliability and Profile Stability. The stability of individual perceptions was measured by administering the URES to the same students on three separate occasions in one men's and one women's residence hall. The residents perceived their environments in similar ways both one week and one month after initial testing. The correlations ranged from 0.67 to 0.75 after one week, and from 0.59 to 0.74 after one month (see Moos and Gerst, 1974). Although the correlations decreased somewhat from the one-week to the one-month interval, the drop-off was quite small, indicating adequate individual stability of perceptions.

Another component of reliability is the stability of the profile for the living group as a whole. The intraclass correlation, which provides a temporal stability index for all ten subscales (Hays, 1973), was 0.96 after one week and 0.86 after one month for the men's unit, and 0.96 after one week and 0.98 after one month for the women's unit. This indicates that the subjective environment can be remarkably stable when the perceptions of the house residents are pooled. Analyses conducted on fifty-two living groups, in which students completed the URES at the beginning of their freshman year and again after a seven-month interval (see Chapter Five), also showed high stability of living group climate (the average intraclass correlation was 0.82).

A related issue is whether the URES profile reflects change. Four of the residence halls in our sample changed from single-sex (three women's and one men's) to coed living units. The URES was given to all four groups before and after the change. The degree of change shown in the profile varied from unit to unit, but the average intraclass correlation for the four units was only 0.27. For example, in the men's unit three subscales increased (involvement, emotional support, and order and organization) and two decreased (independence and competition). The changes in the women's living groups varied somewhat, but, in general, involvement, independence, academic achievement, and student influence increased, whereas traditional social orientation and order and organization decreased. The results indicate that the URES profile is stable when the living unit is stable and is sensitive to change.

Differences Among Living Groups. All ten URES subscales differentiated among the initial thirteen living groups, as well as among fraternities and various other living units on the same and on different campuses (one-way analysis of variance). Estimated Omega Squared (Hays, 1973) indicated that the proportion of variance accounted for by differences among these thirteen living groups varied from 48 percent for traditional social orientation and 45 percent for order and organization to less than 10 percent for academic achievement and competition. These proportions will vary depending on the sample of living units used, but, on the average, differences among living groups account for about 25 percent of the variance in the URES subscales. Goebel (1976) found that each of the URES subscales (slightly modified) discriminated among seven living groups on one campus. The proportion of variance accounted for by differences among the groups varied from 51 percent for involvement to 8 percent for academic achievement (median = 31 percent).

These results resemble those obtained from other measures of educational environments. For example, Centra (1970) derived eight factors from student perceptions of a representative sample of colleges and universities. The proportion of variance attributable to differences among institutions ranged from 21 to 68 percent, with a mean of 35 percent, for the eight-factor scales, and from 3 to 75 percent, with a mean of 21 percent, for the seventy-seven items. The proportion of variance due to differences among colleges was thus quite substantial, although usually still less than that attributed to differences among students within colleges. Centra noted that the proportion of variance due to differences among settings is an important criterion in selecting items for scales assessing educational environments.

Personal Characteristics and Perceptions of Living Groups. Although the URES subscales discriminate among living groups, residents within the same group differ in their perceptions of that group. These differences raise the issue that scales measuring environmental perceptions may reflect background and/or personal functioning characteristics of the perceivers rather than independent attributes of the environment. Data were collected on eighteen living groups (four men's, seven women's, and seven coed) to address this issue. In the fall and again in the spring, 380 of the freshman students in these groups completed the URES and another questionnaire that provided information on their sociodemographic background, such as religious affiliation and mother's and father's education, and on personal functioning indexes, such as interests and activities, coping styles, and self-concepts and moods (see Chapter Five for a description of this questionnaire).

A series of multiple-regression analyses were performed to assess the contributions of five sociodemographic and twenty-four personal functioning variables to perceptions of the social environment after differences among living groups were controlled. Ten multiple-regression analyses (one for each of the ten URES subscales, which were the dependent variables) were run for the fall-term data, and ten separate analyses were run for the spring-term data. There were no consistent relationships between the five sociodemographic variables and the ten URES subscales. In fact, only one result was replicated in the fall and the spring: Students whose fathers had less education saw more emphasis on traditional social orientation. Men saw coed units as somewhat higher on independence and lower on order and organization and innovation in the fall, but these differences were not replicated in the spring. This is consistent with earlier findings indicating close similarity between male and female residents' perceptions of coed living groups (Moos and Gerst, 1974).

With respect to the personal indexes, students who are more extroverted, easygoing, exuberant, or religious and who report participating more actively in a variety of activities see more emphasis on involvement, emotional support, traditional social orientation, and innovation. Students who are high on impulse expression and alienation see less emphasis on these dimensions. Students who are high on cultural orientation, musical interest, and religious concern and who describe themselves as more intellectual see more intellectuality in their living group. Students who report engaging in more hostile interaction, impulse expression, and alcohol consumption and who report more physical symptoms and alienation perceive more emphasis on competition, as do students who obtain lower yearly grade point averages.

These relationships accounted for about 3 to 5 percent of the variance in the URES subscales. Indexes of personal functioning thus show small but consistent relationships with students' perceptions of living group settings. These effects may occur directly as a function of a "perceptual tendency" (that is, intellectual students simply perceive more emphasis on intellectual pursuits) or indirectly as a result of differences in the way students actually function in a setting. For example, intellectual students may participate in more cultural living unit activities, which may lead them to perceive more emphasis on intellectuality (see Chapter Twelve for further discussion).

Content and Concurrent Validity. We obtained some evidence on content validity from semistructured interviews and feedback questionnaires given to students and staff in eight living groups. The interviews covered residents' impressions of their living own groups in each of the ten areas evaluated by the URES. Although these interviews provided mainly impressionistic accounts and vignettes of living group life, they showed close agreement between the URES results and residents' descriptions of their units. Responses to the feedback questionnaire indicated that residents generally felt that the URES profile provided a valid description of their house. Goebel (1976) evaluated fraternities, sororities, and programmatic and living-learning units on one campus and found their URES profiles to fit descriptions given by residence hall directors, prevailing popular notions about the houses, and program descriptions printed in student brochures.

In terms of concurrent validity, we studied fifty-two living groups and found that students in units high on URES emotional support report more supportive interaction (like listening to a friend's personal problems and studying with other people), and that students in units high on URES intellectuality report engaging in more cultural activities (such as attending an art exhibition, visiting a museum, or attending a play). Both our own and Frichette's (1976) results show that living group scores on URES traditional social orientation are highly related to the reported frequency of formal dating activity. Frichette also found that this subscale is unrelated to the amount of informal socializing reported among men and women residing in the same coed residence hall. The traditional social orientation subscale is thus related to formal (traditional) but not informal dating activity. Furthermore, the involvement subscale is closely related to the number of activities that take place in living units but not to activities that take place outside the units (Frichette, 1976). These results provide some evidence of the validity of the URES subscales, but much more work is needed in this area.

Assessing Expected and Preferred Living Group Settings

The Expectations Form (Form E). The URES Form R items and instructions have been reworded to let students, staff, and housing office administrators answer them in terms of their expectations of a living group. To what extent are these expectations accurate? To what extent does providing information about university housing result in more accurate expectations? Do students who hold inaccurate expectations have more difficulty adjusting to the living group? The Expectations Form (Form E) is parallel to Form R (that is, it has 100 items, each paralleling an item in Form R). The scoring keys for the two forms are identical. Form E may be used in conjunction with Form R to identify areas in which students' expectations are accurate or inaccurate. It can also be used alone for assessing the expectations that freshmen, other students, staff, or administrators have about living groups (see Moos and Gerst, 1974, for normative and psychometric data on Form E).

   The Ideal Living Group Form (Form I). The URES Form R items and instructions have also been reworded so that students and staff can answer them with respect to their preferred, or ideal, living group. Form I was developed to measure goals and value orientations. What kinds of residence environments do students and staff consider ideal? In what areas are their goals basically similar? In what areas are they different? Do preceptors, resident assistants, and administrators agree on the characteristics of ideal living groups? Furthermore, actual and preferred living group settings can be compared, thereby giving students and staff an opportunity to identify areas that they might wish to change. Form I is also parallel to Form R. The scoring keys for the two forms are identical.

Diversity of Student Living Groups

   Information about social climate indicates how students see a living group. This information can be used to monitor changes in the social climate of a unit over time and to compare the perceptions of different groups of people (for example, housing administrators, resident assistants, and students). A more complete picture of a living group can be obtained from Form I, which reveals the goals and value orientations of students and staff. The URES can also be completed by observers and other nonresidents (such as parents and student visitors).

Three examples are presented here to illustrate the varied social environments of student living groups (additional examples are given in DeYoung and others, 1974; Moos and Gerst, 1974; and Smail, DeYoung, and Moos, 1974).

Two Coed Living Groups. Figure 2 compares two coed units from a public, state-supported university in a small com-

Figure 2. URES Form R Profiles for Two Coed Units on One Campus

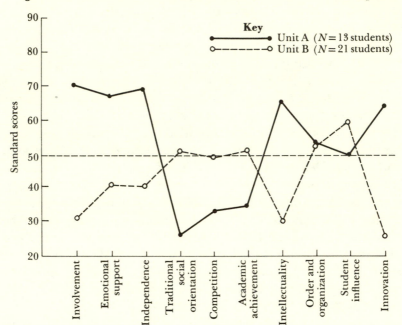

munity. The two units are located in a housing complex composed of a cluster of three-story buildings. Their residents eat in the same dining room, have access to the same recreational facilities within the complex, and live in buildings with mirror-image floor plans. Each unit has one male and one female staff member. All residents of the complex are invited to participate in an active social program and in campuswide intramural activities.

Even though these units are next-door neighbors in architecturally identical surroundings, there are differences in their social environments. Unit A is higher than B and higher than the normative sample on involvement and emotional support. For example, 48 percent of the students in unit B answered true to the involvement item "Very few people here participate in house activities," whereas none of the students in unit A agreed with this item. Similarly, 57 percent of the students in unit B agreed with the item "The people here are often critical of others in the house," compared with only 15 percent of the students in unit A.

The scores on all five personal growth dimensions differed between the two units. Independence was low in unit B, in which only 62 percent of the residents agreed that "People around here don't worry much about how they dress," and high in unit A, in which all the students felt this was true. Traditional social orientation, competition, and academic achievement were average in unit B and low in unit A, but residents in unit A reported much more intellectuality than did residents of unit B. Eighty-five percent of unit A residents responded true to "People around here talk a lot about political and social issues"; only 29 percent of unit B residents agreed with this item. Eighty-five percent of the students in unit A, which scored much higher than unit B on innovation, felt that "Constantly developing new ways of approaching life is important here." Only 14 percent of the students in unit B thought this described their unit.

Impressions based on informal visits to the units, semistructured interviews with students and staff, and attendance at house meetings for giving feedback to residents closely matched the URES profiles. Most of the residents in unit A attended and actively participated in the meetings, which were informal, often humorous, and open to comments and complaints. In contrast, meetings in unit B were poorly attended, covered mainly administrative procedures, and involved little feedback from residents.

A Coed Theme House and a Men's Medical Student House. Figure 3 compares the URES results of a coed theme house and a men's medical student house. The theme house was programmatically organized around the area of international relations. Intellectual discussions of world problems were

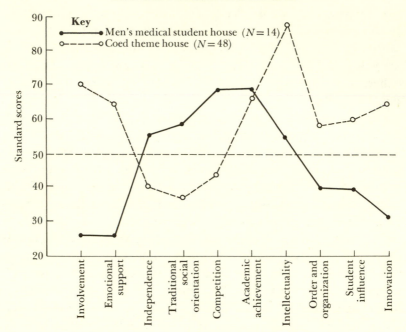

Figure 3. URES Form R Profiles for a Coed Theme House
and a Men's Medical Student House

stressed, it had an active speaker program, and new activities were continually generated. The faculty adviser (who lived in the house and was a strong influence) wanted the students to be the intellectual and academic elite of the university. In contrast, the medical students were disinterested in activities not directly related to their academic pursuits. Many of them commented that the house was more like a hotel than a dormitory.

There are particularly large differences (over four standard deviations) between the two houses on involvement and emotional support, with the coed theme house scoring much higher. These results are illustrated by items like "Very few people here participate in house activities," on which every student in the medical student house answered true, whereas every student in the theme house answered false. There were similar differences on all personal growth dimensions except academic achievement. For example, on traditional social orientation, 94 percent of the theme house respondents answered true to "People here consider other types of social activities to be more important than dating," while only 7 percent of the medical students answered true.

The two living groups are similar on academic achievement, but the theme house stressed intellectuality much more heavily. This difference was reflected on items like "The people in this house generally read a good deal about intellectual material other than class assignments": All but one student in the theme house answered true, as opposed to only 23 percent of the medical students. The high score on intellectuality, both in comparison to the medical student house and the overall average, shows that the theme house residents and staff were successful in developing an intellectual atmosphere.

The theme house also had much higher scores on all three system maintenance and change dimensions. For example, all but two students in the theme house answered true to the item "House officers are regularly elected in the house," while every medical student responded false. Similarly, in relation to student influence, every student in the theme house but only 21 percent of the medical students agreed that "The students formulate almost all the rules here." Overall, the theme house had a warm, supportive, innovative, intellectually stimulating atmosphere. The medical students described their setting as unsupportive, competitive, and achievement oriented. These contrasting social environments should affect the students quite differently.

Expectations and Perceptions of a Student Cooperative. In a third example, we focused on the expected and perceived climate of a small student cooperative in which house members performed most of the functions typically provided by the university administration, including building maintenance, purchasing and cooking, and selecting house officers to handle student affairs and liaison with university officials. Figure 4 shows that there was a high level of involvement and emotional support in the unit and that this level was higher than students initially expected. Over 80 percent of the students agreed that "Trying to understand the feelings of others is considered important by

**Figure 4. URES Expectations, Fall Perceptions, and Spring Perceptions
in a Student Cooperative**

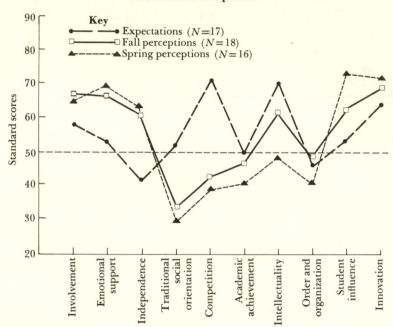

most people in this house." Independence was perceived to be
quite high; for example, 80 percent of the students felt that
"People here pretty much act and think freely without too
much regard for social opinion." Traditional social orientation
was remarkably low. Every student at both the fall and spring
testings stated that "People here consider other types of social
activities to be more important than dating." Competition and
academic achievement were also rather low, and competition
was much lower than students expected.

Incoming students expected and found order and organization to be about average. The high emphasis on student influence and innovation necessary for successful cooperative living
was also evident. The scores in these areas were much higher
than average, increased somewhat during the school year, and
were higher than students expected. This is markedly different
from the usual situation, in which student expectations are

higher than the actual emphasis on these dimensions. Over 90 percent of the students agreed that "The students formulate almost all the rules here" (student influence) and that "New approaches to things are often tried here" (innovation). The house climate was relatively stable during the year, although the stress on academic achievement and intellectuality decreased.

These URES-based descriptions differ from the readily observable indexes, such as the number of residents, type of structure, and the staffing pattern, that are typically used to assess student housing units. The examples show that the perceived sociopsychological climate can be measured reliably and can aid in describing and comparing living groups. Colleges and universities are establishing new types of living arrangements, such as coed housing, dormitories in which 20 to 50 percent of the residents are ethnic minority students, trailer camps, solar-powered ecology houses, and theme houses with equal roles for men and women. The URES may be useful in evaluating the impact of such innovations on students.

Evaluating a Living-Learning Program. Some campuses are developing "living-learning" programs, in which most of the traditional class and seminar teaching is integrated into the residence, with faculty members often living in the house. The hope is that these programs will enhance student achievement and persistence in college. Related to this issue is the concern generated in recent years by the high dropout rate of undergraduate engineering students. Schroeder and Griffin (1976) speculated that the lack of environmental support, such as high-quality advising and teaching and helpful peer relationships, is an important factor. Students who voluntarily withdraw from engineering often describe the lack of group spirit among fellow students and the reluctance of upperclassmen to help new students adjust.

Schroeder and Griffin felt that residential groupings of engineering students would increase persistence and satisfaction with both engineering and residence hall living. These notions prompted the development of a novel environment for freshman engineering students at Auburn University. Three consecutive floors in a men's residence hall were designated as an experimental living-learning center for engineering students. The floors were identical in size, each containing nine double-occupancy rooms. A special lounge was constructed to facilitate group interaction. Wall-to-wall carpeting, comfortable furniture, and a large air-conditioning unit were installed to enhance personal comfort and establish an informal atmosphere. Since entering engineering students must adjust rapidly to the demands of their curriculum, Schroeder and Griffin selected outstanding upperclassman engineering students as resident advisers who exhibited such qualities as commitment to engineering, academic achievement, skills in dealing with people, and enthusiasm for living in the new center. These students served as peer counselors and career role models for the younger students. Preengineering students who signed residence hall contracts were given the choice of entering the homogeneous living-learning center or residing in regular heterogeneous units.

The impact of the living-learning center was evaluated along several dimensions, including persistence in engineering, length of stay in the residence hall, first-year grade point average (GPA), and perceptions of the residence hall environment. URES Form E results indicated that students who selected the living-learning center expected their environment to have a higher degree of commitment and more concern for each other's personal and academic welfare. After two and a half months in the residences, the living-learning students reported that their environment developed more group spirit and commitment, had greater personal concern and emotional support, and focused more heavily on academic and scholarly activities.

The mean first-year GPA for living-learning students was higher than that of their counterparts, although there were no differences between the groups on American College Testing composite scores. Furthermore, 70 percent of the students in the living-learning center were still enrolled in engineering two years after the project was initiated, compared with only 51 percent of the students in the heterogeneous living units. Almost twice as many of the living-learning residents were still residing in the residence halls at this time. Additional indicators, such as the two groups' involvement in intramural activities and volunteer services, strengthened the contention that homogeneous grouping fosters an esprit de corps that carries over into other areas. Using a similar rationale, Richman (1977) found that homogeneous housing assignments for junior college transfer students increased their academic adjustment and led to a more cohesive, involved, innovative, and intellectually oriented living group. These projects illustrate the use of the URES to help evaluate novel residence hall programs.

Changing Residence Hall Climates. While overall programmatic innovations may change the social environment of a residence hall, student-initiated change may be more effective and provide a richer interpersonal learning experience. Such internally generated changes (via encounter groups, student projects, and the like) may be assessed by the URES, and more importantly, the scale itself may be incorporated into a change program (Daher, Corazzini, and McKinnon, 1977). Demonstration studies in other settings indicate that increasing people's knowledge of their environment can help them to plan and implement desired changes (see Chapter Eleven). For example, a comparison of students' actual and preferred living group climates can help them to plan strategies for reducing real-ideal discrepancies. Focusing on the perceptions of students and staff can clarify areas of conflict, confusion, and contradictory expectations. Feedback and discussion sessions can also help to foster greater acceptance of ongoing research and to generate ideas about future research. In this regard, housing office staff lacking extensive facilities or personnel for evaluation may find it feasible to gather information by using easily administered assessment instruments such as the URES.

3

Differences in Living Units and Student Expectations

The URES was applied to a varied group of units to obtain a sample representative of the full range of living group programs. The normative sample includes living groups from campuses in twelve states: California, Colorado, Florida, Georgia, Michigan, Missouri, Montana, Ohio, Oregon, Tennessee, Texas, and Wisconsin. Over 10,000 students and staff in 229 living groups located at twenty-five colleges and universities took Form R of the URES. The schools include a medical school, a fine arts college, and twelve private (eight denominational and four non-denominational) and eleven public colleges and universities.

There are fifty-six men's houses, seventy-four women's houses, sixty-eight coed houses, twenty-four fraternities and sororities, and a smaller number of student cooperatives and special theme and living-learning houses. Most of the houses were composed of students from all four undergraduate years, although the sample includes four freshman women's houses, two freshman coed houses, and several houses composed of graduates and undergraduates. The size of these units ranges from less than 20 to more than 1,000 students (see Moos and Gerst, 1974, for further description).

The data can be organized to highlight the normative social and psychological conditions currently found in student living groups. Table 4 shows some of the URES items with

Table 4. Selected URES Items on Which at Least 70 Percent
of All Students Agree or Disagree

URES Subscale	Majority Response	Item
Emotional support	False	People around here are not very considerate of the feelings of others.
Emotional support	False	It is sometimes difficult to approach the house staff with problems.
Independence	True	People in the house tend to fit in with the way other people do things here.
Competition	False	People here always seem to be competing for the highest grades.
Academic achievement	True	Most people here consider studies as very important in college.
Intellectuality	False	The people in this house generally read a good deal about intellectual material other than class assignments.
Intellectuality	False	Discussions around here are generally quite intellectual.
Student influence	False	The staff here decide whether and when the residents can have visitors of the opposite sex in their rooms.
Student influence	True	The students do not take part in staff selection.
Student influence	False	The students here determine the times when meals will be served.

which more than 70 percent of the residents in living groups either agreed or disagreed (these results are based on 5,437 students in 168 living groups). Students feel that other students and residence hall staff are helpful and supportive and that they can influence visiting hours, but they cannot influence such matters as staff selection and the timing of meals. The majority of students see their peers as feeling that studies are important, but they generally agree that academic competition is deemphasized. Students report that they rarely discuss intellectual matters, which is surprising since this contradicts the notion that the residence hall is usually a kind of living-learning group.

These results describe an "average" student living group, but there is considerable variation among units on one campus and among campuses. Although 77 percent and 81 percent of all students answered false to the two intellectuality items shown in Table 4, the range among living groups varied from 0 to 96 percent and from 0 to 78 percent, respectively. The fact that the range in the percentage of students answering true on 99 of the 100 URES items is over 75 percentage points indicates the diversity of living groups. Social settings vary at least as much as people do. Only by focusing on a representative sample of one type of setting can the range of social environments in otherwise similar types of facilities become apparent.

Comparing Men's, Women's, and Coed Residence Halls

One reason for the variation in social environments is the difference among men's, women's, and coed living groups. In the early 1960s, colleges and universities began to facilitate informal male-female relationships in residence halls. Visiting hours were increased, women's closing hours eliminated, and units with common dining and recreational facilities designed. The goal was to make residential life more enjoyable for students and to help them develop mature heterosexual relationships. Most universities now provide coed facilities, with men and women students living in the same building, if not on the same floor or corridor.

A primary motivation to establish coed living groups is to encourage the development of different social environments. To address this issue, we compared the social environments of forty-one men's, fifty-eight women's, and fifty-one coed residence halls. Since varied atmospheres may develop on different floors of multistory halls, a unit was included in the coed sample only if men and women had rooms on the same floor. Many students commented on the lack of male-female interaction in so-called coed housing, but one especially disgruntled student aptly summed it up: "This coed floor routine is ridiculous; you could live here for twenty years and not know there were girls on the next floor!" Most coed living groups had men and women living in different corridors of one floor, although a few alternated sexes along corridors or in separate sections of each corridor.

The social environments of the three types of living groups are quite different. Women's houses emphasize emotional support, such traditional heterosexual interactions as dating and going to parties, and formal structure and organization (see Figures 5 and 6). Men's houses stress competitive and nonconformist qualities. Coed houses are characterized by more

Figure 5. Mean URES Form R Profiles for Women's and Coed Dormitories

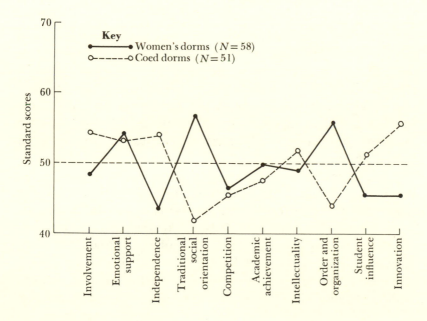

Figure 6. Mean URES Form R Profiles for Men's Dormitories
and Fraternities

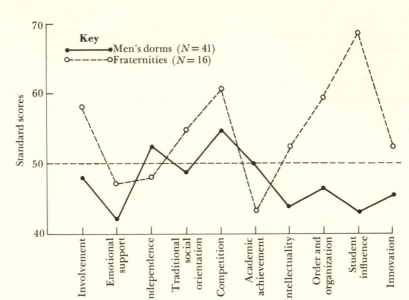

involvement, as much emotional support as in women's houses, and as much independence as in men's houses. However, coed houses do not emphasize competition any more than women's houses. Coed houses are also higher than single-sex houses in intellectuality, student influence, and innovation but lower in traditional social orientation. Residents of coed houses see their settings as stressing involvement, emotional support, independence, and intellectuality.

The results show that students create social environments in coed units that differ from those in single-sex units, and that these differences are consonant with the values underlying the development of coed living. The contrasts among the three types of living groups are illustrated further by students' divergent responses to selected URES items, as shown in Table 5. Some of the conventional wisdom about men's and women's units is supported—women's groups reflect more interpersonal

Table 5. Percentage of Students Answering True on Selected URES Items

	Living Unit			
Subscale	Men's	Women's	Coed	Item
Involvement	63.1	51.4	76.2	There are a lot of spontaneous social activities here.
Emotional support	44.6	70.9	70.8	Trying to understand the feelings of others is considered important by most people in this house.
Emotional support	36.0	61.9	59.1	People here tell others about their feelings of self-doubt.
Independence	75.9	53.7	60.8	People here tend to rely on themselves when a problem comes up.
Traditional social orientation	33.3	54.7	19.9	Dating is a recurring topic of conversation around here.
Intellectuality	31.6	48.0	50.1	The people here are generally interested in cultural activities.
Order and organization	44.4	60.6	30.9	House procedures here are well established.
Order and organization	48.8	60.3	37.7	Around here the staff usually set an example of neatness and orderliness.
Student influence	51.0	59.1	82.8	The students formulate almost all the rules here.

and socially traditional concerns, while men's groups deemphasize these qualities. Certain unexpected similarities also emerge; for example, men's groups are usually considered more spontaneous and academically achieving than women's groups, but no such differences are revealed in this sample.

Comparing Men's Residence Halls and Fraternities. The URES can be used to compare different philosophies, as reflected in the living group programs and organizational structures created on various campuses. In this respect, a comparison of the forty-one men's residence halls with sixteen fraternities drawn from two campuses yields striking results, as shown in Figure 6. The fraternities are much higher on involvement and emotional support; in fact, there is more involvement in the fraternities than in the coed units. As expected, the fraternities are high on traditional social orientation (almost as high as the women's halls) and somewhat lower than the men's halls on independence, although they deemphasize academic achievement and are high on competition, particularly with regard to social status (as opposed to grades).

The fraternities stress rules, scheduling, and established procedures more than the men's halls do, but fraternity residents feel they have more control over the formulation and enforcement of rules and organizational policies. That the fraternities were above average on intellectuality is surprising; this is probably due to the fact that half of these units were drawn from one intellectually oriented private university. However, this biased selection makes the differences between fraternities and men's residence halls on dimensions like traditional social orientation and order and organization even more striking. One explanation for these findings is that the selection and initiation of new members enhance the group loyalty and cohesion in fraternities, since new members' values and interests are more likely to be similar to those of existing members. That fraternities have more control over many of the decisions involved in running the house and that they have greater stability in membership from year to year also increase the degree of support and participation in house activities.

The findings argue against the idea that the differences previously noted between men's and women's living groups are sex related. Men's groups need not be low in involvement and emotional support, as a comparison of the men's and women's residence halls could suggest. This belief is supported by McKinnon's (1976) finding that male students and staff saw more emphasis on involvement in the men's wing of a coed residence hall than female students and staff saw in the women's wing. Women's houses do not necessarily have more emphasis on student-student relationships or traditional social interaction than men's houses. The average social environments of different types of living groups are quite different, but there is considerable variation within each type. Furthermore, the four types of living groups overlap on nine of the ten URES dimensions (all but student influence).

Other Comparisons Among Types of Living Groups

There are many possible comparisons of types of living groups: different coed units on the same campus (Smail, DeYoung, and Moos, 1974) or different floors in a single residence hall can be compared (DeYoung and others, 1974), the discrepancy between expectations and perceptions can be linked to the functioning of individual living groups (DeYoung and others, 1974), all the living groups on one campus can be compared to all those on another (Smail, DeYoung, and Moos, 1974), and so on. All of the possible comparisons cannot be considered, but some important results are summarized briefly here.

Denominational Versus Nondenominational Colleges. We collected data on thirty-four living groups in denominational and forty-two living groups in private nondenominational colleges and universities. Living groups in denominational colleges are much more likely to emphasize traditional social orientation, academic achievement, and order and organization and much less likely to emphasize independence and student influence. Chambers (1976) collected URES data on seven residence halls at two private denominational universities. He found that students perceived more stress on traditional social orientation and order and organization and less on independence and student influence than did the students in our sample of living groups on private nondenominational campuses. These differences are consistent with the prevailing notion that denominational campuses value the traditional aspects of social and academic campus life.

Public Versus Private Colleges. There are some overall differences between living groups on private ($N = 76$) and on public ($N = 99$) college and university campuses. These differences are in the same areas just identified; specifically, public university living groups are more likely to emphasize independence, student influence, and innovation and less likely to emphasize traditional social orientation and order and organization. Despite these average differences, the two samples overlap to a large degree. Also, the social environments of living units within the public and private colleges vary considerably.

Comparisons Among Living Groups on Individual Campuses. The above comparisons are based on samples of living groups drawn from different campuses. It is also of interest to know the extent of such differences among various types of houses on the same campus. For example, Ford (1975) used the URES to compare men's, women's, and coed living units at the University of Northern Colorado. As expected, women's houses were more likely to stress commitment to the house, friendship, and emotional support and had greater emphasis on formal structure and organization than did either men's or coed units. Surprisingly, the coed houses were low on involvement, emotional support, and intellectuality and as high as the women's houses on traditional social orientation. These results probably occurred because the houses were coed by wing or floor rather than by corridor. This setup minimizes male-female interaction and the development of a different social milieu (see Frichette, 1976, for similar findings).

Student cooperatives differ from single-sex and coed (by floor) residence halls. Frichette (1976) applied the URES to randomly selected living groups at Oregon State University and found that cooperatives had much more emphasis on student influence and somewhat more emphasis on academic achievement, intellectuality, and order and organization. The fraternities and sororities on this campus were much higher than cooperatives and single-sex and coed residence halls on involvement, emotional support, traditional social orientation, and order and organization but much lower on independence (the data were combined so that it is not possible to differentiate between the men's and women's houses). These results are consistent with our own, as is the finding that the fraternities and sororities were higher on student influence than either the single-sex or coed (by floor) residence halls.

Goebel (1976) studied four types of living units at Texas Christian University: fraternities and sororities, independent houses, program or theme houses, and a living-learning unit with planned activities and classes offered in the residence. The

URES results showed that the fraternities and sororities emphasized interaction with others, friendship and support, traditional
social orientation, and order and organization and deemphasized competitiveness and individuality. The program houses
stressed individuality, academic competition, and intellectual
stimulation and only moderately emphasized the relationship
areas. The living-learning environment stressed involvement and
emotional support and encouraged intellectual and innovative
ideas but had little focus on academic competition and traditional social orientation. The most heterogeneous of the residence halls, the independent house, stressed the competitive but
not the relationship, intellectual, and innovative aspects of the
environment.

There were predictable differences among the four types
of units on several indexes of college attitudes and behaviors.
Students in fraternities and sororities were more satisfied with
their living units, reported more social relationships, and felt
less alienated than students in the independent house. These differences were linked to social environment and size differences
among the houses (the fraternities and sororities were small, the
independent house large) and to the fact that the fraternities
and sororities carefully selected prospective members to insure
homogeneity, while the students in the independent house were
relatively heterogeneous. Whatever the reasons, fraternities and
sororities are consistently more cohesive and supportive and
have more satisfied and socially active but less independent
students.

A Typology of Student Living Groups

Researchers have recently called for typologies of settings
to parallel typologies of individual differences in ability or personality. The primary purpose of such typologies would be to
identify groups or classes of similar living units within a larger
heterogeneous sample. Empirical classifications usually employ
multivariate statistical procedures to form homogeneous groups
of entities on the basis of similarities and differences on measured characteristics. Cluster analysis provides a multivariate

technique specifically suited to the development of a typology. Although a relatively large number of cluster analysis procedures exist (for example, see Bailey, 1974; Blashfield, 1976), the basic goal is to maximize intragroup similarity and intergroup differences.

My colleagues and I (Moos and others, 1975) used a cluster analysis procedure to identify homogeneous types of living units. We selected a representative set of 100 living groups from the normative sample for analysis because of computer time and cost constraints. The ten URES mean scores for each of the 100 living groups were converted to standard scores with a mean of 50 and a standard deviation of 10. We used the intraclass correlation as the index of similarity between living groups with respect to these standard scores. The intraclass correlation is sensitive to absolute differences in profile magnitude and to differences in elevation among subscale scores, and is a conservative index of profile similarity (Hays, 1973).

This analysis produced a 100 × 100 correlation matrix, which provided a measure of the similarity of each living group to every other living group with respect to their residents' average perceptions of the social environment. The similarity matrix was subjected to the cluster analysis algorithm developed by Carlson (1972) to form groups of living units that maximize the within-cluster homogeneity and the between-cluster variance. The results yielded five clusters of living units. A sixth cluster was identified in subsequent samples. Two of the clusters focus on interpersonal relationships and social activities, two on academic concerns, and two on intellectual and personal growth.

Cluster One: Relationship Oriented. The first cluster is composed of eight living groups. As shown in Figure 7, students in these units feel that involvement and emotional support are strongly valued. Two personal growth dimensions, traditional social orientation and intellectuality, are moderately above average, indicating that there is some stress in these houses on dating and other heterosexual activities and on cultural, artistic, and scholarly pursuits. The other three personal growth dimensions are below average, and the focus on academic achievement is well below average. These houses also show slightly above

Figure 7. Mean URES Form R Profiles for Relationship Oriented and Traditionally Socially Oriented Clusters

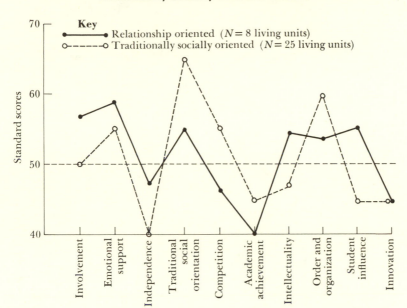

average emphasis on order and organization and student influence and slightly below average emphasis on innovation. These units are characterized by a supportive relationship orientation.

Cluster Two: Traditionally Socially Oriented. Figure 7 also shows the profile of the second cluster, which is labeled traditionally socially oriented. The twelve units in this cluster place above average emphasis on traditional social orientation and order and organization. They are well below average on the personal growth dimensions of independence, academic achievement, and intellectuality and on student influence and innovation. These houses give priority to dating, going to parties, and other traditional heterosexual interactions, as well as to aspects of formal structure and organization, such as rules, schedules, established procedures, and neatness.

Cluster Three: Supportive Achievement Oriented. The thirteen living groups in the third cluster, labeled supportive

Figure 8. Mean URES Form R Profiles for Supportive Achievement Oriented and Competition Oriented Clusters

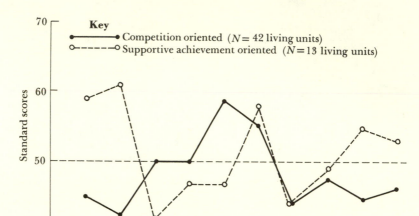

achievement oriented, place their highest emphasis on the relationship dimensions of involvement and emotional support and on the personal growth dimension of academic achievement (see Figure 8). These living groups stress academic achievement, but in contrast to the competition oriented units, they do so within a basically supportive, noncompetitive context. The other personal growth dimensions in these units are all well below average. The emphasis on student influence and innovation is somewhat above average, but there is very little focus on independence.

Cluster Four: Competition Oriented. The fourth and largest cluster, which is composed of forty-two living groups, is labeled competition oriented. As shown in Figure 8, the striking characteristic of these units is the high stress on competition, with somewhat above average emphasis on academic achievement. These units have very little involvement or emotional support. They are about average on independence and traditional social orientation. Intellectuality is below average, as are order and organization, student influence, and innovation.

Cluster Five: Independence Oriented. The fifth cluster, which consists of twenty-five living groups, is identified as independence oriented. Figure 9 shows that these units are high on

Figure 9. Mean URES Form R Profiles for Independence Oriented and Intellectually Oriented Clusters

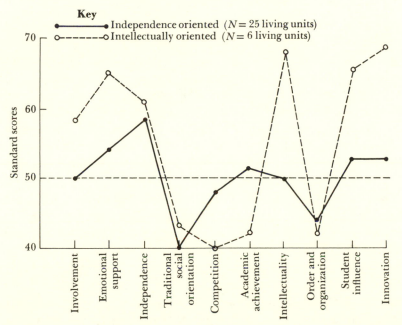

independence; that is, they encourage a wide diversity of student behaviors without specific social sanction and do not value socially proper or conformist behavior. As might be expected, traditional social orientation is low. These living groups are low on order and organization, but they are slightly above average on emotional support, student influence, and innovation.

Cluster Six: Intellectually Oriented. Although it did not emerge in the cluster analysis, a sixth type of living group was identified in subsequent samples. This type, which is relatively uncommon ($N = 6$), is labeled intellectually oriented. It consists primarily of theme houses and living-learning and cooperative units composed largely of students in the humanities and social sciences. These living groups are high on intellectuality and independence and in both the relationship (involvement and emotional support) and system maintenance and change (student influence and innovation) areas (Figure 9). They have much less emphasis on traditional social orientation, competition, and academic achievement. Intellectual and cultural activities are not stressed in most living groups, but some units are organized predominantly around these areas to the apparent detriment of traditional academic goals.

The six clusters differ in sex composition. Competition oriented units are most likely to be male (twenty-six of the thirty-one men's units fell into this cluster), independence and intellectually oriented units are most likely to be coed, and traditionally socially oriented units are most likely to be female (eleven of the twelve units in this cluster were women's units). Supportive achievement and relationship oriented units are almost exclusively female and coed. The results suggest that a greater variety of social environments may exist in women's and coed units, which are represented in all six clusters, than in men's units, which are represented in only four (see Moos and others, 1975, for further details).

Living Groups and the Clark-Trow Typology. There are some similarities among the four college student subcultures identified by Clark and Trow (1966) and the six types of living group environments described here. Clark and Trow's collegiate subculture, one of the four they identified, is composed of students with strong interests in social life, parties, athletic events, and dating. These students do not ignore grades, since they are necessary to remain in school and to obtain a degree, but academic activities are generally secondary to interpersonal relationships and social activities. Collegiate subculture students probably would develop either relationship or traditionally socially oriented living units. The academic subculture is composed of students who are interested in coursework, frequently engage in reading and other intellectual activities, identify with the values of faculty members, and enjoy the company of students involved in and excited by academic pursuits. These students would be likely to create supportive achievement or competition oriented living units.

The vocational subculture consists of students who emphasize career training and vocational preparation and who view the degree as a "union card" necessary for upward mobility. These students show little interest in intellectual activities that cannot be readily related to their anticipated field of employment and resist academic demands beyond those required to obtain their degree. They are likely to develop either supportive achievement or relationship oriented living groups. The nonconformist subculture is composed of students who are detached from and somewhat hostile to the college administration and to the vocational and social aspects of campus life. These students are interested in individuality and tend to be campus radicals, to be interested in the counterculture, and to focus their energies on changing the university and the larger community. They are likely to create independence or intellectually oriented living groups.

Although the Clark-Trow typology seems to describe the major types of student subcultures adequately, investigators have devoted very little work to the kinds of social environments created by these different student groups. The mix of the four subcultures in a living unit may affect the degree to which the unit is oriented toward achievement, intellectuality, or competition. In turn, this orientation can influence how students of each subculture change. Further work that would clarify these relationships and their connections with the overall campus environment may enhance our understanding of the differential impacts of college residential settings (see, for example, Long, 1977; Terenzini and Pascarella, 1977).

A major reason for developing a typology of living groups is to identify students who may adapt better in one type of residence than in another. For instance, students who come from cohesive families providing much supportive interaction might feel especially isolated and lonely in a competition oriented unit, which lacks involvement and emotional support. A unit that emphasizes dating might be appropriate for a student with good social skills but anxiety provoking for a shy, introverted student. A fun-loving athlete might feel uncomfortable in a unit where students often discuss literary and cultural topics. A university housing office that has categorized its living groups could help to place students (particularly incoming and transfer students and students who wish to change living groups during the academic year) into units that satisfy their personal preferences.

Expectations of Student Living Groups

The development of Form E of the URES, which yields information about students' and staff members' expectations of living groups, was mentioned in Chapter Two. We gave Form E to freshmen (N = 1,424) after they knew their residence hall assignments but prior to their entrance to college. Form E also has been given to freshmen at Auburn University (Schroeder and Griffin, 1976; West, 1976) and to freshmen, upperclassmen, and staff in a coed residence hall at Michigan State University (McKinnon, 1976).

These samples are not as varied as would be desirable, but the results give a good indication of students' expectations of residence halls. We compared entering students' expectations with the actual characteristics of their living groups as measured by the URES Form R, which students completed in the fall quarter of their freshman year. Entering students expected much more involvement, traditional social orientation, competition, intellectuality, order and organization, and innovation and much less independence in their living groups than actually developed. Some initial expectations differed substantially from later reality. For example, 80 percent of the students expected many discussions about political and social issues, and 66 percent expected much concern about intellectual awareness, whereas only 56 percent and 38 percent, respectively, thought these characteristics accurately described their living groups.

Conversely, some areas pleasantly surprised students. More than 50 percent felt it would be difficult to approach house staff with problems, that discussions would frequently turn into verbal duels, and that people would always be trying to win arguments and appear more intellectual than others, whereas only about 20 percent felt these items actually characterized their units. West (1976) compared entering male students' initial expectations and later perceptions of a newly developed living unit program at Auburn University and concluded, in conformity with our results, that freshmen found more diversity and freedom (independence) and less emphasis on dating and cultural, academic, and intellectual activities than they had expected.

The results are consistent with previous findings showing that freshmen often have stereotyped and idealized expectations of college and that they are not fully aware of the degree of freedom they will have there (Feldman and Newcomb, 1969). Little is known about how differences between students' expectations and actual college environments affect functioning. Some studies have found such differences to be related to lower academic achievement and morale and to a greater likelihood of dropping out, but others have not (McKinnon, 1976; Pace, 1969; Stern, 1970). Since the reality of a setting can cause disappointment when expectations are overly optimistic, thereby prompting chronic complaining and low morale, procedures to provide prospective students with more accurate and realistic information should be developed.

Sources of Variance in Expectations

Freshman students' expectations of college living groups vary much less than their later perceptions of these groups, indicating that the heterogeneity of actual living group social environments is greater than students expect. Specifically, the standard deviations (over living groups) of the Form E subscales are lower than those of the Form R subscales. Some of the sources of variation in students' expectations about college living groups are examined in this section.

Differences in Expectations Among Campuses. Students of a large, state-supported public university differed from those in a medium-sized denominational school in their expectations concerning residence halls. Students entering the denominational school expected more emphasis on traditional social orientation, academic achievement, and order and organization and less on emotional support, independence, student influence, and innovation. Each of these seven differences characterized the social environments that actually developed in the residence halls on the two campuses (see Smail, DeYoung, and Moos, 1974).

Data obtained on the URES in other universities support the notion that students entering different campuses have varied expectations of residence halls. For example, students entering Auburn, a medium-sized, science-oriented southern university, expected much less emphasis on involvement, emotional support, achievement, intellectuality, and student influence and much more emphasis on dating than did the students on the two campuses we studied (West, 1976). Students entering Michigan State University expected more emphasis on emotional support, academic achievement, and student influence and less emphasis on dating and competition than students entering Auburn (McKinnon, 1976). In general, these differences seem to reflect accurate information about the residence halls on these campuses.

Differences in Expectations of Men's, Women's, and Coed Units. We found consistent differences in the expectations entering freshmen held of men's, women's, and coed units. Students expected women's and coed houses to be higher in involvement, emotional support, and intellectuality than men's houses. They expected coed houses to be higher in innovation than men's houses, and women's houses to be higher in order and organization than coed houses, which were expected to be higher than men's houses. Men's houses were expected to be higher in traditional social orientation and competition than either women's or coed houses. Although most of these differences were consistent with (but much less extreme than) the differences that actually developed, there were still substantial discrepancies between students' expectations and the later reality of these three types of living groups.

Differences in Expectations of Freshmen, Upperclassmen, and Staff. McKinnon (1976) compared freshman students' expectations of a large coed residence hall with the expectations of upperclassmen, almost all of whom had lived in the hall the previous year. The coed hall was composed of men's and women's wings separated by a cafeteria and classroom building. Each student was assigned to a two-person suite in a floor section housing forty-seven other students and one undergraduate staff member. McKinnon also obtained expectation data from thirty residence hall staff members, most of whom were returning to their positions in the hall for a second year.

Entering freshmen expected more emphasis on involvement, emotional support, academic achievement, intellectuality, order and organization, and student influence than did upperclassmen. Their expectations were overly positive; that is, the emphasis that actually developed in each of these areas (the students completed Form R of the URES in the middle of their freshman year) was less than what they had initially expected. Although upperclassmen generally had lower and more accurate expectations than freshmen, they did have inaccurately high expectations on certain dimensions, especially traditional social orientation, competition, and order and organization. The staff members had relatively accurate expectations, although they expected more traditional social orientation and competition than they perceived later. The fact that all three groups expected more stress on traditional social orientation and competition than developed indicates that students' behavior shifted significantly in these areas from previous academic years. In general, students' values in these areas have altered considerably over the past decade.

Personal Characteristics and Expectations of Living Groups. We related five sociodemographic and twenty-four personal functioning characteristics to each of the ten Form E subscales (with differences between campuses and types of dorms partialed out) in order to identify the correlates of individual differences in students' expectations (see Chapter Two for a description of the variables included). With respect to background variables, religious affiliation and parental education had no effects on students' expectations. However, there was a small but consistent sex difference in students' expectations of coed living groups, with men expecting more emphasis on academic achievement and less on innovation.

Some of the personal functioning characteristics were correlated with entering students' expectations. Students who described themselves as more extroverted, easygoing, and exuberant and who reported engaging in more social participation, dating behavior, and student body involvement had more positive expectations in several areas, particularly involvement, emotional support, intellectuality, order and organization, and innovation. Students who described themselves as alienated, hostile, and impulsive expected less emotional support and order and organization and more traditional social orientation and competition. Students who entered college measuring high on alcohol consumption, complaints of physical symptoms, and medication use expected a more competitive atmosphere.

These relationships account for between 3 and 15 percent of the residual variance (mean = 7.5 percent) in expectation subscale scores (that is, residual after school, type of residence hall, and sociodemographic effects were partialed out). Personal functioning characteristics relate more highly and consistently to students' expectations than to students' perceptions of the actual residence hall milieu. Since expectations are largely attitudinal and have less of a reality referent than perceptions of an actual environment, they should be more affected by students' personal characteristics.

Ideal Student Living Group Environments

In Chapter Two I described a form of the URES (Form I) used to obtain information about students' and staff members' views of ideal living groups. This form has been given to 920 students and ninety-one staff members at three universities. Two campuses were medium-sized private universities, and the third was a medium-sized, state-supported public school. The data are sparse and conclusions must be tentative, but the results are intriguing because of the rather large differences in value orientations.

Students and staff on all three campuses wanted very high emphasis on involvement and emotional support, slightly above average emphasis on intellectuality, and very little emphasis on competition. However, students at the two private universities wanted much more independence, student influence, and innovation and much less traditional social orientation, academic achievement, and order and organization. Residence hall staff showed similar cross-campus differences on five of these six dimensions (staff members on all three campuses showed similar ideals concerning academic achievement). Students and staff on each campus generally agreed with each other about their preferred residence hall environments, although staff wanted more intellectuality and less independence and traditional social orientation. These results make sense, given that staff are drawn primarily from students who have lived in the residence halls in previous semesters. This line of reasoning is supported by Ford's (1975) finding that entering and upperclass students' values about residence halls are similar.

Another issue is the extent to which men and women differ in their values about ideal student residences. Both our own and Ford's (1975) data indicate that women want more involvement, emotional support, academic achievement, intellectuality, order and organization, student influence, and innovation and less traditional social orientation. These findings are based on relatively small samples and need replication, but they support the notion that there are extensive individual and group differences in the kinds of living groups students prefer.

The most important aspect of the findings concerns the relatively large differences between actual and ideal living groups. Students and staff want much more emphasis than they currently have on the relationship dimensions of involvement and emotional support, on the personal growth dimensions of academic achievement and intellectuality, and on all three system maintenance and change dimensions (that is, they want more emphasis on order and organization *and* on student influence and innovation). These real-ideal discrepancies, which are generally similar for the three campuses that we compared, show that there is considerable student and staff dissatisfaction with residence hall environments. This supports the use of the

URES and similar techniques to initiate feedback to students and staff and to develop systems-oriented change strategies in living groups. The first priority is to determine the types of residence hall programs preferred by students and staff on each campus. Information about these preferences may help to formulate new programs, to select residence hall staff likely to implement desired programs, and to place students into the types of living settings they desire.

4

Architectural, Organizational, and Contextual Influences on Living Groups

To what extent can architectural and organizational characteristics influence the social environment that develops in a living group? To what extent do the aggregate characteristics of the students who enter a living group affect the social environment? In examining the determinants of the six major types of social environments, I focus here on the relationship between living group social climates and three other domains of environmental

67

variables: physical and architectural variables, organizational structure and functioning variables, and human aggregate variables. In Chapter Five I discuss the impacts of these six types.

Although there is little work relating these domains of variables to each other in student living groups, colleges and universities have been characterized along such dimensions as affluence, size, type (private versus public), masculinity versus femininity, realistic (technical) emphasis, homogeneity, and the like (Astin, 1977; Astin and Panos, 1969). For example, some investigators have related perceived environment scales, such as the College Characteristic Index (CCI) and the Institutional Functioning Inventory (IFI), to such objective indexes as number of books in the library, average faculty salary, faculty-student ratio, and so forth (Centra, Hartnett, and Peterson, 1970; Stern, 1970). Chickering (1972) measured the environments of thirteen small colleges with the College and University Environment Scale (CUES) and the Experience of College Questionnaire (ECQ). The ECQ assesses the aggregate characteristics of students by asking them about their experiences in such areas as academics, extracurricular activities, and relationships with peers. The CUES and ECQ scales obtained roughly consistent results, but they differed sufficiently to lead Chickering to conclude that studies of college environments should use both types of measures.

Centra (1970) compared three methods of assessing the college environment: student perceptions, student self-reports of their aggregate behavior and experience as measured by the Questionnaire on Student and College Characteristics (QSCC), and objective institutional data. He used multiple-method factor analysis, a technique that removes method variance by focusing on correlations between rather than within different methods of measurement. Centra concluded that "each method seems to tap *some* information not predictably obtained by other methods. Quite likely, then, there are certain kinds of information that can be obtained by only one method even when it appears that two or more methods assess the same domain" (Centra, 1970, p. 39).

Interrelating Multiple Measures of Living Group Settings

The studies just cited indicate that architectural, organizational, and human aggregate variables influence the social environment; thus, including these three domains when evaluating environments enables us to obtain a more complete and differentiated picture of the total setting. Feldman (1971) suggested that certain characteristics of environments may conceptually and empirically precede others; that is, some aspects of environments may be causally dependent on others. In keeping with Feldman's logic, a simplified model of the relationships among four sets of characteristics of student living groups and of their relationship to the institutional context is shown in Figure 10. The model is simplified because a unidirec-

Figure 10. A Model of the Determinants of Living Group Climate

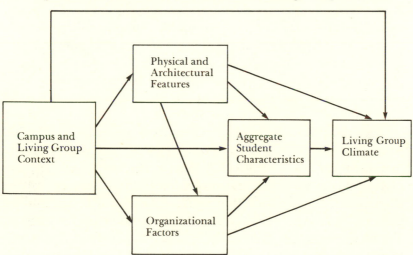

tional causal flow is depicted, even though the four sets of factors can influence each other.

The model suggests that physical and architectural variables can affect social climate directly (more cohesive climates may develop in living groups with a high proportion of double rooms), and indirectly through their impact on organizational functioning (small settings facilitate student interaction and the development of common interests and activities, which encourage the formation of student committees, thereby creating cohesion and support). Physical and architectural variables can also affect social climate indirectly by affecting the types of people who decide to enter a particular setting. Living groups with a high proportion of single rooms may be more attractive to introverted students, who are presumably less likely to develop a cohesive climate. The existence of a library or special study rooms in a living group may attract academic-minded students, who value competition and academic achievement.

Organizational structure and functioning variables can also influence social climate directly (living groups with many student government committees have more student control), and indirectly by affecting the types of students who select an environment (students with active social and political interests are more likely to enter theme houses, thereby creating more emphasis on independence and intellectuality). Human aggregate variables also can affect social climate directly. For example, women tend to develop somewhat more cohesive and conventional social environments than do men.

As already noted, each of these effects can be bidirectional, since the social climate of a living group can affect the type of people who select the setting (shy, introverted students may wish to enter emotionally supportive living groups), the organizational structure and functioning of the setting (greater student influence may result in the formation of new student committees), and certain physical and architectural parameters. For example, students in an intellectually oriented living group may decide to use a lounge originally intended for social purposes as a library and quiet room. Students who wish to increase cohesion may partition a large dining room to control noise levels and allow for more privacy and small-group interaction (Holahan, 1977).

The institutional context (that is, the characteristics of the college or university in which a living group is located) can affect each of the four sets of environmental descriptors. Living units at universities differ architecturally; for example, some campuses have more high-rise units. The degree of student control varies among colleges, and this factor can change organizational and social climate factors. The reputation and overall environment of a college influence the types of students who enroll, thereby affecting the aggregate personal and behavioral patterns of its living groups.

The underlying notion is that the impact of architectural, organizational, and human aggregate factors on behavior results in part from the mediating effects of the social environment they help to create. Architectural characteristics do not usually have a direct impact on behavior. They are important because they affect perceptions, attitudes, and values and thereby change the characteristics of the social environment, which in turn directly influence behavior. For example, Bickman and others (1973) found that smaller low-rise dormitories are seen as more cheerful, friendly, relaxing, spacious, and warm than larger high-rise dormitories, and that more helping behavior is shown in the low- than in the high-rise units. Furthermore, aspects of the social environment, such as cohesion and support, may mediate the adverse effects of stressful environmental characteristics, such as overcrowding. Although cohesive student groups are less likely to form in crowded dormitory settings, they markedly reduce the degree of crowding and stress experienced when they do form (Baum and Valins, 1977).

Some writers have suggested that contextual (human aggregate) variables, such as school socioeconomic status and school ability level, may produce variations in intervening aspects of the educational process, such as organizational functioning or social climate, and that the effects of these contextual variables may be mediated in part by the interpersonal or social processes (social climate) they help to create (Alwin and Otto, 1977; McDill and Rigsby, 1973). For example, DeCoster (1968) found that homogeneously assigned high-ability students reported that their living units were more conducive to study, that informal discussions had more educational value, and that there was a more academically oriented atmosphere.

Our interest in these issues and in identifying the determinants of living group social environments led my colleagues and me to develop ways of measuring their architectural, organizational, and human aggregate characteristics. We constructed a Residence Hall Information Form (RHIF) to focus on the architectural and organizational characteristics of living groups. The section of the RHIF relating to architectural characteristics includes questions covering: (1) the number of rooms in the house, (2) the proportion of single rooms, (3) the age of the building, (4) library or study areas, (5) recreational facilities, such as recreation rooms or lounges, (6) dining hall or dining area, and (7) snack bar or vending machine area. We focused on these variables to test specific hypotheses, including the following: Less cohesive climates develop in older and larger living groups and in living groups lacking a dining hall or snack bar; living groups with more library or study areas and fewer recreational facilities develop more achievement oriented climates; and living groups with a greater proportion of students in single rooms develop more competitive environments.

Another section of the RHIF covers the organizational structure and functioning of the living group. It is composed of questions about the frequency of regularly scheduled house meetings, lectures by outside speakers, and intramural activities (such as competing with other houses athletically or scholastically). Other questions cover how much control students have in selecting house officers and defining their functions, regulating study or quiet hours, and regulating meal times. Data were also obtained on the number of faculty and nonstudent resident positions in the house. We selected these organizational variables to test the ideas that the frequency of house meetings is related to student cohesion, that an emphasis on guest lecturers helps to foster an intellectual orientation, and that student decision-making power relates to an orientation toward independence and intellectuality.

We obtained RHIF data by observing and interviewing residence staff members of eighty-seven living groups drawn from the normative sample. Twenty-three units housed males, twenty-eight housed females, and thirty-six were coed. The sample included units for freshmen only, units for upperclassmen only, and units with all classes represented. Forty-eight of the units were from public state colleges or universities, and thirty-nine were from private schools (see Moos, 1978a, for further details).

To relate architectural and organizational characteristics to living group social environments, we first derived scores to index the similarity between each of the living groups and the six types of social environments. The index of similarity was a profile correlation between a living group's ten URES subscale standard scores and the ten URES mean subscale standard scores of each type of living group (see Figures 7, 8, and 9 in Chapter Three). Six climate types scores were thus derived for each of the eighty-seven living groups, indexing how similar their social environment was to each of the previously identified types. We then calculated the relationships between the architectural and organizational characteristics just described and each of the six climate-type scores (Pearson correlation coefficients) to determine the extent to which different social environments develop in living groups with varying architectural and organizational characteristics. To review, the six types of living group social environments are relationship oriented, traditionally socially oriented, supportive achievement oriented, competition oriented, independence oriented, and intellectually oriented.

Architectural and Organizational Correlates of Social Climates

The architectural characteristic with the most pervasive relationship to social climate was the proportion of single rooms in the living group. Living groups with a larger proportion of single rooms were oriented more toward competition and less toward supportive achievement, independence, intellectuality, and relationships (see Table 6). Housing students in single rooms may inhibit social interaction and a feeling of friendship, a concern for others in the house, open and honest communication, spontaneity, and planning for new activities.

Larger living groups were less likely to develop supportive

Table 6. Architectural and Organizational Characteristics of Living Groups with Different Social Environments

Characteristic	Type of Social Environment					
	Relationship Oriented	Traditionally Socially Oriented	Supportive Achievement Oriented	Competition Oriented	Independence Oriented	Intellectually Oriented
Architectural						
High percentage of single rooms	Low	—	Low	High	Low	Low
Large number of rooms	—	—	Low	—	Low	—
Facilities for studying	—	Low	—	Low	High	High
Recreational facilities	High	Low	High	Low	High	High
Presence of snack bar	High	—	High	Low	High	High
Organizational						
Guest lectures	—	Low	High	—	High	High
Intramural activities	—	Low	High	Low	High	High
Control of house officers	Low	Low	—	—	High	High
Control of meal times	Low	—	Low	High	—	—
Control of study hours	—	Low	—	—	High	High
Staffing	—	—	—	Low	—	High

achievement or independence oriented social environments. Ford (1975) compared small (housing less than 100 students), medium (100 to 300 students), and large (300 to 600 students) residence halls and found that students in smaller units saw more emphasis on involvement, emotional support, academic achievement, order and organization, student influence, and innovation. These results, which are consistent with those found in other types of institutional settings (Moos, 1976c, chap. 8), support the idea that more cohesive and satisfying social environments develop in smaller living groups (see the following discussions of suites and megadorms). However, size may not always be strongly related to living group social climate, since the negative effects (less overall friendliness and cohesion) are sometimes balanced by positive effects (greater student heterogeneity and diversity), which increase the likelihood that students will be able to find compatible friends.

Neither the age of the building nor the presence of a dining hall or dining area was related to any of the six types of social climates. These results cast doubt on the notion that newer residence halls with dining facilities will create more positive social environments. The other three variables (study areas, recreational facilities, and a snack bar or vending machine) were associated with more cohesion, achievement, independence, and intellectuality and with less traditional social orientation and competition. These variables were also associated with more emphasis on student influence, which is found in settings oriented toward independence and intellectuality. This is consistent with West (1976), who found that residence hall floors having group rooms that residents could personalize and control had more emphasis on emotional support, academic achievement, and intellectuality.

Regarding organizational characteristics, the frequency of house meetings was not related to social climate, but more frequent student activities (guest lecturers and scholastic and athletic intramural events) were related to more emphasis on supportive achievement, independence, and intellectuality and less on traditional social orientation (see Table 6). As expected, living groups in which students exercised more control tended to be more independence, intellectually, and competition oriented and less relationship, supportive achievement, and traditionally socially oriented. Houses that had more faculty and nonstudent residents placed more emphasis on intellectual and cultural activities (which is associated with theme houses) and less emphasis on the competitive aspects of residence hall life.

Suites Versus Dormitories. Gerst and Sweetwood (1973) used the URES to study the extent to which the social climate in small suites differs from that in traditional large dormitories. The suites, housing ten students each, had five double rooms with a common bathroom and two study areas. Students were asked about their perception of their suite and of the entire dormitory. Suites were seen as much more involving, supportive, student controlled, and innovative than the dormitories. Since suites are smaller and involve more face-to-face interaction among members, that they should be viewed as having more emphasis on the relationship dimensions is not surprising. Furthermore, the smaller size may allow students to organize and carry out new activities and to experiment with innovative styles of relating. One would also expect more student autonomy in suites, which do not have staff members as residents. Although the results indicate that more cohesive and student-controlled social environments tend to develop when students are housed either in double rooms or suites, significant interpersonal problems, such as isolation and lack of privacy, may arise when an "incongruent" student is placed in a suite.

Baron and others (1976) illustrated the importance of social density by evaluating the impact of the triple occupancy of men's dormitory rooms that had previously been used for double occupancy. Residents of these triples felt more crowded, perceived less control over room activities, expressed more negative interpersonal attitudes, and experienced more negative room ambience. The authors noted that students in triples may have problems in dealing with overload because of the greater unpredictability of social contacts, more diversity of personal characteristics, and increased difficulty in negotiating amount and use of space.

The Social Environment of Megadorms. A recent study used the URES to investigate the influence of high- versus low-rise building design on the social environment. The sample consisted of second-semester freshmen living in university owned and operated residence halls at the University of Texas. Freshmen were chosen to limit the effect of self-selection into specific living groups, which was more likely to occur among upperclassmen. Two high-rise towers (one for each sex) were compared with four low-rise residence halls (two for each sex). The effect of floor level in the towers was studied by contrasting the lower floors (one to five) with the upper floors (seven to ten). The low-rise building had an average population of 250 students, compared with 1,500 for each of the high-rise towers (Wilcox and Holahan, 1976; see also Holahan and Wilcox, 1978).

Residents of the high-rise buildings rated their environments lower on involvement, emotional support, order and organization, and student influence but higher on independence. Women in the low-rise buildings perceived their environments as much higher on traditional social orientation than women in the high-rise building. In addition, high-rise residents cn floor levels seven to ten rated their floors lower on involvement, emotional support, student influence, and innovation than did residents on floors one to five. The results support the assumption that physical features of the residential setting can affect the quality of students' social life, including the degree of commitment they feel for one another, their patterns of interaction and emotional support, and their level of involvement in organizational functioning. It is important to realize that these somewhat negative aspects of high-rise dormitories are not necessarily unavoidable. They can be modified by policy revisions, such as resident assistant training programs, orientation programs, increased social contact between students and residence hall staff, additional social functions at the floor level to facilitate friendship networks, and greater administrative responsiveness to students' requests for specific roommates or roommate changes.

Architectural or organizational variables do not determine the formation of certain social climates. Although architectural characteristics are relatively constant and, for the most part, antedate the social climate, quite different social environ-

ments can emerge in architecturally identical settings. Furthermore, the development of certain social climates can modify
students' reactions to their living unit architecture. Gerst and
Sweetwood (1973) found that students who described their
dormitories or suites as highly involving, supportive, innovative,
and student controlled saw the dormitory architecture as more
attractive, harmonious, beautiful, and interesting. Students living in the same physical spaces may evaluate these spaces differently, depending on their own social environment. Architectural
variables may influence the social environment, and the social
environment may in turn influence how students evaluate the
architecture.

Another consideration that contradicts a causal explanation is the fact that students often select their own living
groups. Most students know the architectural and organizational
characteristics of a residence hall (such as where it is located on
campus, its proportion of single rooms, and whether it is a
theme house) and select a living group partly on this basis. Students inclined toward academic achievement who do not wish
to create a cohesive and innovative living group environment
may choose to live in units with a high proportion of single
rooms. Architectural characteristics may mediate the development of social environments by providing information that
influences certain types of students to select particular living
groups.

Testing Holland's Theory in Student Living Groups

In related work, Jim Hearn and I (Hearn and Moos, 1976)
focused on the influence of a set of aggregate student characteristics on social climate. Specifically, we tested one aspect of
Holland's (1973) theory of vocational choice by investigating
the relationship between choice of major and living group social
environment. Holland theorized that people's vocational and
college major choices are expressions of their personalities, and
he categorized personalities and occupations into six groups:
realistic, investigative, social, conventional, enterprising, and
artistic. He further theorized that each group represents a different personality type.

Holland extended his theory to the concept of environmental types: "Because people in a vocational group [major field] have similar personalities, they will respond to many situations and problems in similar ways, and they will create characteristic interpersonal environments" (Holland, 1973, p. 9). He proposed six types of environments corresponding to the six personality types. The type of environment is determined by the modal personality type for the occupational category in which the highest proportion of people in a setting are classified. In this way an average background characteristic of a group (that is, its dominant vocational preference or major field choice) create a characteristic environment with unique demands, rewards, and opportunities.

Realistic environments (majors such as engineering and physical education) reward people for displaying such realistic values as respect for power and material possessions and reinforce such personality traits as thriftiness and conformity. Investigative environments (majors such as mathematics and biological and physical sciences) reward such investigative values as intellectualism and empiricism and reinforce such personality traits as introspection, precision, and rationality. Social environments (majors such as education and social work) reward humanistic and ethical activities and reinforce such traits as friendliness, responsibility, and tact.

Conventional environments (majors such as accounting, business, and economics) reward people for displaying business and economic achievement and reinforce conscientiousness, obedience, and self-control. Enterprising environments (majors such as political science, history, and public administration) reward enterprising values like political and economic success and reinforce such traits as ambition, self-confidence, and acquisitiveness. Artistic environments (majors such as art and English) reward artistic activities and values and reinforce emotionality, independence, nonconformity, introspection, and originality.

Although Holland's theory is widely used, the validity of these environmental descriptions has rarely been tested. The proportion of students in the six categories of majors has been related to the College Characteristics Inventory (CCI) to ascertain whether the dominant major field orientations of thirty-six

colleges and universities affected their social climates as predicted by Holland's environmental model. Many of the relationships did support Holland's descriptions. Students at institutions with a realistic orientation expressed a preference for the
practical and concrete rather than the abstract and disliked
humanistic and reflective experiences. Schools scoring high on
investigative orientation emphasized introversion at the expense
of social and interpersonal skills. Institutions with a conventional orientation emphasized sports and social activities and
discouraged academic and scholarly pursuits (Holland, 1973).

Pace (1969) used a sample of 100 colleges and universities to relate the five CUES subscales to the proportion of students majoring in the six Holland categories. Schools characterized by a conventional orientation emphasized practicality
and showed little concern for propriety, scholarship, or community. Institutions with more investigative majors emphasized
scholarship and placed little stress on practicality. Schools with
a social orientation stressed community and propriety and deemphasized scholarship. Colleges with more artistic majors
stressed awareness, propriety, and community, whereas those
with more realistic majors placed much less emphasis on these
factors. Studies of overall university climates thus have tended
to support Holland's theory of environmental types.

Social Climate and Major Choice. Jim Hearn and I studied
the relationships between living group social climates and major
subject choices in a sample of freshman students in fifty-two
living groups on two university campuses (see Chapter Five for
descriptions of the students and living groups). We obtained
data on major subjects by categorizing students' probable college majors into the six Holland categories. The similarity between the descriptions of the characteristic interpersonal environments formed by the six Holland types and our six social
climate orientations prompted several expectations. For example, investigative personalities are thought to be independent,
critical, introverted, reserved, and so on. Living groups with a
high proportion of investigative majors should thus be more
independence oriented and less traditionally socially oriented.
We calculated correlations between the proportion of

entering students who planned to major in each of the six Holland categories and the type of social climate that developed in their living group. As shown in Table 7, the results generally fulfilled expectations. For example, living groups with a high proportion of investigative majors were oriented toward supportive achievement and independence but were not relationship or traditionally socially oriented. Living groups with a high proportion of conventional majors emphasized traditional social orientation and competition and deemphasized supportive achievement and independence. Living groups with a high proportion of social majors stressed relationship, traditional social orientation, and (perhaps surprisingly) intellectuality and deemphasized independence; living groups with more enterprising majors were high on competition but low on supportive achievement.

Conceptual Aspects of Holland's Theory. Although the Holland typology of majors was predictably related to living group social climate, some results were contrary to expectations. For example, living groups with a high proportion of artistic majors emphasized traditional social orientation and deemphasized independence. The freshman students in artistic majors at our two campuses were more likely prospective teachers (that is, conventional and social types) than prospective creative artists. Also, only a small proportion of the students were in the artistic category (about 11 percent), and they may have had minimal impact on living unit climate. Fortunately, the overall sample included two "perfect" units, that is, units in which all the major choices were in one of Holland's categories. One unit was a male medical students' house (see Figure 3 in Chapter Two), and the other was a coed dormitory at a college of arts and crafts that was composed entirely of prospective artists.

The artistic students' living group emphasized independence more highly than the medical students' group. There were somewhat higher levels of involvement and support in the artistic students' unit, although both units were below national norms, as Holland would forecast. The artists, also not surprisingly, were much lower on traditional social orientation, where-

Table 7. Human Aggregate Characteristics of Living Groups with Different Social Environments

			Type of Social Environment			
Characteristic	Relationship Oriented	Traditionally Socially Oriented	Supportive Achievement Oriented	Competition Oriented	Independence Oriented	Intellectually Oriented
Sex Composition						
Male	Low	—	Low	High	—	Low
Female	High	High	High	Low	Low	High
Coed	—	Low	High	Low	High	High
Type of Major						
Realistic	Low	Low	—	High	High	Low
Investigative	Low	Low	High	Low	High	—
Social	High	High	—	Low	Low	High
Conventional	—	High	Low	High	Low	—
Enterprising	—	—	Low	High	—	—
Artistic	—	High	—	—	Low	High

as the medical students' unit was more than four standard deviations higher on academic achievement. This is consistent with Holland's idea that the rebellious, disorganized, antiorganizational personality of artistic types precludes such dedication to academic concerns as evidenced by medical students, who are investigative types. The artistic students' unit was more than three standard deviations above the medical students' unit on innovation. This again fits into the Holland scheme, with artists being seen as original and nonconformist. The social environments of these two perfect units thus were consistent with predictions derived from Holland's theory of environmental types.

We were also somewhat surprised to find that living units with a high proportion of investigative majors were high on supportive achievement. Since investigative majors were often in the majority in their living groups, they may have created a homogeneous environment with mutually compatible interests and orientations and been able to maintain high levels of involvement and support despite their presumed tendencies toward introversion. Very few of the living groups were dominated by one major type. This may account for the lack of some expected relationships between social climate and major choice, particularly for the less popular majors, such as artistic fields. The characteristics of the people in an environment may have a stronger and more lasting influence on the social climate when that environment is dominated by one vocation or profession (like banks or law firms). It is also possible that although freshman students initially relate to each other on common academic concerns, later interpersonal relationships form around such factors as extracurricular interests and activities. This may affect student living groups, in which many activities are organized around social concerns, intellectual and cultural interests, and athletic participation.

The results are relevant to occupational behavior on both the environmental and the individual level. Holland's concepts are supported in a rather basic, nonhierarchical, non-task-oriented setting. This suggests that personality types are important in determining the environmental character of the occupational world, since the intervening complexities of occupational roles, norms, and structures are not involved in student living groups. On the individual level, the college residence may present students with information about how they would fit into an occupational structure dominated by personalities of a particular Holland type. Students majoring in engineering might find that the environment of their residence, if it is comprised predominantly of engineering majors, seems too materialistic and conforming. This partial preview of the occupational world could thus lead to changes in major and subsequent career plans.

Living groups are composed of varying proportions of students having different majors. Thus, hypotheses about the relationships between the degree of homogeneity of majors and social climate can be tested. Astin and Panos (1969) found that students' career choices and fields of study conform more and more to the dominant or modal choices of their peers as time passes. They considered this "progressive conformity" to result from a process that discourages students who are planning relatively popular careers from abandoning their initial choice and encourages those who are planning less popular careers to switch to more popular ones.

The Institutional Context

The college or university context of a living group may also affect its social climate. In Chapter Three we learned that social climate differs somewhat among residence halls located in public, private denominational, and private nondenominational institutions. In work focusing on the relationship between the overall campus and the dormitory environment, Brown (1973) gave students in four living groups at Montana State University the URES and the CUES. He found some relationship between students' perceptions of the college and of their dormitories but noted that several aspects of residence hall environments were quite different from the social milieu of the university setting. The relationship between living group and campus environments probably varies from campus to campus, depending on such factors as the size of the student body, the size and diversity of living groups, and the social environment of the university itself. Because the social environments of living groups on a campus usually vary widely, studying these groups separately provides information that cannot be obtained from measures of the overall campus environment alone.

We obtained information about the location of student living groups from the Residence Hall Information Form (RHIF). We assessed the centrality of a unit by the number of minutes required to walk from the unit to the student union. Less centrally located units had more emphasis on social interaction and a feeling of friendship, academic achievement, independence, student control of house rules, and intellectuality. They had less emphasis on competition and on dating, party going, and other traditional heterosexual activities. Living groups located closer to the center of campus seem to establish social environments more in keeping with traditional college concerns (competitive and socially oriented), whereas those located toward the edge of campus or off campus are more likely to establish cohesive settings that stress the personal growth areas of achievement, independence, and intellectuality. These differences, which are consistent with the social environment differences that we identified between residence halls and off-campus apartments and houses (Moos and Lee, 1979), are probably due primarily to student self-selection.

An Integrative Framework

To integrate the foregoing material with the conceptual framework presented earlier, we used four sets of environmental variables to predict the type of social environment created in a living group. The analysis was conducted on fifty-two living units for which we had complete data on all sets of environmental variables. We combined and deleted variables on the basis of simple correlations in preliminary analyses and thereby arrived at the following sets of predictors: (1) *institutional context*—a dummy variable identifying the campus on which the living group was located; (2) *architectural characteristics*—a set of three variables assessing the total number of rooms, the proportion of single rooms, and the number of physical facilities in the living group (recreational areas, snack bars or vending machines, and study areas); (3) *organizational characteristics*—a set of two variables assessing student decision-making power (a combination of scores measuring student control over house officers' functions, meal times, and study and quiet hours) and student activities (a combination of house meetings, guest lectures, and intramural activities); and (4) *human aggregate characteristics*—a set of four major choice variables (the proportion of students in realistic, investigative, social, and artistic majors) and two dummy variables indexing whether the living group was composed of all male or all female students.

We conducted multiple-regression analyses in which the six climate-type scores were the dependent variables, and the twelve indexes described above were the predictors. The order of entry of the four sets of predictors was varied systematically so that the unique and shared variance accounted for by each set could be identified. A considerable proportion of the variance in the type of social environment that develops in a living group can be predicted from these four sets of environmental variables and their interactions (see Table 8). The set of six human aggregate variables accounts for more of the unique variance than do any of the other three sets of predictors. Although the institutional context, architectural characteristics, and organizational characteristics account for relatively small proportions of unique variance in supportive achievement and competition orientations, they account for appreciable proportions of unique variance in the other four types, particularly the relationship oriented type.

In all cases, the combinations of two sets of environmental characteristics (first-order interactions) and the various combinations of three sets and all four sets (higher-order interactions) accounted for considerable variance. This variance was due almost entirely to the first-order interactions of school and organizational factors (one campus had fewer student activities and allowed students less control), school and human aggregate factors (one campus had more social and conventional majors, and the other had more realistic and investigative majors), and

Table 8. Determinants of Living Group Social Climate

			Type of Social Environment			
Effect	Relationship Oriented	Traditionally Socially Oriented	Supportive Achievement Oriented	Competition Oriented	Independence Oriented	Intellectually Oriented
Unique						
Institutional context	3.1	4.9	0.9	0.4	5.3	2.2
Architectural characteristics	3.6	1.3	2.4	1.6	3.3	3.1
Organizational characteristics	5.8	2.7	0.6	0.9	2.3	2.2
Human aggregate characteristics	12.4	10.8	17.1	23.9	12.2	25.9
Shared						
First-order interactions	2.7	12.1	18.4	15.7	11.7	6.2
Higher-order interactions	13.4	38.5	3.4	0.0	34.8	4.0
Total variance accounted for	41.0	70.3	42.8	42.5	69.6	43.6

Note: Percentage of variance explained in living group climate; $N = 52$ living groups.

organizational and human aggregate factors (students majoring in social and conventional areas tended to be in living groups with fewer activities and less decision-making power). The second-order combination of school, organizational, and human aggregate factors was also important (following from the above, living groups on the campus that allowed students less control and had fewer intellectual and scholarly activities were more likely to have students majoring in social and conventional areas). The architectural variables contributed little or no additional shared variance. The relatively small sample of living groups limits the generalizability of these results, but they confirm the model presented earlier.

As the model suggests, all four sets of environmental variables have unique effects on social climate. In addition, there is substantial shared variance among the external context and the organizational and human aggregate factors in relation to social climate. The results provide little evidence for shared (indirect) effects of architectural factors on social climate through the other three sets of environmental variables, probably because of the limited range of architectural variables. The general notion that these four sets of environmental variables are important in determining the type of social environment is supported. Although the proportion of variance accounted for is considerable (ranging from 40 percent to 70 percent), it would be useful to identify additional variables in each of these four sets of environmental predictors to help explain a living group's social environment.

The specific results must be considered preliminary, but it is instructive to note the combination of characteristics related to particular types of social environments. For example, supportive achievement climates are more likely to develop in living groups with certain architectural characteristics: a smaller number of rooms, a lower proportion of single rooms, and better recreational and leisure-time facilities. These living groups also tend to have a higher proportion of women and of investigative majors and more scholarly and intellectual activities, but they do not necessarily have greater student decision-making power. The above architectural characteristics are related to the emergence of independence and intellectuality oriented climates, but these climates are also more likely to develop in settings where students have more decision-making power. In addition, faculty and nonstudent residents help to create intellectually oriented settings. However, the determinants of these two types of social environments differ somewhat, since independence oriented settings are more likely to be coed and to be composed of realistic and investigative majors, whereas intellectually oriented settings are more likely to be either women's or coed units and to have more social and artistic but fewer realistic majors (see Tables 6 and 7).

The competition and traditionally socially oriented units present contrasting examples. They both have fewer facilities and fewer intellectual and scholarly activities, but competition oriented environments are more likely to develop in men's living groups with a higher proportion of single rooms and with more realistic and enterprising majors, whereas traditionally socially oriented milieus tend to emerge in women's living groups with more social and artistic majors.

The findings provide guidelines by which housing office staff can understand the social environment likely to emerge in a living group. However, since particular architectural, organizational, or human aggregate characteristics need not necessarily lead to certain types of social climates, the relationships presented here should not be construed rigidly. In fact, they may be used to help select living groups whose social climates should be actively changed. Male students in realistic, conventional, and enterprising majors who live in units having a high proportion of single rooms tend to develop competition oriented environments. Housing office staff might wish to select empathic, relationship oriented faculty residents to live in these settings to help students develop more activities and enhance their sense of community.

Several methods of evaluating student living groups (and other types of institutional settings) need to be developed. Varied types of measures provide somewhat overlapping but generally different perspectives on an environment. Furthermore, information about relatively objective architectural and organizational characteristics may be most useful for comparing settings and for planning long-term changes. Information on the aggregate characteristics of their prospective peers may be most helpful to entering students, so that they know about the stimuli that they are likely to encounter. It is important for new students to know how much time other students in their prospective living group spend studying, since that will give them specific ideas about the kinds of behaviors that may be required. Data concerning the daily activities and experiences of students can also provide useful information for program planners and decision makers. Evidence that a program does not foster the desired objectives (for example, a living-learning residence hall in which students report few scholarly or intellectual discussions) may constitute sufficient reason to initiate change. Information about social climate may be most valuable in providing meaningful feedback to students and residence hall staff and in facilitating short-term environmental change.

5

Effects
of Living Groups
on Student Attitudes
and Behavior

Students change considerably during their college years. In general, they develop more positive self-images (as reflected in greater interpersonal and intellectual competence, enhanced self-reliance and autonomy, broader interests in political, social, and cultural affairs, and more liberal and cosmopolitan attitudes) and show less interest in religion, status, and other traditional values (Bowen, 1977; Feldman and Newcomb, 1969; Nelsen and Uhl, 1977). Although there is some controversy on this point, Astin (1977) argued that many of these changes are attributable to the impact of college rather than to maturation, since resident students change more than commuters, students with high interpersonal involvement on campus change more than less involved students, and students who stay in college for four years change more than those who drop out. In this chapter I focus on the differential impacts of student living groups on freshman students' personal and social development as measured by some of the indexes just mentioned.

The work combines two approaches to studying change in college students (Feldman, 1972). The construction of the URES proceeded from a social-organizational approach, in that the focus was on analyzing the environmental characteristics of living groups. In the personality oriented or developmental approach used in most studies, investigators first identify changes in students and only then examine different features of the environment that might be responsible for these changes. My approach was to develop concepts and methods to measure the environment (social-organizational approach) and then to examine the impact of the environmental dimensions thereby identified on entering students in a longitudinal study conducted during their freshman year (developmental approach).

The College Experience Questionnaire

One of the major criticisms of college impact research is that most studies have used a limited range of outcome criteria. These criteria are usually linked to indexes of academic performance, such as grade point average, achievement test scores, and motivation to pursue advanced degrees. These variables are important, but a much wider range of changes must be considered. Chickering (1969) identified seven developmental issues that confront students during college: achieving competence, managing emotions, becoming autonomous, establishing identity, developing more open interpersonal relationships, clarifying purposes, and developing integrity. Feldman and Newcomb (1969) listed nineteen areas of interest in studies of college impact, such as students' self-concepts, intellectual and religious orientation, sociability and friendliness, readiness to express impulses, and psychological well-being (see also Bowen, 1977).

My colleagues and I developed a College Experience Questionnaire (CEQ) to assess student stability and change in several of these areas. In addition to covering sociodemographic characteristics, such as sex, ethnicity, religion, and parents' education and occupation, the CEQ contains items reflecting four areas of personal functioning in which college life might have an impact on students: styles of coping with college life; personal interests and values; self-concept, mood, and health-related indexes; and aspiration and achievement levels. (The first version of this form was called the Biographical and Experience Questionnaire.) Some of the items were adapted from Astin's (1968) Inventory of College Activities. The items are combined into subscales on the basis of content validity and empirical item intercorrelations (see DeYoung, 1975). The present analysis focuses on the indexes described in the following sections.

Styles of Coping with College Life. Six subscales assess styles of coping with college life. These subscales fall into two conceptual categories: active behavioral coping and tension reduction. Four subscales measure active behavioral coping (item examples are in parentheses), as follows: (1) *social participation* (listening to a friend's personal problems, studying with other people, discussing sex with friends, telling jokes, playing cards or dice), (2) *dating behavior* (picking up a date at a party or dance, going to a party, arranging a date for another student, having a blind date), (3) *athletic orientation* (participation in intercollegiate sports, participation in intramural athletics, self-description as "athletic"), and (4) *student body involvement* (attending a school political rally, voting in a student election). Two subscales measure coping styles related to tension reduction: (5) *hostile interaction* (arguing with other students, losing one's temper) and (6) *impulse expression* (oversleeping and missing class, breaking school rules without getting caught, cutting class, cheating on examinations, driving a car at high speed).

Personal Interests and Values. Three subscales assess personal interests and values: (1) *religious concern* (praying, reading the Bible, attending church), (2) *cultural orientation* (attending a public lecture, attending a public concert or ballet, visiting a museum, attending an art exhibition), and (3) *musical interest* (listening to jazz or folk music, playing a musical instrument, listening to classical music).

Self-Concept, Mood, and Health-Related Indexes. Seven indexes assess relevant variables in these following areas: (1) *easygoing* (calm, cooperative, happy, easygoing); (2) *exuberance* (feeling "on top of the world," particularly excited about something, pleased about accomplishing something); (3) *alienation* (feeling very lonely or remote from other people, angry at some minor frustration, depressed or very unhappy, bored, vaguely uneasy without quite knowing why), (4) *physical symptoms*—a summary score based on the student's complaints on each of fifteen items (such as back pain, cold sweats, common cold, constipation, diarrhea, dizziness, fever, and headaches), (5) *medication use*—a summary score based on the student's ratings of their use of each of ten medications (such as No-Doz, aspirin, laxatives, sleeping pills, tranquilizers, and special prescription medications), (6) *health center utilization*—a score, derived from records kept throughout the academic year by the health centers on the two campuses, based on such things as the number of visits per quarter for each student and the chief reason for each visit, and (7) *alcohol consumption* (the frequency with which the student drank wine, beer, and hard liquor).

Each of the items in the subscales assessing styles of coping, personal interests and values, and alcohol consumption are rated on four-point scales, ranging from "never" to "often," that indicate the frequency with which the student participated in the activity during the past year. The items on the self-concept subscales are rated on four-point scales, varying from "not at all" to "quite accurately," that indicate "how well the term describes the way you see yourself." The items on the mood, physical symptoms, and medication use subscales are rated on four-point scales, ranging from "never" to "frequently," that indicate the degree to which the student experienced the feeling in question (or how often he or she took each of the medications) during the past month.

Aspiration and Achievement Levels. (1) *Aspiration level* is assessed by the question "What is the highest academic degree that you intend to obtain?", with choices ranging from associate in arts to doctorate; (2) *academic orientation* is assessed by two items, which ask whether the student entered a project in a state or regional science contest or was a member of a scholastic honor society; and (3) *achievement level* is measured by obtaining from the registrar's office the student's grade point average for each quarter and for the overall freshman year.

Sample of Students and Living Groups. The work was carried out on two campuses. Campus A is a large, state-supported public university in a medium-sized rural community. Undergraduates are not required to live on campus, but because of geographic and financial factors, many students, including most entering freshman students, live in the residence hall system. Campus B is a smaller, church-affiliated private university in a busy urban area. Entering freshmen are required to live on campus unless they live with relatives in the surrounding community. A description of the two campuses and of their residence hall facilities is presented elsewhere (DeYoung, 1975).

Freshman students at the two universities were asked to complete the questionnaire when they entered college and again during the spring quarter of their freshman year. They also completed Form E of the URES, which was mailed to them about a month before the beginning of the fall quarter with information on the type of house (coed or single sex) to which they had been assigned. Assignments to single-sex or coed living groups were based on students' preferences, which were indicated in a prior questionnaire. Assignments to specific living units were made by housing office staff. Freshmen completed Form R of the URES shortly after they moved into their new living units and again at the end of the spring quarter of their freshman year.

The students resided in fifty-two living groups. Thirty-five of the units were on Campus A, and seventeen on Campus B. There were eighteen men's, eighteen women's, and sixteen coed units. The analyses are based on 846 students who completed the questionnaires at the beginning and the end of their freshman year. The student dropout and turnover rate (that is, transfers into and out of living groups) was approximately 25 percent. Our sample represents about 65 percent of the students who lived in the same unit for the entire school year. The entering characteristics of these students were almost the same as those of the rest of the students in the sample, indicating that they constitute a representative sample of the overall group (see Nielsen, Moos, and Lee, 1978, for a discussion of the effects of nonresponse bias).

Specifying Living Group Effects

In general, we expected that the six types of living group social environments would maintain or further accentuate individual characteristics congruent with the dominant aspects of the setting. For example, relationship and traditionally socially oriented units should facilitate the social aspects (social participation, dating behavior, and student body involvement) of college life. Supportive achievement and competition oriented settings should enhance the academic aspects of college, but competition oriented settings should have stressful effects on students, because of the lack of emphasis on involvement and support. We also expected that intellectually oriented settings would facilitate cultural orientation, that independence oriented settings would inhibit religious concern, and that both of these settings would enhance aspiration and achievement levels, because of their emphasis on personal growth.

It is necessary to control for a student's initial status before attempting to relate differential change to living group social climate. The best predictor of a student's final scores on a variable is the student's initial score on that variable. In addition, men and women may change differentially during the freshman year over and above what would be expected from their initial status. A multiple-regression analysis was carried out in which initial student standing on each of the variables and the student's sex were used as predictors of the final student standing on each variable. Earlier analyses indicated that sociodemographic indexes did not account for additional variance in the outcome criteria, so they were not included in the final regressions.

For each student we calculated expected final standing

(spring) scores and residual scores (representing the difference between the actual spring score and the expected spring score) on each subscale. We then derived living group mean residual scores by averaging the standardized residual scores of the students residing in each of the fifty-two units. A positive mean residual indicates that students in that unit had scores averaging higher than predicted, whereas a negative mean residual indicates the reverse.

Are these differential changes associated with the social environment of the living group? To answer this question, we correlated the mean residual scores for each of the outcome criteria with the climate-type scores, which measure the living group's similarity to each of the six types of social environments previously described (see Figures 7, 8, and 9 in Chapter Three). The spring URES data were used to derive the climate-type scores, since we thought it a better measure of the type of social environment that emerged during the year. There was a high negative correlation between the independence oriented and the traditionally socially oriented type of social climate in this sample, but the results for both types are shown in order to illustrate the overall findings more clearly.

Students in relationship oriented groups focused their activities much more on social than on academic concerns (see Table 9). For example, relationship oriented units facilitated social participation, athletic orientation, student body involvement, and impulse expression, as well as religious concern and cultural orientation. Students in these units also showed less academic orientation and lower achievement levels than expected. These settings tended to enhance social interaction and its concomitants (such as impulse expression) and to detract from students' academic concerns.

Independence oriented living groups had quite different effects. They inhibited religious concern, dating behavior, and student body involvement and enhanced musical interest. Students in these settings had a greater academic orientation and higher grade point averages than expected, but their aspiration levels were somewhat lower than expected. Living groups high on traditional social orientation had just the opposite effects.

Table 9. Correlations Between Types of Residence Hall Environments and Mean Residual Scores on Outcome Criteria

Outcome Criterion	Relationship Oriented	Traditionally Socially Oriented	Supportive Achievement Oriented	Competition Oriented	Independence Oriented	Intellectually Oriented
Coping styles						
Active behavioral						
Social participation	0.26[a]	0.10	-0.01	-0.06	-0.05	0.14
Dating behavior	0.21	0.33[b]	0.23[a]	0.01	-0.31[a]	-0.19
Athletic orientation	0.29[a]	0.16	-0.04	-0.17	-0.17	0.15
Student body involvement	0.42[b]	0.53[b]	-0.38[a]	0.09	-0.48[b]	0.24[a]
Tension reduction						
Hostile interaction	0.14	0.16	-0.02	0.06	-0.14	0.14
Impulse expression	0.36[b]	0.27[a]	-0.29[a]	-0.06	-0.21	0.28[b]
Personal interests and values						
Religious concern	0.23[a]	0.58[b]	-0.06	0.16	-0.64[b]	0.06
Cultural orientation	0.31[a]	0.18	-0.34[b]	-0.07	-0.17	0.39[b]
Musical interest	-0.19	-0.43[b]	-0.06	-0.09	0.40[b]	0.07
Self-concepts and moods						
Easygoing	-0.06	-0.07	0.10	0.01	0.02	-0.22
Exuberance	-0.16	-0.07	-0.10	0.19	0.05	-0.06
Alienation	-0.08	0.10	-0.07	0.16	-0.10	0.13
Aspiration and achievement						
Aspiration level	0.16	-0.20[a]	0.12	-0.06	-0.19[b]	0.12
Academic orientation	-0.38[b]	-0.56[b]	0.26[a]	-0.12	0.55[b]	-0.23[a]
Achievement level	-0.39[b]	-0.46[b]	0.33[b]	-0.06	0.40[b]	-0.26[a]

Note: $N = 52$ living groups.

[a] $p < 0.05$.

[b] $p < 0.01$.

These units are composed of students who emphasize such activities as dating, partying, and student body involvement, who are competitive around social status, and who demonstrate the correlates of an active social life, such as high impulse expression and low academic achievement.

Supportive achievement oriented social environments had still different influences on students. These units facilitated dating behavior, academic orientation, and achievement level but inhibited cultural orientation, student body involvement, and impulse expression. These students may have less time to engage in extracurricular activities, such as student government and the student newspaper, and in behavior such as cutting class, which is not consistent with their emphasis on achievement. The intellectually oriented settings had a set of unique impacts, enhancing cultural orientation, student body involvement, and impulse expression but inhibiting academic orientation and achievement levels. An emphasis on intellectuality may be associated with strong peer pressure to participate in activities with other living group members, which would affect academic performance adversely.

Although five of the six types of social environments had differential influences on their students, the competition oriented units had no such effects. This is an important finding, because these were the most prevalent settings in the typology analysis (42 of the 100 living groups), and they were composed primarily of men. Thus, some living groups (perhaps those that are low on cohesion and fail to integrate students into the social and interpersonal aspects of college life) may have less influence on personal and academic development, and living groups may have fewer effects on men than on women (see Moos, DeYoung, and Van Dort, 1976, for results of earlier analyses conducted separately on each of the ten URES subscales).

Commonality Analysis of Personal and Environmental Factors. Inferences about the differential effects of colleges on students have been based primarily on the increments in explained variance. This method is asymmetric in that it attributes variance shared by two or more sets of variables to the set that is entered first in the regression analysis (such as student background and personality characteristics); thus, it may overestimate the first set's contribution by crediting that set with both its unique and shared variance. In contrast, the increment in explained variance attributed to the set of variables added last (such as environment-related variables) represents only the explained variance that is unique to that set of variables and not the variance that is shared with the variables entered earlier.

Consequently, inferences about the relative effects of environment-related variables, social background characteristics, and the initial value of the outcome criterion may be misleading (Coleman, 1975). Such inferences have important policy implications for residence hall programs. For example, if the unique variance attributed to program-related variables is small, and if the variance that is shared with student background and personality variables is attributed only to this latter set of characteristics, then researchers and administrators may conclude that the effects of residence hall programs are negligible. As a result, they may recommend less expensive and more uniform living group settings.

We conducted a series of analyses to estimate the portion of the predictable variance in each of the outcome criteria unique to environmental variables, unique to personal variables, and shared by personal and environmental variables. Three sets of environmental variables were included: (1) the climate-type scores used in the preceding analyses, (2) the initial residence hall mean score on the relevant outcome criterion (for example, the living group's initial mean score on religious concern was used in the analysis predicting the student's level of religious concern during the spring term); and (3) the overall context, as measured by whether the living group was male, female, or coed and by the campus on which it was located. The intent was to estimate the extent to which the social climate of the living unit, the relevant human aggregate or contextual variable, and the school context and type of dormitory could explain stability and change in the outcome indexes. (Achievement level was not included in these analyses because we did not have information on students' average grade point average at entrance to college.)

Regression analyses, in which the order of entry of the environmental and personal variables sets was varied systematically, were conducted for each of the outcome criteria. The proportion of variance in each criterion attributable to differences among the fifty-two living groups was also determined. This was obtained from one-way analyses of variance in which the proportion of variance in each criterion due to between-group differences (that is, differences among the fifty-two units) and within-group differences (that is, differences among students within each of the units) was calculated.

The proportion of predictable variance varied considerably, ranging from 9.6 percent for academic orientation to 62.1 percent for religious concern (see Table 10). The set of personal variables uniquely accounted for the major portion of the variance of every outcome criterion. Almost all of the unique variance due to the set of personal variables was accounted for by the intake value of the outcome criterion. Relatively small proportions of the variance were uniquely associated with the set of environmental variables; this proportion was less than 2 percent for seven of the fourteen outcome criteria (however, this proportion was notably higher for student body involvement, cultural orientation, and academic orientation). Personal and environmental variables shared a considerable proportion of the *predictable* variance in each of the outcome criteria. This proportion was over 10 percent for nine of the fourteen criteria and over 20 percent for social participation, impulse expression, religious concern, and academic orientation.

The results show that college living settings have some influence on differential change (unique variance) but that most effects occur because students create settings that help them to maintain their preferred characteristics (shared variance). For example, students who are high in religious concern create living group environments that are high in traditional social orientation, and such settings help them to maintain or consolidate their initial religious values. Feldman and Newcomb (1969) noted that processes favoring consolidation may be a common source of the impact of college on students, and Chickering and McCormick (1973) posited that such consolidation is most

Table 10. Proportion of Variance in Student Outcomes Accounted for by Personal and Environmental Factors

Outcome Criterion	Total Predictable Variance	Variance Unique to Personal Variables	Variance Unique to Environmental Variables	Variance Shared by Personal and Environmental Variables	Variance Accounted for by Living Group Differences
Coping styles					
Active behavioral					
Social participation	28.8	18.6	2.1	8.1	15.5
Dating behavior	29.5	23.2	2.3	4.0	11.9
Athletic orientation	25.6	22.3	1.1	2.2	6.2
Student body involvement	23.6	12.2	7.2	4.2	17.1
Tension reduction					
Hostile interaction	30.4	26.2	2.1	2.1	9.2
Impulse expression	40.3	28.5	2.2	9.4	16.0
Personal interests and values					
Religious concern	62.1	47.6	1.7	12.8	16.1
Cultural orientation	37.8	28.6	3.4	4.8	14.7
Musical interest	48.6	41.4	0.7	6.5	10.0
Self-concepts and moods					
Easygoing	39.1	36.4	0.5	2.3	4.9
Exuberance	27.3	24.0	0.6	2.7	6.4
Alienation	30.0	26.9	0.9	2.3	6.9
Aspiration and achievement					
Aspiration level	41.6	34.8	0.8	6.0	11.1
Academic orientation	9.6	2.9	3.8	2.9	10.6

likely to occur when the college setting provides a safe, congruent, "womblike" environment. Living groups thus affect both stability and change in students. They help to stabilize students' congruent characteristics and to change their deviant characteristics to conform to the norms of the setting (see also Vreeland and Bidwell, 1965).

The proportion of variance related to the set of environmental factors is low to moderate compared with the total predictable variance in the outcome criteria, but it is considerable when evaluated with respect to the proportion of variance attributable to differences among living groups (see Table 10). The environmental variables explain over half (unique and shared variance) of the variance among living groups for all but two of the criteria. The milieu characteristics we measured thus account for a substantial portion of the effects that can be attributable to living group differences.

Living Group Social Climate and Student Health

There is considerable current interest in the relationship between social environment and physical well-being. The evidence indicates that social-environmental factors are related to psychophysiological processes. Associating different psychosocial stimuli with specific effects is difficult, but the stimuli associated with support, cohesion, and affiliation are generally thought to enhance normal development and reduce recovery time from illness. Evidence also exists that such factors as responsibility, competition, work pressure, time urgency, and change increase the likelihood of stress and disease (Kiritz and Moos, 1974; Moos, 1979).

In this respect, the prevalence of physical symptoms among college students is quite high. For example, Comstock and Slome (1973) found that of 1,200 students who reported on health problems they experienced during the school year, over 70 percent complained of colds, sore throats, or headaches. Almost 40 percent experienced upset stomach, diarrhea, or vomiting, and a surprising 28 percent experienced injuries. Between 10 and 50 percent of the students on our two campuses complained of physical symptoms at some time during their freshman year (Moos and Van Dort, 1977). Mechanic and Greenley (1976) pointed out that the high levels of physical and emotional symptoms among students probably reflect situational stresses characteristic of college life. An important issue, therefore, is to identify the student background and environmental or stress factors related to the prevalence of symptoms and to the use of health services in college settings.

To address this issue, multiple-regression and correlation procedures, similar to those previously described, were used to relate the six climate-type scores to mean residual physical symptoms (N = 52 living groups). Students in competitive and intellectually oriented living groups had more complaints than expected, whereas those in supportive achievement oriented units had fewer complaints than expected. Students in relationship and intellectually oriented units reported using medications more often than expected. Students in competition and intellectually oriented units visited the health center more often than expected for such relatively minor symptoms as respiratory and gastrointestinal complaints, and students in competitive units used the health center more often than expected for psychiatric and personal counseling services. (Expected health center use was derived from a student's sex, initial physical symptom score, and propensity to use health services as indexed by the extent to which the student reported using the services of a physician or personal counselor during the preceding year.)

The URES Symptom Risk Subscale. Our interest in social-environmental influences on health led Bernice Van Dort and me (Moos and Van Dort, in press) to construct a new URES subscale, the symptom risk subscale, to assess the degree to which the social environment of a living group is related to and enhances students' complaints of physical symptoms. In brief, for each URES item we calculated the proportion of students answering true for each of the fifty-two living groups. We computed correlations between the mean physical symptom score for all the students in a living unit and the proportion of students in the unit who answered true to each URES item. We conducted these analyses separately for men's, women's, and coed living groups so that we could identify consistent social environment correlates of students' complaints of physical symptoms. The results enabled us to construct a twelve-item URES symptom risk subscale related to mean physical symptom complaints and to greater-than-expected increases in these complaints in all three types of living groups (see Moos and Van Dort, in press, for details). The twelve items in the symptom risk subscale and their scoring direction are given in Appendix A.

The social environments of living groups in which students complain of more physical symptoms are low in involvement, emotional support, and student influence and high in competition. These units lack a sense of loyalty and cohesion and are low in student participation and social activities. Students report difficulty in approaching house staff with problems and relatively little influence on discipline and on the rules, policies, and operation of the residence. Students feel they are in an academically competitive environment (for example, some students try to appear smarter and to outdo others in intellectual matters).

An emphasis on the competitive aspects of academic life combined with little or no social support and cohesion seems to create stress effects that manifest themselves in students' complaints of physical symptoms and in health center utilization. Thus, competitive living groups may not have their expected effects on academic achievement because the anxiety and strain they create hinder students' functioning. The fact that students in supportive achievement oriented units had fewer complaints than expected supports the notion that cohesion and support can buffer against some of the stressful aspects of college life.

Findings in other settings also indicate that an emphasis on competition and responsibility without sufficient social support can lead to dissatisfaction and strain. For example, the social environments of military basic training companies are related to sick call rates. Men in companies with high rates of sick call feel little support from officers or other enlisted men. They note that their work is repetitive and boring, that they enjoy little if any autonomy, and that the officers are very strict, supervise them too closely, and ridicule them publicly. One adaptation to such a noxious social environment is to become ill and withdraw from daily activities (Moos, 1975, chap. 12).

We were surprised by the finding that students in intellectually oriented living groups showed more physical symptoms and a higher use of medication and of the health center than expected. Since students' academic and intellectual abilities are central to their self-concept, and since intellectual emphasis in a living group often has competitive overtones, many students may find the focus on this area stressful. Students in these units may demand conformity regarding cultural and intellectual matters (that is, they may socially isolate those who have less interest or different opinions in these areas) and thereby elicit anxiety and alienation. These speculations are consistent with DeCoster's (1966, 1968) finding that some low-ability students were negatively affected by living in settings where most of their peers were highly able academically.

Kaplan, Cassel, and Gore (1977) noted that social support is important in ameliorating stress and promoting health. They believe that social supports protect a person from the effects of noxious psychosocial stressors. This is consistent with our finding that an environment high on either achievement or competition and support has a quite different impact from one high on achievement or competition but low on support. They concluded that as a preventive measure important psychosocial factors should be changed (such as increasing social supports) and that illness should be detected as early as possible.

Identifying High-Risk Students. These considerations raise the issue of identifying "high-risk" students; that is, students who are likely to complain increasingly of physical symptoms or to become ill during their college years. Several previous studies attempted to characterize students who are at risk for academic failure, psychiatric disturbance, and student health center utilization (Greenley and Mechanic, 1976). For example, Burke (1974) found that "perceived morbidity" (assessed by self-reported days of restricted activity and self-reported symptoms) was related to student health center utilization.

In addressing this issue, Dean Nielsen and I (Nielsen and Moos, 1977) identified characteristics that distinguished students whose physical symptoms increased during the academic year from those whose symptoms did not. Students whose symptoms increased (high risk) were higher than their low-risk counterparts in hostile interaction, alienation, overload (having too much to do), alcohol consumption, and aspirin and vitamin use. They were less likely to describe themselves as extroverted or intellectual, had lower educational aspirations, completed fewer academic units, and earned lower grade point averages. Students who complained of physical symptoms thus evidenced poorer social and academic adjustment to college. Also, students who later seek college counseling services score higher on alienation, social nonconformity, and discomfort at entrance to college than students who do not (Bruch, 1977).

These findings in conjunction with such environmental assessment techniques as the URES can help to identify entering students who may need health and counseling services, to provide information on high-risk students functioning in high-risk environments (such as competitive or intellectually oriented living groups), and to determine less stressful settings for these students. This information should help college counselors and health center staff to assist illness-prone students.

The Impact of Coed Living

Since coed student housing has become quite popular, there is a need to study its effects systematically. Although there is relatively little research on this issue, Brown, Winkworth, and Braskamp (1973) found that men who live in coed halls were more involved with women on a casual basis, had fewer strictly "masculine" interactions with other men, engaged in fewer formal dating activities, and attained greater ease in dealing with women. Women living in coed halls spent more time going to plays, musical performances, and special lectures, were more likely to become involved in a floor activity or project, spent less time talking about sex, dating, or sports, and developed more informal relationships with men.

Researchers have drawn conflicting conclusions about changes in sexual behavior in coed living groups. Duncan (1974) suggested that coed living is more likely to lead to platonic relationships and healthy attitudes toward sex because of strong community feelings. However, Reid (1974) found increased sexual activity in coed residences, along with more frequent casual relationships between men and women. Reid also found that women living in coed halls had more positive, less stereotyped images of femininity and showed more interest in their careers.

Because personality factors are associated with students' selection of housing arrangements, it is reasonable to assume initial differences between the men and women who choose coed housing and those who choose unisex housing. For example, Schroeder and LeMay (1973) found that students who chose coed halls were higher on indexes measuring inner-directed support, existentiality, and capacity for intimate contact. This suggests that students who choose coed residence halls are more mature, exhibit greater flexibility, and are more able to develop meaningful interpersonal relationships. Coed residence halls also facilitated interpersonal growth, as shown by increases on the capacity for intimate contact index. The authors concluded that coeducational living enhanced the development of healthy, mature relationships.

Jean Otto and I (Moos and Otto, 1975) investigated the initial differences between students entering coed and students entering single-sex living groups and identified differential effects of these living arrangements. We also conducted analyses on a subsample of the units used in the studies just described. The results are based on freshmen in ten women's, ten men's, and seventeen coed units.

Initial Differences. The two groups of men were similar in background characteristics except that more men in coed units had fathers with a college degree. This difference was consistent with their higher academic and career goals (46 percent of the men entering coed units wanted to obtain a doctoral degree versus only 34 percent of the men entering men's units). There were only slight group differences in the other indexes. The men in the coed units were more likely to report drinking beer and to describe themselves as easygoing and feeling "on top of the world."

Like their male counterparts, more women in coed units had fathers who graduated from college. In addition, more of them sought a doctoral degree. They were more likely to have discussed sex, argued with others, told jokes, attended a play, bought a book, and visited a museum. They had also engaged in more behavior reflecting impulse expression than the women in the women's units. The women in the coed units saw themselves as more cooperative, calm, easygoing, and happy, and reported fewer physical symptoms and less use of medications.

Change for Men in Coed and in Single-Sex Units. The men in the men's units maintained about the same aspiration levels throughout the academic year, whereas those in the coed units lowered their aspiration levels somewhat. Specifically, fewer coed men selected a medical or doctoral degree as their ultimate goal, and more selected a master's degree. The men in the coed units also developed more negative attitudes toward demanding careers, whereas those in the men's units showed more interest in such careers. For example, fewer men in coed units felt they had the ability to become a physicist or engineer, whereas more of them developed positive attitudes toward being a high school teacher. The two groups of men showed similar changes on the other indexes, but the men in the coed units increased more in impulse expression and in their use of No-Doz and prescription medications.

Change for Women in Coed and in Single-Sex Units. There were no changes in aspiration levels for the women in the women's units, but those in the coed units showed a substantial drop. Specifically, a higher percentage of the coed women sought only a bachelor's degree, and fewer expected to work toward a doctoral or medical degree. The women in the coed units also developed more negative attitudes toward demanding careers. For example, more of them felt that becoming an engineer would be too costly, that they did not have the necessary ability to be an engineer, that the requirements for becoming a physicist were too stringent, and the like.

The women in the women's units were more likely to

increase their participation in such traditional social activities as dating and partying. There were no differential group changes in either personal interests and values or in self-concepts and moods. However, the women in the women's units increased much more in impulse expression and alcohol consumption (for example, cutting class, oversleeping and missing class, and drinking hard liquor) than did the women in the coed units. The two groups differed somewhat in their use of medications and health supplements, but these differences were not particularly consistent.

Health, Grade, Transfer, and Dropout Data. A greater proportion of the men in the coed units used the health center for orthopedic and urogenital problems and for preventive treatment (that is, immunizations and physical examinations). The men in the coed units averaged 4.8 visits per student during the year, whereas those in the men's units averaged 4.0 visits per student. The differences between the two groups of women were somewhat larger (6.4 visits versus 5.1 visits, respectively). For example, women in the coed units visited the health center more frequently for respiratory, digestive, endocrine, dermatological, and orthopedic problems. In addition, 21 percent of the women in the coed units visited the health center to obtain birth control information, whereas only 14 percent of those in the women's units used these services.

The two groups of men did not differ in the percentage of dropouts (6.3 percent and 7.1 percent for the coed and single-sex units, respectively) or transfers out of the living groups (3.2 percent and 4.7 percent, respectively). However, a greater proportion of the women in the coed units dropped out of school (9.7 percent versus 6.8 percent) or transferred out of their living group (7.0 percent versus 2.6 percent, respectively). Indexes of academic achievement did not differentiate between the two male or the two female groups.

The coed living groups had a relatively high emphasis on involvement and emotional support, as well as on independence and innovation (which was higher than in the women's units) and intellectuality (which was higher than in the men's units). The social environments of the coed units were thus more heterogeneous than those of the single-sex units; that is, they emphasized several nonacademic areas of personal development. The sense of community in these units, in conjunction with this diversity and the relatively lower press for academic achievement and competition, may result in a disproportionate emphasis on independence and the pursuit of nonacademic intellectual activities (see Chapter Three). This may help to explain the unexpected finding that aspiration levels and interest in more difficult careers decreased for men and women in coed units.

The fact that students in coed units used the health center more often than their counterparts in single-sex units and that almost 17 percent of the women in the coed units either transferred out of their living unit or dropped out of school, suggests that there is some stress in coed living, especially for women. This stress may be due to the greater diversity of necessary roles (more casual *and* more intimate heterosexual relationships) and to the heterogeneity of personal growth goals. Furthermore, there is a potential conflict between such goals as independence and intellectuality and other normative pressures, such as those for achievement from peers and professors in the students' major department and those for conformity from the students' family.

Coed units raise problems in adapting to college for at least some students. In this respect, Astin and Panos (1969) found that both men and women had a higher chance of dropping out of college if they attended a coed institution and that highly able women students were more likely to drop out if they attended an institution with a relatively large percentage of men in the student body. Women in women's colleges are more likely to become involved in student government, to attain positions of leadership, to focus on academic activities and develop high aspirations, and to persist to graduation (Astin, 1977). These findings are consistent with the hypothesis that the more diverse influences in coed units can be stressful and can prove at least temporarily detrimental to academic pursuits.

The Importance of Student Living Groups

Living groups influence students in each of the seven developmental areas identified by Chickering (1969). Indepen-

dence and supportive achievement oriented living groups maintain and enhance aspiration and achievement levels and thereby
the development of competence and the clarification of students' purposes and goals. Living groups that facilitate (relationship and traditionally socially oriented) or inhibit (independence oriented) religious concern affect a student's autonomy
and sense of personal identity. Living groups that enhance (relationship and traditionally socially oriented) or inhibit (independence and supportive achievement oriented) active styles of
coping with college life affect such tasks as achieving competence, establishing identity, and developing more open interpersonal relationships.

Several of the mood and health-related indexes and measures of tension-reduction coping styles are related to the task
of managing emotions. Student living groups have impacts on
this area; specifically, units that emphasize supportive achievement inhibit impulse expression and the development of physical symptoms. Living groups that emphasize traditional social
orientation maintain and facilitate impulse expression, whereas
those that emphasize competition and intellectuality increase
physical symptoms and health center use.

Some investigators have speculated on the effects of students' integration into either the social or the academic aspects
of college. For example, concentration on academic pursuits
may isolate students from peer group effects on behavior that
normally accompany college attendance and lead to less-than-
expected change in such dimensions as liberalism, hedonism,
artistic interests, and religious concern (Astin, 1977). In this
respect, relationship and traditionally socially oriented living
groups emphasize and enhance the social aspects of college,
whereas competition and independence oriented units both
focus on the academic aspects but in different ways. Competitive units focus on achievement via conformity (working hard,
studying long hours, and emphasizing grades) and seem to insulate students from both social and academic peer group influences; independence oriented units emphasize achievement via
independence, which insulates students from social, though not
from intellectual and academic, influences. Furthermore, social

and academic pursuits can be combined in at least two ways with quite different effects. One case emphasizes the traditional aspects of achievement within a generally cohesive setting (supportive achievement), whereas the other case emphasizes the broader intellectual and cultural milieu. The distinction between academic and social aspects of college is important, but it may overlook differences in how students function and are integrated into these two areas.

The basic results are consistent with those found in studies of college and university impact. Colleges emphasizing such relationship dimensions as faculty-student interaction, peer cohesion, and enthusiasm in teaching have a positive impact on students. Colleges emphasizing such personal growth dimensions as humanism, a broad intellectual orientation, independent study and criticism, high standards, and controversy and challenge also have students who tend to do better academically (Astin, 1977; Bowen, 1977; Moos, 1976c, chap. 10). Astin and Panos (1969) found that the educational and vocational development of college students depended primarily on their personal characteristics and family background. However, certain characteristics of the college's social environment had an important impact. For example, students were more likely to complete four years of college if they attended an institution that enrolled academically superior students and that had a cohesive peer environment, characterized by many close friendships among students.

These findings indicate the need to consider the connections between living groups and the college campuses of which they are a part. A supportive living group may protect students from the stressful effects of a competitive college setting. A living group in which achievement and studying are valued may enhance the impact of a college setting that strongly values academic concerns, but the potential effects of such a college setting may be countered by the norms of a relationship oriented unit (a focus on social activities) or an intellectually oriented unit (a focus on intellectual but not on academic matters). Studies of college impact need to consider the mediating influences of student living groups.

6

Analyzing College Student Drinking Patterns

Many students begin or increase their use of alcohol during the freshman year. Moderate or heavy alcohol use is associated with poor academic or social functioning and may lead to other problem behavior (such as drug use), disciplinary action, and interruption or termination of a student's college career. Because alcohol use is readily changeable and is influenced by both personal and social factors, it provides a useful model for analyzing student-environment relationships.

Note: This chapter is coauthored by Bernice S. Moos.

114

Abstaining, Moderate-Drinking, and Heavy-Drinking Students

The search for etiological patterns of alcoholism has focused primarily on characteristic profiles of young drinkers and abstainers. The following sociodemographic factors show moderate correlations with teenage drinking: social class (higher socioeconomic status adolescents tend to drink more, although the results are inconsistent), religion (Catholics tend to drink more than Protestants and Jews), sex (boys drink more than girls, although this effect is decreasing), and parental drinking (Davies and Stacey, 1972; Straus and Bacon, 1962; Wechsler and Thum, 1973). Male adolescent problem drinkers participate less in religious activities and engage in more deviant behavior, such as aggression, lying, and stealing, than either moderate drinkers or abstainers. Drinking is also related to participation in such social activities as dances, parties, and dating. Students who drink more have lower aspiration levels and perform poorer academically than nonproblem drinkers or light drinkers, and male adolescent problem drinkers are more frequently truant from school than are abstainers (see Jessor and Jessor, 1977, for a review of this area).

Results derived from personality tests and self-descriptions have yielded the most consistent differences between drinkers and abstainers. Williams (1970) used the Adjective Checklist and found college-age male problem drinkers to be relatively independent, aggressive, impulsive, anxious, and depressed. Jones (1968, 1971), analyzing personality ratings of young men and women, concluded that male problem drinkers are less self-controlled and more hostile, expressive, assertive, and gregarious, while female problem drinkers are more unstable, hostile, and impulsive than moderate drinkers or abstainers. Jones also reported that male abstainers are more over-controlled, emotionally bland, introspective, and moralistic than drinkers; similarly, Sanford and Singer (1968) noted that college-age male abstainers are more responsible and self-controlled and less dominant, sociable, and flexible than drinkers.

Most of the studies on college student drinking patterns are limited because they are based on small samples or focus exclusively on men. More extensive and reliable information is necessary to formulate needed profiles of individuals who are at risk for alcohol abuse and for dropout or academic failure and who are more likely to need college health and counseling services. The purpose of the first analysis was to provide more comprehensive information on college men and women drinkers and abstainers through cross-sectional comparisons on a broad spectrum of personal functioning variables.

Drinking Classifications. Of the 846 freshman students who returned the initial questionnaire (see Chapter Five), we classified 299 as abstainers, 279 as moderate drinkers, and 175 as heavy drinkers. Drinking was classified according to self-ratings on four-point scales, ranging from "never" to "often," of the frequency of drinking wine, beer, and hard liquor during the student's senior year in high school. We classified students as heavy drinkers if they had drunk wine, beer, and hard liquor often or if they had drunk two of the three types of alcoholic beverages often and drunk the third at least occasionally. Students who had consumed no wine, beer, or hard liquor or who had drunk one type of alcoholic beverage no more than once or twice were classified as abstainers. Drinking frequencies of students considered moderate drinkers were between those of heavy drinkers and abstainers.

Separate questions regarding quantity and frequency of alcohol consumption were included in a later version of the questionnaire. Frequency and quantity-frequency measures correlated 0.98, indicating that the frequency indexes provide data essentially identical to that provided by combined quantity-frequency measures. The proportions of abstaining, moderate-drinking, and heavy-drinking students are similar to those obtained in other recent studies of drinking patterns among college students (Engs, 1977), and, as would be expected, the proportion of heavy drinkers is somewhat higher than the proportion of problem drinkers (19 percent) identified in a recent nationwide survey of junior and senior high school students (Donovan and Jessor, 1978).

Personal Interest and Coping Style Variables. Men and women abstainers reported higher religious concern than moderate and heavy drinkers. Heavy drinkers engaged in more social activities and dating than moderate drinkers, and moderate drinkers socialized and dated more than nondrinkers. A much higher proportion of drinkers than of nondrinkers reported attending parties, picking up a date at a party or dance, and arranging a date for another student. Heavy drinkers also were more expressive, as shown by their greater frequency of both supportive interaction (discussing sex with friends and telling jokes) and hostile behavior (arguing with other students and losing their temper). The most consistent and sizable differences between abstainers, moderate drinkers, and heavy drinkers were obtained on variables reflecting impulse expression. Heavy drinkers broke school rules without being caught (82 percent), drove a car at high speed (51 percent), overslept and missed class (32 percent), and cheated on exams (30 percent) much more frequently than moderate drinkers. Moderate drinkers engaged in each of these activities proportionately more than nondrinkers. The extent of group differences is illustrated by the relatively low proportion of nondrinkers who engaged in the above activities (20, 10, 3, and 2 percent, respectively).

Self-Concepts, Mood, and Health. Heavy drinkers rated themselves as more dominant, rebellious, and outgoing and less cautious than nondrinkers. Affective self-descriptions showed that drinkers were somewhat more content with their lives but were prone to more frequent mood fluctuations than abstainers. Men and women who drank frequently described themselves as more energetic, easygoing, and exuberant than did abstainers. However, heavy drinkers more frequently reported alienation, complained of more physical symptoms, engaged in more preventive and remedial health measures, and went to doctors and personal counselors more frequently than did abstainers.

Academic Variables. Heavy-drinking men and women had lower educational aspirations than abstainers. Academic performance was more closely associated with drinking among men than among women. The average number of academic units completed differentiated female heavy drinkers from female abstainers, whereas cumulative grade point averages (GPAs) did not. However, male heavy drinkers completed significantly fewer units and earned lower cumulative GPAs than did male nondrinkers. Furthermore, male heavy drinkers were more likely than abstainers to transfer to other living groups within the university (11 percent versus 5 percent) and to drop out of school during their freshman year (10 percent versus 4 percent). Female heavy drinkers (12 percent) were more likely than female abstainers (6 percent) to drop out of school (see Moos, Moos, and Kulik, 1976, for details).

The results of these analyses generally corroborate those of earlier studies of drinking in college. They extend the scope of our knowledge by focusing on both men and women students and by examining a comprehensive array of personal functioning and academic variables. Comparisons of men and women heavy drinkers and their abstaining counterparts are quite similar on most of the variables studied. However, while only some variables reflecting alienation were differentially associated with male drinking patterns, female heavy drinkers reported greater frequencies than female nondrinkers on *every* variable measuring alienation. Similarly, several items reflecting more frequent physical complaints and greater use of medications and health services did not differentiate male heavy drinkers from male abstainers but did differentiate female heavy drinkers from female abstainers.

These findings suggest that the female heavy drinker is more deviant in some respects than is the male heavy drinker. The female heavy drinker may be more likely to drink for escapist or rebellious reasons, especially since American society continues to be more permissive concerning heavy drinking by men than by women. Cahalan, Cisin, and Crossley (1969) did in fact find that 64 percent of female heavy drinkers, compared with 48 percent of male heavy drinkers, drank to escape worries, anxieties, depression, and the like. While neither causality nor directionality can be specified, alcohol consumption by men, and to an even greater extent by women, likely influences alienation and physical symptoms, and alienation and physical symptoms can in turn increase consumption of alcohol as a form of escapism. At the same time, however, drinking has short-term facilitative effects on social interaction and may lead to the more frequent feelings of exuberance reported by male and female heavy drinkers compared with their abstinent counterparts.

Sanford and Singer (1968) suggested that women who drink frequently may do so to conform to the situation, such as drinking on dates. Men, however, are more likely to want to drink frequently because it is more sex-role appropriate in the company of both men and women. Drinking by men thus may be attributed more to dispositional factors, whereas drinking by women may be relatively more influenced by situational factors. As a result, personal characteristics that can lead to frequent drinking and to failures in academic performance are more closely associated with heavy drinking among men than among women. However, the finding that female as well as male heavy drinkers are more likely to drop out of college than nondrinkers indicates that both sexes can be adversely affected by frequent drinking.

Predicting Changes in Student Drinking Patterns

The cross-sectional nature of these comparisons does not allow us to make predictive inferences. We cannot say whether the characteristics that differentiate heavy drinkers motivate the use of alcohol or result from alcohol consumption. In an effort to make more compelling arguments for causal inference, several investigators have conducted predictive studies to examine personality, behavioral, health, and environmental factors that antedate the onset of drinking patterns. For example, Jones (1968, 1971) found that personality characteristics of male and female junior high school students differentiated individuals who developed problem-drinking patterns in adulthood from those who became moderate drinkers and abstainers. Males who later became problem drinkers were more undercontrolled, rebellious, expressive, and assertive; females who became problem drinkers were less responsible, conventional, consistent, and emotionally controlled. Loper, Kammeier, and Hoffman (1973) found that a group of hospitalized male alcoholics had reported themselves to be more gregarious and impulsive and less conforming and healthy as prealcoholic college freshmen than had a nonalcoholic control group.

Jessor and Jessor (1977), conducting longitudinal studies of high school and college men and women, found the onset of drinking to be related to the following set of personal and behavioral attributes: lower value on academic achievement, greater tolerance of deviant behavior, less religiosity, less involvement with parents and with friends whose ideologies are similar to those of the parents, more friends who drink and who approve of drinking, and less involvement with church and grades. These attributes constitute a readiness to begin drinking and relate to the time of drinking onset: the greater the readiness, the earlier the onset.

In view of the fact that neither youth nor adult levels of alcohol consumption are static, it is surprising that longitudinal studies have focused on increases and neglected decreases in drinking levels. One exception is a longitudinal study of high school students (Kandel, 1975), which identified four stages in drug use. The stages were: beer, wine, or both; cigarettes or hard liquor; marijuana; and other illicit drugs. Kandel concluded that the legal drugs were necessary intermediates between the nonuse of alcohol and the use of marijuana, since essentially no one progressed directly from nonuse to illegal drug use and no one progressed from beer and wine to illicit drugs without taking up hard liquor or cigarettes. However, a particular drug did not invariably lead to other drugs higher up in the sequence; many adolescents stopped at a particular stage. Furthermore, many regressed to an earlier stage. Kandel found the above sequence to be reversed for regression in drug use; that is, adolescents first stopped using illicit drugs, then marijuana, and so on.

Information concerning factors that may influence increases and decreases in alcohol consumption is necessary to understand youth drinking more completely and to develop profiles of individuals who are risks for future alcohol abuse. The following analysis differs from analyses of previous longitudinal studies in that it explores initial group differences in indexes of personal functioning that antedate increases and decreases in freshman-year drinking patterns. The aim is to make more compelling causal inferences by demonstrating that a drinking group's relative initial status on a set of variables corresponds to its subsequent level of alcohol consumption. By focusing on students who are abstainers at entrance to college, we can identify factors that precede the onset of drinking.

We studied 174 students classified as abstainers and 119 students considered heavy drinkers at the beginning of their freshman year who completed the CEQ at the end of their freshman year. Of the abstainers, 103 (59 percent) remained abstainers and 71 (41 percent) became drinkers. Most students reported greater alcohol consumption at the end of the year, but some students did report less drinking. Of the initial heavy drinkers, 85 (71 percent) remained heavy drinkers, and 34 (29 percent) drank substantially less during the year (see Moos, Moos, and Kulik, 1977, for details). In sum, we identified four groups of students: those who remained abstainers (abstainers), those who began drinking (increasers), those who remained heavy drinkers (drinkers), and those who decreased their heavy drinking (decreasers).

Group Differences at the Beginning of the Freshman Year. Increasers exhibited more social participation and impulse expression and less religious concern prior to the onset of drinking than abstainers. Increasers also described themselves as less cautious than abstainers. Decreasers saw themselves as less extroverted and easygoing and engaged in less social participation, dating, student body involvement, and impulse expression than students who remained heavy drinkers. The most noteworthy aspect of the results was the overall ordinal pattern. In almost every instance abstainers and drinkers were at opposite ends of the continuum of CEQ scores, while increasers and decreasers occupied intermediate positions closest to their initial drinker classifications. Thus, eight months before assessing drinking-pattern changes, increasers were consistently more similar to the drinking groups than were abstainers, and decreasers were consistently more similar to the abstinent groups than were drinkers.

Group Differences at the End of the Freshman Year.
These initial group differences became more pronounced with
time. Increasers exhibited less religious concern and more social
participation, supportive interaction, dating behavior, student
body involvement, hostile interaction, and impulse expression
than abstainers. Increasers also saw themselves as more dominant and extroverted. Decreasers saw themselves as less extroverted, easygoing, and rebellious and exhibited less social participation, dating behavior, student body involvement, and
impulse expression than drinkers. Abstainers had higher GPAs
than increasers, whereas drinkers had lower GPAs than decreasers.

These results suggest the existence of antecedent behavior
and self-concept differences among college students who develop different drinking patterns. Unlike previous predictive
studies, similar behavioral and self-concept variables differentiated not only abstainers who became drinkers from abstainers
who remained abstinent but also heavy drinkers who decreased
their consumption from those who remained heavy drinkers.
This pattern allows for more compelling causal inferences, since
variables hypothesized to influence drinking should be predictive for decreases as well as for increases in consumption
(Kandel, 1975).

The results show that three sets of personal characteristics are associated with student drinking patterns. First, alcohol use is related to a set of variables indicating a lack of commitment to conventional values: lower religious concern, lower
aspiration levels, less interest in academic achievement, and
greater likelihood of engaging in impulsive behavior. Greater
religiosity also is associated with less tolerance for deviant behavior, less incidence of deviant behavior, and less use of marijuana (Jessor, Jessor, and Finney, 1973). Religious beliefs are
especially influential in enhancing personal control among high
school and college students. The religious student is more resistant to all types of problem-prone or deviant behavior and
thus to both excessive drinking and marijuana use. Second, alcohol use takes place during such informal social activities as dating and partying, and students who describe themselves as more

sociable, extroverted, and dominant and who participate in these activities are more likely to begin drinking and to drink more heavily.

Third, students who drink more are less well integrated into the academic aspects of college life, are more likely to encounter stressful situations, and are more prone to experience the effects of stress, such as alienation, physical symptoms, and medication use. This relates to the notion that alcohol use can be an attempt to escape from anxiety or depression, to obtain substitute satisfaction (such as social cohesion instead of academic success), or to cope with a perceived or actual failure in attaining academic or social goals (Braucht and others, 1973; Jessor and Jessor, 1977). These three sets of factors are influenced by the social environment of the student's living group (see Chapter Five). This fact, together with the important role of peer group influences, and the large changes in alcohol consumption during the student's freshman year led us to attempt to specify social-environmental influences on drinking patterns.

Characterizing Living Groups with a High Risk for Drinking

Studies of peer influence suggest that student living groups may have considerable impact on the drinking practices of their members. Associations between peer context and youth drinking have been demonstrated in both cross-sectional and longitudinal studies. Alexander and Campbell (1967), for example, found that male adolescents were more likely to be drinkers when their friends drank than when they did not; that the more drinking friends an adolescent had, the more likely he was to drink frequently; and that the greater the number of drinking friends a nondrinker had, the more likely he was to experience peer pressure to drink.

Having friends who drink heavily is related to more drinking and problems associated with drinking for male and female college students (Orford, Waller, and Peto, 1974). Heavier use of alcohol by college students is also associated with perceptions of more favorable attitudes of friends and other students toward drug use. Similarly, Forslund and Gustafson (1970) reported that the strongest influence on high school seniors' decisions to drink is peer pressure, and a longitudinal study of drinking onset by Jessor and Jessor (1977) indicated that greater peer approval and modeling of drinking antedates the transition from abstainer to drinker for both males and females (see also Braucht and others, 1973).

With respect to college living units, Rogers (1958) found varying drinking frequencies in residence groups and inferred that different reference norms were operating. In the case of conflicting reference norms (for example, fraternity pledges who live in dormitories but who have contact with fraternity norms), drinking patterns approximated the norms with which the student was in closer contact (in this case, the dormitory). Among fraternity actives, 79 percent were drinkers; among fraternity pledges living in the fraternity, 61 percent; among fraternity pledges living in men's dorms, 56 percent; and among the men's dorm residents, 40 percent. Gusfield (1961) reported that 60 percent of fraternity members, compared with 32 percent of nonmembers, were high users of alcohol and that greater attachment to the fraternity culture, as evidenced by more close friends in the fraternity, was associated with heavier drinking.

Social Climates of High Drinking Living Groups. What kinds of social environments characterize high-drinking living groups? There are some indications that drinking patterns vary in different types of living groups. Men and women in single-sex units are more likely to drink on dates and at parties, whereas students in coed living units drink more at meals and in informal social gatherings, which often are organized around intellectual and cultural interests. Accordingly, we focused separately on eighteen men's, eighteen women's, and sixteen coed living groups. We computed correlations between the mean level of alcohol consumption and the six climate-type scores for all three kinds of units.

Quite different social environments were associated with drinking in single-sex and coed living groups. The men's and women's units where alcohol consumption was greater were high on relationship and traditional social orientation and low on independence. In contrast, coed social environments associated with drinking had a relatively high emphasis on independence and intellectuality and a lack of emphasis on academic achievement and traditional social orientation. We undertook an additional analysis (similar to the one described in Chapter Five for developing the symptom risk subscale) to specify further the social-environmental characteristics associated with alcohol consumption in single-sex and coed living units. The proportion of students answering true was calculated for each URES item for each living group. We then correlated each of the items with the living group's mean alcohol consumption score.

A set of fourteen URES items related highly and consistently to alcohol consumption in men's and women's units (see Appendix A for the specific items). The average correlations between these items and the mean level of student drinking were 0.59 and 0.45 in the men's and women's units, respectively. Examination of the items, all of which come from four URES subscales (traditional social orientation, order and organization, student influence, and innovation) indicated that the social milieus of high-drinking single-sex living units were characterized by frequent dating and parties, by clarity and specificity of house officer functions and financial policies, by reliance on staff rather than students for establishing and enforcing rules, and by a feeling of predictability about the house.

A separate, nonoverlapping set of fourteen items was related highly to alcohol consumption in the coed living units (see Appendix A). The average correlation of these items and student drinking was 0.53. All but one of the items come from the URES support, independence, academic achievement, and intellectuality subscales. The items indicated that the social climate of high-drinking coed units was relatively concerned with and supportive of the feelings of others, indifferent to social etiquette and opinion, unconcerned with dating and studying, and actively focused on creative pursuits and extracurricular intellectual and cultural matters.

Social-Environmental and Contextual Effects on Drinking. Since peer pressure to drink and belonging to high-drinking reference groups should lead to an increase in drinking, we focused next on the extent to which initial mean levels of drinking reported by students in a living group (an index of peer pressure to drink) and the six climate-type indexes were related to greater-than-expected increases in alcohol consumption. We investigated this issue by conducting correlation and regression analyses similar to those described in Chapter Five.

The initial aggregate level of alcohol consumption for the living group was related to greater-than-expected increases in individual drinking in both men's and women's, but not in coed, living groups. Students who enter single-sex living groups in which other students consume more alcohol increase their drinking beyond what would be expected from their initial drinking levels. This progressive conformity effect held for drinking levels of all three kinds of beverages; that is, greater-than-expected alcohol use was related to initial aggregate levels of consumption of wine, beer, and hard liquor in the men's and women's living groups. This shows a living group contextual effect in which average initial levels of drinking increase the likelihood of further increases in drinking during the year. With respect to social climate, there were greater-than-expected increases in alcohol consumption in relationship and traditionally socially oriented men's and women's houses and in supportive achievement oriented women's houses. However, none of the six social climate orientations were related to changes in drinking patterns in the coed houses. Thus, both the context and the social climate influence consumption in single-sex but not in coed living groups.

Understanding Student Drinking

We have identified four sets of factors related to student drinking: lack of commitment to conventional values, participation in informal social activities, indexes of stress (such as alienation and physical symptoms), and contextual (high aggregate drinking levels) and social-environmental (relationship and traditional social orientation) conditions in the living unit. Do each of these sets of factors influence drinking independently of the other three sets? For example, do living group climate and context conditions influence later drinking levels after initial drinking and the three sets of personal factors related to drinking have been accounted for? To answer these questions, we used correlation and regression analyses, in which composite indexes measuring each of the four sets of factors were used, in conjunction with high school (initial) levels of alcohol consumption to predict spring-term (final) alcohol consumption.

Each of the four sets of variables was predictive of later drinking levels (simple correlations), and all but the stress-related indexes had independent predictive effects on drinking (multiple-regression analyses). Stress is related not only to alcohol use but also to the other sets of variables, especially to lack of commitment to conventional values, and it does not have an effect independent of them. Separate analyses limited to initial abstainers showed similar results, supporting the expectation that the climate and context variables influence the onset as well as the level of alcohol use. The findings for the two sexes were comparable, although the effects of the environmental variables were stronger on women than on men (see Igra and Moos, 1978, for details).

Climate, Context, and Student Drinking. Previous studies of the relationship between college living groups and alcohol consumption have been limited primarily to comparisons between fraternity and nonfraternity drinking practices. Our work represents a step toward delineating the specific environmental conditions differentially associated with drinking patterns in student living groups. The social climate correlates of drinking in men's units are similar to those in women's units but differ from those in coed units. High-drinking single-sex living units have social environments similar to those that have traditionally characterized fraternities and sororities (involvement and cohesion, dating and partying, and clear rules and regulations). These living groups affect drinking and the personal characteristics related to drinking; that is, they enhance social participation and impulse expression and inhibit academic orientation and achievement levels. High-risk single-sex units thus influence student change in alcohol consumption and in two of the three sets of personal factors (all but stress-related indexes) related to increases in alcohol consumption.

The fact that women in achievement oriented settings increased their alcohol consumption more than expected is consistent with the notion that they are under greater stress in settings oriented toward academic performance, perhaps because of a belief that intellectual and academic success may lead to a loss of popularity and femininity (Horner, 1972). Women who deemphasize social activities and opt to compete academically may need some release from the traditional stress and thus increase their drinking. Alternatively, these women may consume more alcohol because they identify more strongly with the heavier-drinking masculine subculture on campus.

The milieus that relate most closely to alcohol consumption in coed units are characterized by relative nonconformity, that is, independence, indifference toward dating and studying, and greater concern for creativity, personal feelings, and extracurricular intellectual matters. However, coed living units did not enhance drinking beyond what was expected from students' initial drinking levels. The emphasis on independence and intellectuality in these settings may have neutralized one another, since our earlier results (see Chapter Five) indicated that independence oriented units enhance aspiration and achievement levels but inhibit social participation, whereas intellectuality oriented units have roughly the opposite effects. Students in coed units also show more tolerance for some types of individual differences and are unlikely to demand conformity in such personal characteristics as alcohol consumption.

We do not know the extent to which the quite dissimilar drinking-related social climates of single-sex and coed living units are attributable to sex composition as a mediating variable, to selection biases that may have led to average personality constellation differences, or to the fact that having both men and women in a living unit supports the establishment of different social environments and drinking habits. Housing men and women together probably influences the emergence of different drinking-related norms (less social pressure to drink and more freedom to be independent), which in turn are reinforced by the social-environmental characteristics of coed houses (less emphasis on dating and partying).

The evidence indicates that more homogeneous environments (such as living groups composed mostly of high-drinking students) have more uniform and consistent influences with fewer conflicting pressures and are more likely to affect student change. The pressure on abstainers or very light drinkers in homogeneous high-drinking settings is particularly strong, and as a result many of them conform to the majority. Homogeneous environments maintain and accentuate students' development in consonant areas. Incongruent students conform to the majority, and students who are initially in the majority further accentuate their attitudes and behavior in the areas reinforced by subgroup norms. In this way, the qualities students bring to a living group persist and become accentuated, provided they are shared by their peers in the unit. If students are in proximity to other students who drink, they are more likely to have friends who drink; thus, they are more likely to drink themselves, provided that the living unit is cohesive and that there is a demand for conformity in alcohol consumption. A heterogeneous unit (for example, a living group in which some students are abstainers, some are moderate drinkers, and some are heavy drinkers) has many more conflicting influences, providing each student with a wider choice of friends. Students have a better chance to find other students with similar attitudes and values, and the pressure to change is likely to be less consistent in such a setting.

Characterizing Environmental Resistors

Many students who do not wish to drink avoid settings where frequent drinking occurs by associating with abstaining or low-drinking friends, participating in religious activities, selecting living groups where drinking is likely to be infrequent, and so on. But what happens if such a student inadvertently selects or is placed into a setting where other students drink heavily? Most students under these conditions will conform to the press of the environment and increase their alcohol consumption, but some students will not. Studies of these "environmental resistors" and of their coping methods should be particularly informative. What personal characteristics are related to the lack of progressive conformity in alcohol consumption? What distinguishes men and women whose alcohol consumption level becomes more like that of other students in their living unit from those whose alcohol consumption level does not?

To investigate this issue, we categorized students who entered college as abstainers or mild drinkers into four groups. Students whose alcohol consumption levels were low in the fall and spring were categorized as abstainers. Those whose scores were low in the fall but high in the spring were categorized as increasers. We then examined the students' alcohol consumption levels in the context of the average alcohol consumption level of the other students in their living groups. We categorized men's units as "low risk" if the average alcohol consumption of their residents was below the median for the men's units in the fall and spring. We categorized units as "high risk" if they were above the median for their respective groups. Coed units were not used in these analyses, since they showed little or no press for conformity in alcohol consumption.

Four groups emerge when abstainers and increasers are analyzed in the context of the average alcohol consumption level in their living unit. We focus here on identifying the unique characteristics of environmentally resistant students, that is, abstainers in high-drinking settings. We compared these students with abstainers in low-risk settings and with drinking-prone students (increasers in low-risk settings) and conforming students (increasers in high-risk units).

As expected, abstainers in high-risk settings differed from the two groups of increasers on roughly the same sets of variables that distinguished abstainers from increasers in our earlier analyses. However, we found that the abstainers in high-risk settings (the environmental resistors) differed from the abstainers in low-risk settings on several personal functioning indexes and that the characteristics of the thirty male and twenty-nine female environmental resistors were somewhat different. The men who resisted the press of the environment (as compared to their abstaining counterparts in low-risk settings) described themselves as more extroverted, easygoing, intellectual, and interested in athletics at the beginning of their freshman year.

They were also higher on cultural orientation and religious interest and participated more actively in student body activities. These men had somewhat lower, more realistic expectations of the social environments of their living units. In the spring the environmentally resistant men again described themselves as more extroverted and easygoing and professed more interest in culture and religious concern. In addition, they had higher educational aspirations and were less likely to have used medical and personal counseling services.

The female environmental resistors described themselves as more extroverted and as higher in social participation in both the fall and spring of their freshman year. However, these women, in contrast to the environmentally resistant men, complained of more physical symptoms in the fall and reported engaging in more hostile interaction and impulse expression in the spring. They also had lower yearly GPAs than did their abstaining female counterparts in low-risk settings.

The environmentally resistant men resemble the moderate drinkers and differ from other abstainers and light drinkers in that they are integrated into the social aspects of college life. But they differ from the other two groups of men on three characteristics (religious concern, intellectual self-concept, and educational aspirations), which may give them the self-confidence to resist the pressure to increase their alcohol consumption. The environmentally resistant women participated in social activities but did not differ from women abstainers in low-risk settings on the other dimensions associated with resistance among men. The reasons why these women do not increase their drinking are unclear, but the fact that they show some problems in personal, social, and academic adjustment suggests that they are experiencing stress.

These findings are intriguing but must be viewed with caution due to the small number of students evaluated, the fact that we did not measure a broad range of personality characteristics, and the conceptual problems involved in defining resistance to environmental pressure. For example, since most students in college drink, both groups of abstainers are resisting the overall press of the environment, although there are stronger

pressures on the abstainers in high-risk living groups. Furthermore, the results for women focus more on the stress effects of
living in an incongruent setting (abstaining in a high-drinking
unit) than on the personal or environmental characteristics that
enable students to resist strong pressures to conform.

Following Brothers and Hatch (1971), we speculate that
the high cohesion, support, and organization in the women's
units, in combination with the lower emphasis on independence, create a demand for social conformity. Women seem to
depend on support from other women in their living unit,
whereas men are more absorbed in independent outside activities, such as academic and athletic pursuits, which help to insulate them from living group influences (Newcomb and others,
1967). Thus, such personal characteristics as a greater need for
affiliation and conformity and such social-environmental characteristics as more emphasis on cohesion and support combine
to make it more difficult and stressful for women to resist the
environmental influences that they themselves have created.

Sex Differences in Environmental Impact

Several of our findings suggest that women are more subject to environmental influences than men. Coed living units
have stronger effects on women than on men, especially with
respect to stress-related indexes (Chapter Five). Women who
resist environmental influence in alcohol consumption seem to
exhibit some stress-related consequences. In this respect, we
also found that the overall influence of the context and the
social climate in a living unit was stronger on women than on
men. Although the total predictable variance in spring-term
alcohol consumption was virtually identical for women (47 percent) and men (46 percent), the proportion of unique and
shared variance accounted for by living group factors (social
climate, contextual, and campus) was larger for women (14 percent) than for men (8 percent). About half of this variance was
related to the social climate of the living group, whereas the
other half was related to the aggregate initial level of student
drinking.

Residence hall environments may affect women more because the college setting represents a bigger change from the home environment for women than for men. High school girls usually are more sheltered and function less independently in their social and heterosexual activities than high school boys do. Women show greater increases in alcohol consumption during their first year in college than men, suggesting that college environments have more influence on those sex-related personal factors that undergo the most changes during the freshman year. Whatever the reason, the freshman-year living group can exert an important influence in shaping young women's social and academic behavior. Hearn (1978) followed many of these same students into their senior year and found that the environment of the major department had a stronger influence on the self-concepts, moods, and graduate school plans of women.

This evidence is consistent with other studies suggesting that women are more susceptible to environmental influences than men. McDill and Rigsby (1973) demonstrated that high school boys' college plans and academic achievement are influenced significantly by internal attributes (ability level and motivation), whereas high school girls' educational aspirations and outcomes are influenced more by external attributes (the constraints of socializing agencies, such as home and school). The effect of the father's education on college plans is stronger for girls than boys, probably because it is a measure of the home pressure to attend college and girls are more conforming to parental desires concerning higher education than boys (Alexander and Eckland, 1974). Our work on adult problem drinkers also supports these notions, in that more women than men alcoholic patients are married to heavy-drinking spouses, suggesting that drinking press within the family has a more profound influence on women than on men (Bromet and Moos, 1976).

Witkin and others (1977) described individual differences in cognitive styles that relate to the issue of sex differences in environmental impact and to the characteristics of individuals who resist environmental pressure. They distinguish between relatively "field independent" people, who are able to overcome the organization of a perceptual field or to restructure it, and relatively "field dependent" people, who tend to adhere to the way that a perceptual field is organized. These individual differences carry over into social and interpersonal areas.

Field dependent people are more likely to attend to and make use of prevailing social frames of reference. They look more at the faces of others, attend more to verbal messages with social content, and take greater account of external social referents in defining their attitudes and feelings, particularly under conditions of ambiguity. Field dependent people are better liked, tend to be seen as warm, tactful, and considerate, and are socially outgoing and affectionate.

Field independent people have a more impersonal and independent orientation. They are likely to be described as cold and distant, as individualistic and solitary, and as interested in abstract and theoretical issues. Field independent people experience their needs and feelings as being more distinct from the needs and feelings of others. According to Witkin and his colleagues, these independent needs and feelings provide internal frames of reference to which the field independent person can adhere in dealing with the social world. There are small but persistent sex differences in these indexes beginning in adolescence, with women tending to be more field dependent than men. This supports the idea that women are more likely to be influenced by the social environment and to conform to external social forces than men.

We need to identify other personal characteristics related to the ability to resist environmental pressure. For example, Lefcourt (1976) noted that an internal locus of control (the belief that one has control over the outcomes of one's activities) can help one to resist submitting to authority. When people believe that they are responsible for their own life fortunes, they are more likely to resist attempts to bypass their beliefs and values and are more discriminating about what external stimuli they will allow to influence them.

Feldman and Newcomb (1969) concluded that the impact of the college environment is greatest on those students who are open to change, concerned about social acceptance, and sensitive and responsive to the normative pressures of their college peer groups. However, a rather different perspective on this issue is afforded by the environmental docility hypothesis (Lawton and Nahemow, 1973), which proposes that less competent individuals, such as students who consume much alcohol and enter college with fewer academic or social skills, are more likely to be influenced by environmental characteristics. Some people may resist all environmental influences, and some environments may be powerful enough to influence almost everyone. But most people show a blend of conformity and resistance, and most environments influence some people but not others. In order to increase understanding of stability and change in student drinking patterns, a conceptual framework must be implemented that focuses on the reciprocal influences of personal and social factors when encountering environmental influence.

7

Social Environments of Secondary School Classes

Most educators believe that the classroom is an important locus for student personal and academic growth, and that it has a distinct atmosphere that mediates growth. Some recent developments have reinforced this notion, prompting increased interest in the classroom as a unit of study. For example, investigators who have focused on school systems have found only relatively small differences among schools in student achievement and other criteria. They have suggested that experiences within a school, such as contact with outstanding teachers and particular classes that create intensive individual interest, may have more influence than differences in overall school programs (Alexander and McDill, 1976; Peng, Bailey, and Ekland, 1977; Shea, 1976).

136

The variation of instructional patterns among classes in a school and between teachers using the same instructional materials also necessitates a focus on classroom differences. There are often large differences in how much each teacher talks and in the adequacy of coverage of specific topics among teachers who are presumably using the same teaching style. For example, there are four organizational patterns in team teaching (team leader type, associate type, master teaching-beginning teacher type, and coordinated team type), and each type can result in a different classroom environment, even though the same teaching technique is used. Furthermore, instructional methods such as team teaching often are not implemented properly, so that the classroom practices labeled team teaching and those labeled solitary-teacher teaching may hardly differ (Armstrong, 1977).

The influence of the classroom socioecological system on teacher behavior and student learning has recently become clearer. Copeland (1978) used an ecological perspective to analyze the relationship between the behavior of a regular classroom teacher and a student teacher's use of skills acquired during microteaching. A regular teacher's consistent use of a target skill (such as asking focused questions) causes that skill to become a functional part of the classroom's ecological system. The pupils become accustomed to the skill and develop appropriate responses to its use. When a student teacher attempts to use the skill in such a classroom, the attempt is ecologically congruent with the system, and the use of the skill is likely to be reinforced. When a student teacher attempts to use a skill in a class in which that skill is not part of the ecological system, its use is not appropriate, is not reinforced, and may produce aversive consequences. The use of a skill recently learned by a teacher or student may develop or decline, depending on the nature of the social-ecological system of the class in which it is used.

These ideas have led to the construction of methods for assessing the qualities of classrooms. A considerable amount of work has focused on developing detailed coding categories for teacher verbalizations and classroom activities as indicators of the learning environment (Van Horn, 1976; Wilson, Spelman, and Trew, 1976). Other approaches have used global observational scales and self-report or perceptual indexes to focus on the social-emotional climate, or atmosphere, of classes. Recently developed techniques include a Classroom Climate Inventory, composed of self-report items, peer nominations, and teacher judgments (Barclay, 1974), a Learning Structure Questionnaire to assess the learning environment on teacher-centered, class-centered, and self-directed dimensions (DiMarco, 1974), and a Learning Environment Inventory (LEI), which has been extensively used and related to such variables as class size, curriculum, and achievement (Anderson and Walberg, 1974).

The Classroom Environment Scale (CES), which was developed by Edison Trickett and me (Trickett and Moos, 1973), offers a somewhat different approach from the normative patterns emphasized in previous research. It focuses on the psychosocial environment of junior high and high school classes, and conceptualizes that environment as a dynamic social system that includes not only teacher behavior and teacher-student interaction but also student-student interaction. In addition, we used a conceptual framework to inform the selection, development, and organization of the dimensions to be evaluated. Previous work has lacked the guidance of theoretical or conceptual frameworks producing isolated findings that are difficult to organize into a coherent body of knowledge about classroom functioning.

Rather than relying on the ratings of outside observers, we defined the classroom environment in terms of the shared perceptions of the people in that environment. This has the dual advantage of characterizing the class through the eyes of the actual participants and of soliciting information about its long-standing attributes in a manner more parsimonious than observational methods. A phenomenological approach provides important data that the objective observer who counts cues or behaviors may miss (Walberg, 1976). For example, students often ignore frequently occurring stimuli and modify their actions in light of how they expect the teacher to behave. Teachers may be inconsistent in their day-to-day behavior, but they still usually project a consistent image and develop a coherent classroom environment. Furthermore, the "same" behaviors or stimuli used in different settings may lead students to different perceptions, attitudes, or behaviors.

Walberg (1976) also noted that certain kinds of social environments, as indexed by student and teacher perceptions, may be worthy goals in their own right, quite independently of how they relate to student achievement or other criteria. Students are a good source of information about a class, since they have encountered many different learning environments, are in a class for many hours, and have enough time to form accurate impressions of the classroom milieu. Because of the recent emphasis on accountability and on obtaining information about the preferences and reactions of consumers of instructional procedures (that is, students) the development of perceptually oriented measures of classroom environments is a high priority (McLaughlin, 1976; Stubbs and Delamont, 1976).

Developing the Classroom Environment Scale

In constructing the Classroom Environment Scale (CES), our basic strategy was to identify which aspects of the psychosocial environment of classrooms were salient to students and teachers. The conceptual framework embodied in our previous work and in the literature on educational and organizational psychology aided in delineating three sets of variables. Relationship variables included affective aspects of student-student and teacher-student interactions. System maintenance and change variables involved aspects of rules and regulations of the classroom and teaching innovations. Personal growth, or goal orientation, variables were conceptualized as relating to specific functions of the classroom environment. We designated the academic function of the classroom as a critical area and placed special emphasis on the "academic style" in classes.

Given this framework, we used several strategies to select initial dimensions for the CES. We reviewed prior research and literature for descriptions of classroom milieus. We observed classes in each of several high schools and conducted structured interviews with teachers and students. Interviews with students focused on their perceptions of the important aspects of classroom settings and on how their classes differed from one another. Interviews with faculty focused on their teaching styles and the kinds of classroom environments they tried to create.

We identified conceptual dimensions on the basis of these data and wrote questionnaire items we thought to be indicators of the dimensions. Consistent with our work in student living groups, the choice of items was guided by the general concept of environmental press. Each item had to identify aspects of an environment that either were characteristic of or could exert a press toward involvement, task orientation, innovation, and so forth. A press toward involvement is inferred from the following kinds of items: "Students put a lot of energy into what they do here" and "Most students in this class really pay attention to what the teacher is saying." A press toward task orientation is inferred from these items: "Almost all class time is spent on the lesson for the day" and "The teacher sticks to classwork and doesn't get sidetracked." A press toward innovation is inferred from these items: "The teacher thinks up unusual projects for the students to do" and "New ideas are always being tried out here."

The details of the development of the CES are given elsewhere (Moos and Trickett, 1974; Trickett and Moos, 1973). In brief, we used several criteria to select the final items and subscales for the 90-item Form R of the CES, which was derived from extensive analyses of three previous forms. We chose items that related highly to their own subscale (eighty of the ninety items had item-to-subscale correlations of 0.40 or above, and every item correlated more highly with its own subscale than with any other), that differentiated among classes, and that were not characteristic of extreme classes only. We also tried to include an equal number of true and false items on each subscale to control for acquiescence response set. Five of the subscales have an equal number of items scored true and false, three subscales have a six-four split, and one has a seven-three split.

Three Domains of Classroom Environments. Table 11 lists the nine CES Form R subscales and gives brief definitions of each. The involvement, affiliation, and teacher support sub-

Table 11. Brief CES Subscale Descriptions

Subscale	Description
Relationship Dimensions	
1. Involvement	Extent to which students are attentive and interested in class activities and participate in discussions.
2. Affiliation	Student friendship and the extent to which students help each other and enjoy working together.
3. Teacher support	Help, interest, trust, and friendship the teacher shows toward students.
Personal Growth or Goal Orientation Dimensions	
4. Task orientation	Importance of completing planned activities and sticking to the subject matter.
5. Competition	Emphasis placed on students competing with each other for grades and recognition, and the difficulty of achieving good grades.
System Maintenance and Change Dimensions	
6. Order and organization	Emphasis on students behaving in an orderly manner and on the organization of assignments and class activities.
7. Rule clarity	Emphasis on establishing and following a clear set of rules and on students knowing what the consequences will be if they do not follow them.
8 Teacher control	How strictly the teacher enforces rules and the severity of punishment for rule infractions.
9. Innovation	How much students contribute to planning class activities, and the number of unusual and varying activities planned by the teacher.

scales measure relationship dimensions. These dimensions assess the extent to which students become involved in the class, the extent to which students support and help one another, the amount of friendship and loyalty in the class, and how supportive teachers are of students. The task orientation and competition subscales assess personal growth, or goal orientation, dimensions. They measure the emphasis on two important, academic-style dimensions differentiating among classes. The next four subscales assess system maintenance and change dimensions. Order and organization, rule clarity, and teacher control are maintenance oriented since they relate to keeping the classroom functioning in an orderly, clear, and coherent manner. The final subscale, innovation, assesses the degree of variety, novelty, and change in the class milieu.

The Ideal and Expectations Forms. Like the URES, the CES has three forms: (1) a 90-item Form R (real form) to assess the actual classroom, (2) a 90-item Form I (ideal form) to assess teacher and student conceptions of an ideal classroom, and (3) a 90-item Form E (expectations form) to assess expectations about a new classroom. Students and teachers answer the same items. The CES Form R and its scoring key are given in Appendix B.

We developed Form I to measure goals and value orientations. What kinds of learning environments do teachers and students consider ideal? In what areas are their goals similar? In what areas are they different? To what extent do teachers, principals, administrators, school board members, and parents agree on the characteristics of ideal classes? We developed Form E to assess teachers' and students' expectations about a new class. This form makes it possible to focus on the accuracy of expectations and on the extent that expectations about classes become more realistic when information about them is provided. Form I and Form E are parallel to Form R; that is, each one of their 90 items corresponds to an item in Form R. The scoring keys for the three forms are identical. The Form I and Form E items and instructions are given in the CES Manual (Moos and Trickett, 1974).

The CES is used most often to assess teachers' and students' perceptions of their own classroom environment, but it can also be used to obtain observers' impressions of classroom functioning. Parents can fill out the CES on the basis of observations of their children's classes. Teachers can fill out the scale for other teachers' classes. The majority of CES items are observable and ratable during a class session, but raters feel more comfortable when completing the scale after sitting in on three to five class sessions.

CES Form R Normative Sample and Test Statistics

We have applied the CES to a sample of well over 500 junior and senior high school classes. We drew the classes from a wide range of schools, including middle-class suburban schools, medium-sized rural schools, small private schools, integrated inner-city alternative schools, inner-city black schools, and vocational schools. Schools were located primarily on the East and West coasts. Classes were sampled from over fifty public schools (both general and vocational) and eighteen private schools, and over 10,000 students and 500 teachers completed Form R. We usually sampled classes randomly within schools, but in some schools a few teachers preferred not to participate. In these cases we generally succeeded in securing a representative group of classes.

Subscale Internal Consistencies and Intercorrelations. Internal consistencies for the subscales were calculated using Kuder-Richardson Formula 20 and average within-classroom variances for the items, as suggested by Stern (1970). The subscale internal consistencies are all acceptable, ranging from 0.86 for teacher control and 0.85 for involvement to 0.67 for competition. The average item-to-subscale correlations are quite high for all nine subscales, and all nine significantly differentiate among classes.

The intercorrelations among the subscales average about 0.25, suggesting that the subscales measure distinct though somewhat related aspects of classroom environments. The three relationship dimensions show moderately high intercorrelations, indicating that they tend to fluctuate together, but even these correlations account for less than 25 percent of the subscale variance. Trickett and Wilkinson (in press) compared the pattern and magnitude of subscale interrelations obtained with the individual versus those obtained with the entire group (the classroom) as the unit of analysis. The correlations based on classes averaged somewhat higher than the individual-based results, but the pattern of relationships obtained in the two analyses was almost identical. (See Moos and Trickett, 1974, for the subscale means, standard deviations, and intercorrelations and for information on test-retest reliability and profile stability).

Factor Dimensions. In related work, Trickett and Quinlan (in press) factor-analyzed the CES items using a sample of 229 classes. They identified six factors, which were basically similar to six of the CES subscales, although some items from different subscales merged into one factor. The six factors assessed student affiliation, the friendliness and supportiveness of the teacher (teacher support), student competition, the emphasis on rules and clarity of expectations, the organizational aspect of class policies and procedures, and the focus on an innovative, student-oriented teaching approach. Although the involvement, task orientation, and teacher control subscales did not emerge as separate factors, the findings support the multidimensionality of the CES and indicate that the scale does not contain a general factor that cuts across various subscales.

Personal Characteristics and Perceptions of Classes. We used two sets of twenty-four classes each to focus on the extent to which students' personality characteristics were related to their perceptions of their classes. Regression analyses were conducted to estimate the proportion of the variance of the CES subscales related to the personality characteristics of internal-external control and exploration orientation. Students high in internal control and those high in exploration orientation showed a slight tendency to see their classes more positively, but this effect was small and accounted for an average of less than 2 percent of the subscale variance. Perceptions of classes did not differ by sex; that is, on the average, boys and girls saw their classes similarly. These findings are consistent with results we reported earlier (Moos and Trickett, 1974) and with the results of Nielsen (1977) and Paige (1978), who found little or no evidence of relationships between students' background and personality characteristics and their perceptions of classroom environments (see Chapter Twelve for further discussion).

Content and Concurrent Validity. What are the relationships between the perceived learning environment and other ways of assessing classroom settings, such as interviews and behavioral observations by outside observers? Classroom observations and interviews were conducted with teachers in thirty-eight classes, representatively sampled from two suburban schools serving similar student populations. Information was obtained over a one-month period on the number of hours of free class time and on the frequency with which student-suggested topics were discussed, students engaged in special projects, and students worked together in small groups. We also monitored the use of special materials and teaching aids (such as a slide or film projector, record player, or tape recorder) and of objectively identifiable methods of reward (announcing who did best on tests or assignments or displaying a student's work on the bulletin board) and punishment (students sent to the office, sending notes to parents, assigning extra work, or detention after school).

These indices were correlated with students' mean CES subscale scores from the thirty-eight classes. The most striking results were the very high relationships between teacher control and the frequency of specific rewards ($r = 0.63$) and punishments ($r = 0.74$). These two indices, which were closely related to each other, were higher in classes seen as competitive and clear about rules but lower in classes where the teacher was seen as supportive. Teachers who give specific rewards also tend to give specific punishments and to run highly structured classes. Students appear to perceive rewards of the type included in our assessment as a method of teacher control.

Most of the other relationships followed our predictions, although there were some surprises. Students who work in small groups see their classes as high in affiliation. Students have more free time and are more likely to initiate discussion topics and engage in special projects in classes high in innovation and low in task orientation and organization. The use of teaching aids was positively related to teacher control, as well as to competition and rule clarity. The control-oriented teachers apparently used rewards and punishments to develop structured classroom settings and used more structured teaching aids to try to engage students in the learning process.

We also obtained data on three related aspects of classroom policy that affected the physical characteristics of the classes: (1) the amount of open area (that is, the area not filled by desks, bookcases, and other furniture), (2) the type and flexibility of desk arrangement (such as in rows, in a large circle or square, or in small groups facing each other), and (3) the degree to which the use of space was structured (individual assignment of drawer and shelf space, bulletin board space, and the like).

As expected, open space, the flexibility of desk arrangement, and individual space allocation were more prevalent in classes high in innovation and involvement and low in task orientation, competition, and order and organization. Much more work is needed, but these results provide initial evidence on the validity of some of the CES subscales.

In a related study, Kaye, Trickett, and Quinlan (1976) used principals' nominations and student CES scores to select four types of classes: high control-high support, high control-low support, low control-high support, and low control-low support. Five tape-recorded sessions of each class were rated according to the Flanders (1967) system. The authors took the categories of "accepts feelings," "praises or encourages," "accepts or uses ideas of students," and "amount of student-talk initiation" to be indicators of teacher support, and the category "criticizes or justifies authority" to be an indicator of teacher control.

Teachers whose classes were high in CES teacher support more often praised or encouraged students and accepted or used student ideas. Teachers high in CES control praised or encouraged students less and had less initiation of talking by students in their classes. CES teacher control was not related to the use of authority statements, but authority-related interactions were infrequent (averaging about 2.5 percent of class time), suggesting that the intensity of these interactions may compensate for their lack of frequency: "It may take only a moment to expel a student from class, but that moment has an intensity and salience that leaves a clear and enduring impression on students" (Kaye, Trickett, and Quinlan, 1976, p. 375).

Kaye, Trickett, and Quinlan (1976) noted the desirability of using multiple methods to capture the qualities of classroom environments and of trying to tailor the methods used to the particular nature of the dimensions to be measured. For example, many of the ways in which teachers convey personal interest in students (such as meetings after class and impromptu conversations in the hall) are not directly observable in class but are indicative of support. The timing of observations is another important issue, due to changes in the salience of different environmental dimensions over time. Teacher support, involving trust and personal concern for students, tends to evolve slowly, since it takes time to establish supportive relationships in the school context, whereas the issue of teacher control is likely to be dealt with early in the life history of a class.

The problem of validating students' perceptions is complicated by the fact that there is a lack of stability in important clusters of teacher behaviors, such as teacher questioning, negative feedback, student-centered teaching style, interpersonal behavior, and indirect teacher control or classroom management (Shavelson and Dempsey-Atwood, 1976). Scott (1977) found that less structured class settings permitted greater freedom of expression of individual differences by teachers and that there was more variation in one teacher's behavior in different class subsettings (such as morning greeting and large-group activity) than between different teachers in the same subsettings. Furthermore, attraction for the teacher and the development of a particular kind of classroom environment is a function of the teacher's verbal and nonverbal behavior. These issues led Walberg (1976, p. 156) to question whether we should validate students' perceptions with observers' accounts of behaviors or validate observers' accounts of behaviors with students' perceptions, since perhaps "what is objectively counted or measured should be weighted and justified by what is subjectively perceived."

Comparing Students' and Teachers' Views of Classes

Research in other settings has indicated that role differences are related to perceptions of the environment. People who have more authority and responsibility in a setting tend to see the setting more positively. These findings suggested an overall comparison of students' and teachers' perceptions of classrooms. The results show that teachers generally perceive classroom environments more positively than their students do, although there are only small differences in several areas, most notably task orientation, competition, teacher control, and innovation (see Figure 11). The biggest differences are on involve-

Figure 11. Mean CES Form R Profiles for Students and Teachers

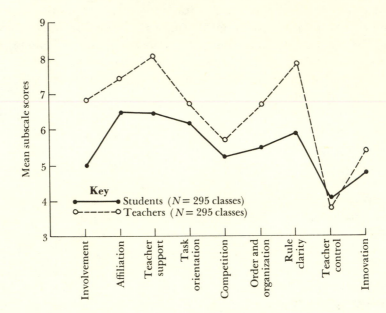

ment, teacher support, and rule clarity, with teachers perceiving much more emphasis on all three areas than students.

Notwithstanding these results, teachers and students tend to agree on the *relative* emphasis on various areas. For example, correlations between students' and teachers' CES subscale scores over classrooms averaged about 0.50, ranging from 0.65 for innovation and 0.57 for involvement to 0.44 for order and organization and 0.42 for competition (see Pond, 1973, for similar results on a sample of 100 classes).

We calculated CES profile similarity scores between teachers and students in each of our classes (these were rank-order correlations between teachers' and students' nine CES subscale scores). These scores measure the degree of agreement between students and teacher with respect to perceptions of the classroom social environment. The average student-teacher congruence was considerable (mean $r = 0.47$, SD = 0.34). Teacher-student agreement varied widely from class to class, from over

0.90 to essentially zero, the latter indicating a total lack of congruence with regard to the perceived class milieu. The degree of teacher-student agreement is one measure of the development of a coherent classroom culture.

Comparing Real and Ideal Classrooms

We have given the CES Form I to students in fifty and to teachers in forty-two classes. The subscale means and standard deviations are reported in Moos and Trickett (1974). Students and teachers tend to agree on the characteristics of ideal class settings. The main exceptions are that teachers want more emphasis on task orientation and rule clarity than students do. However, there is considerable variation among students and among teachers in their conception of ideal learning environments, particularly in the areas of task orientation, competition, order and organization, and teacher control. This variability supports what many educational practitioners feel: different students want and presumably need different types of classroom environments.

In a further analysis, we contrasted students' and teachers' perceptions of their actual and ideal class settings. There are some large real-ideal discrepancies; that is, students and teachers want much more emphasis on involvement, affiliation, teacher support, order and organization, and innovation than they have in their classes (see Figure 12 for the results for students). It may seem surprising that students want more emphasis on order and organization, but this is consistent with the finding that students are more satisfied in classes with more emphasis in this area (see Chapter Nine). In general, the real-ideal discrepancies for teachers are similar to those shown by students. The exceptions are that teachers want somewhat more task orientation and teacher control than exist in their classes, whereas students want somewhat less.

These results are illustrated by comparing the differences between the proportion of students who answered selected CES items true for their real classes and the proportion answering true for their ideal class. For example, over 90 percent of stu-

Figure 12. Student Perceptions of Real and Ideal Classroom Settings

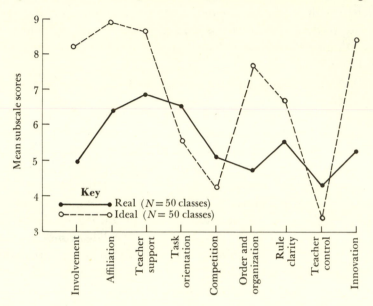

dents would like a teacher who focuses on what students want to talk about, whereas only 57 percent feel this is true of their actual teacher. Over 50 percent of students feel they have little to say about how class time is spent, whereas more than 85 percent want to help determine what happens in class. More than 60 percent of students feel that the teacher often has to tell students to calm down and that students fool around a lot in class and interrupt the teacher, whereas only about 20 percent want this to be true in their ideal learning environment.

Feldman (1976) noted that the dimensions associated most consistently with superior college teachers are stimulation of interest, clarity, preparation and organization, and enthusiasm for the subject matter. Such characteristics as friendliness, concern, and respect for students, helpfulness, and openness to their opinions are frequently mentioned when students freely describe their ideal or best teachers. However, when students respond to a preset list of variables, these descriptions are rated as less important, indicating that they are not necessarily the most salient characteristics of ideal teachers. Grush and Costin (1975, p. 65) also found that college students put a premium on classroom structure (organization and clarity of expectations), which, they noted, "should be reassuring to faculty members who might question the reasonableness of student judgments."

Students' values concerning preferred teaching styles vary according to their personal characteristics. Student-centered instruction is preferred by students who reject traditional sources of authority, have strong needs for demonstrating their personal independence, and have a desire for academic achievement. A student with authoritarian needs is likely to be unhappy in a student-centered class. Students' attitudes toward cooperation and competition are related to their preferences for different types of classroom settings. For example, students' competitiveness is positively related to wanting rules and wanting teachers to enforce rules, to keep students quiet, and to communicate clear goals and instructions (Johnson and Ahlgren, 1976). Students' preferences are also influenced by such factors as ability level, grade point average, and whether their dominant learning modality is auditory or visual (Barrall and Hill, 1977).

Student learning styles may be especially important in influencing classroom environment preferences. Kolb and Fry (1975) found that students who prefer different learning styles all may be satisfied with a particular class but for quite different reasons. Convergent thinkers generally preferred more order and structure and did not like open-ended peer discussions and group autonomy. Divergent thinkers reported open-ended unstructured homework papers and self-diagnostic activities to be helpful, and least preferred course requirements and peer interactions in class. Accommodators preferred a lack of structure, a high amount of peer interaction, and no authority figure, whereas assimilators were most dissatisfied with just these areas, but found activities requiring some conformity to directions or rules helpful.

The issue of student preferences in learning environments is important, since allowing students a choice of classroom setting may be an effective method of individualizing instruction.

However, one problem with this procedure is that students may prefer learning environments that are not sufficiently challenging. In this connection, Kolb and Fry (1975) distinguished between compensatory and preferential models of person-environment matching. If the goal involves acquisition or further specialization of knowledge or skills that require a particular learning style, then one would try to select or design environments to match the preferences of the learner. If, however, the goal is to integrate styles by acquiring less preferred or less dominant modes of thinking, then it is important to determine what factors are compensatory or needed to help acquire new ways of learning. For example, divergers who *prefer* open-ended, self-directed activities also report *needing* time limits and constraints. The distinction between what students like or want and what they need is critical to efforts to design "ideal" learning environments. To make matters more complex, students' notions about ideal learning environments change over time as they experience different classroom settings and their consequences. The types of learning environments considered ideal by students, teachers, parents, and others involved in the educational process must be focused on to clarify these issues.

Toward a Typology of Classroom Environments

The extensive differences we found among classes led us to develop a typology of their social environments. The need to develop a typology of classroom settings is apparent from research indicating that dimensions of classroom environments may interact with each other and affect students differently, and that the congruence between student and classroom characteristics accounts for some of the variance in student behavior and development (Hunt, 1975; Solomon and Kendall, 1976). We identified homogeneous groups or types of classes using the multivariate cluster analysis procedures by which the typology of student living groups was developed (see Chapter Three). We then analyzed a representative group of 200 classes drawn from the national sample. The range of subject matter, grade level, and type of school found in the normative group was represented in this sample.

The procedure developed by Carlson (1972) yields clusters that maximize the homogeneity within clusters (the social environments of classes in each cluster are similar to one another) and the heterogeneity between clusters (the social environments of classes in different clusters are different from one another). The Carlson method is agglomerative and hierarchical; that is, it begins with individual objects and successively combines and recombines them into larger and larger clusters. The number of clusters is not predetermined, and cluster membership does not overlap (see Bailey, 1974, for a description and classification of clustering techniques).

The analysis yielded nine clusters that accounted for 196 of the classes; four classes could not be located in any cluster. Later analyses indicated that the unstructured affiliation cluster ($N = 6$) was highly related to the innovation oriented cluster, and that the structured task ($N = 8$) and structured competition ($N = 14$) oriented clusters were highly related to the control oriented cluster. These three clusters were thus dropped from the present analysis. The original unstructured task oriented cluster was renamed supportive task oriented to reflect its characteristics more accurately (see Moos, 1978b, for methodological details and descriptions of the original clusters). These changes resulted in six clusters of classes: innovation oriented, structured relationship oriented, supportive task oriented, supportive competition oriented, unstructured competition oriented, and control oriented.

Cluster One: Innovation Oriented. The average student standard score profile for the first cluster, labeled innovation oriented, is shown in Figure 13. The forty-four classes in this cluster showed above average emphasis on innovation and on all three relationship dimensions, indicating that students perceive moderate to substantial emphasis on teacher-student and student-student interaction and on variety and change in the classroom. They see relatively little task orientation and complain of a lack of clarity in classroom goals and procedures. They also perceive relatively low levels of teacher control.

Cluster Two: Structured Relationship Oriented. The twenty classes in the structured relationship oriented cluster emphasize student interaction and participation and are rela-

Figure 13. Mean CES Form R Profiles for Innovation Oriented and
Structured Relationship Oriented Clusters

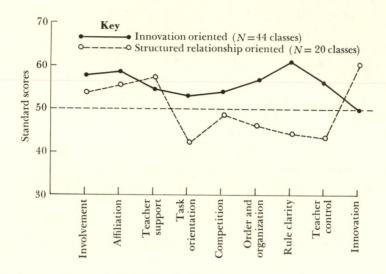

tively high in student interest and involvement and in teacher support (see Figure 13). These classes also emphasize organization, clarity of rules and procedures, and the number and extent of rules governing student conduct.

Cluster Three: Supportive Task Oriented. The thirty-nine classes in the supportive task oriented cluster are characterized by their emphasis on the accomplishment of specific academic objectives (see Figure 14). This type of class stresses teacher support and organization, but lacks emphasis on the maintenance dimensions of rule clarity and teacher control. The results indicate that task orientation may often occur in a basically supportive but somewhat unstructured classroom setting. These classes have little emphasis on student participation and interaction or on innovation.

Cluster Four: Supportive Competition Oriented. The eleven classes in the supportive competition oriented cluster

Figure 14. Mean CES Form R Profiles for Supportive Task Oriented and Supportive Competition Oriented Clusters

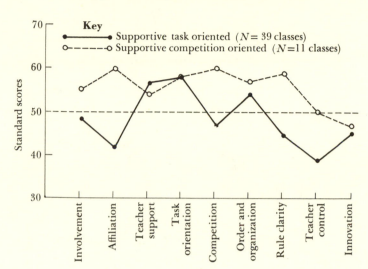

stress competition but in a context where students feel friendly toward each other, help each other with homework, and enjoy working together (see Figure 14). These classes emphasize organization and clarity, but deemphasize teacher control. They are similar to the structured relationship oriented cluster except that they are higher on task orientation and competition and lower on teacher control.

Cluster Five: Unstructured Competition Oriented. Although the seven classes in the unstructured competition oriented type are high on task orientation and competition, they are average or below average on all three relationship dimensions, as well as on organization, clarity, control, and innovation (see Figure 15). These classes occur infrequently and are unique in that they emphasize goal orientation and deemphasize everything else.

Cluster Six: Control Oriented. The sixth and largest clus-

Figure 15. Mean CES Form R Profiles for Unstructured Competition
Oriented and Control Oriented Clusters

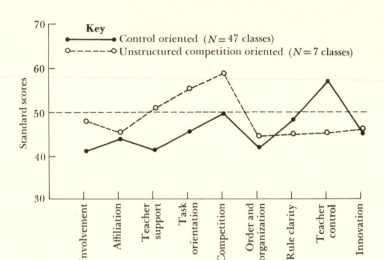

ter, composed of forty-seven classes, is labeled control oriented.
The striking feature of these classes is the high teacher control
without any emphasis on the other dimensions of classroom environments (see Figure 15). Students feel that these classes lack
supportive teacher-student and student-student relationships,
and they perceive little stress on task orientation or classroom
organization.

Utility of Conceptualizing Types of Classes. The cluster
solution makes good conceptual and empirical sense. The first
two groups of classes emphasize involvement and student-
student and teacher-student relationships. One of these groups
is relatively unstructured and stresses openness and change,
whereas the other is relatively structured because of the considerable focus on clarity and organization. The second two groups
emphasize different aspects of classroom goal orientation within
a generally cohesive framework focused primarily on teacher

support. The last two groups are similar in that they both lack emphasis on the relationship areas. One of the clusters stresses goal orientation (primarily competition), but does so within a framework lacking both cohesion and structure. The final cluster, control oriented, primarily emphasizes stability and organization.

The identification of forty-seven classes (over 23 percent) oriented almost exclusively toward teacher control of student behavior is striking. The most salient characteristics of these classes are strict rules for student behavior that are determined by the teacher. Since control of behavior is emphasized to the virtual exclusion of substantive learning, these classes may be appropriate targets for change and for understanding why teachers use less effective teaching strategies.

Solomon and Kendall (in press) developed a conceptually similar typology from cluster analysis of a 249-item observational instrument. They identified six types of classes (two formal, two mixed, and two informal), which are roughly similar to the six types just described. One type of formal classroom was highly controlled, orderly, cold, and impersonal (control oriented), whereas the other was cold and unfriendly but moderately permissive and oriented toward academic participation (unstructured competition oriented). One type of mixed class was fairly high on structure and warmth and moderate on academic emphasis (structured relationship oriented), whereas the other was high on academic emphasis and moderate on both warmth and structure (supportive task or supportive competition oriented). Both types of informal classes were warm, friendly, innovative, and lacking in task orientation (innovation oriented), but one type was much lower in order and control than the other.

Bennett (1976) offered a typology of classroom management styles, consisting of fourteen types of classes, most of which he placed along a formal-informal style dimension. His formal classes are somewhat more maintenance and control oriented, whereas the informal classes are somewhat more relationship oriented. These typologies all indicate that the relative emphasis on personal relationships and system structure is especially important in discriminating among classroom social environments.

The results have implications for school and classroom impact research, for comparisons between open and traditional instruction, and for the identification of consistent aptitude-treatment interactions. There are several relevant dimensions of classrooms, and these dimensions may interact with and mediate each other's potential effects. The relationship between task orientation or competition and learning outcomes may vary among studies because other relevant variables, such as affiliation and teacher support, also vary. Generally, competitive classes can have negative effects on students' self-esteem and continuing motivation (Johnson and Johnson, 1974; Maehr, 1976), unless they emphasize affiliation and support. Focusing on types of classroom environments can help future researchers to take these interactions into account.

One advantage of a typology is that it allows investigators to select classes to study with some assurance that they are distinctive and represent important and reasonably representative types. Attempts to replicate studies on different samples of classes may be unsuccessful partly because of differences in the social environments of the classes studied. Findings obtained using mainly innovation or structured relationship oriented classes may or may not generalize to task oriented or control oriented classes. The six classroom types provide information on the range of environmental variation within which replications of specific findings can be expected to occur.

8

Architectural, Organizational, and Contextual Influences on Classroom Learning Environments

We need a unifying conceptual framework to focus on the determinants of classroom social environments. Researchers generally consider the important sets of variables, such as physical

Note: This chapter is coauthored by Edison Trickett.

and architectural, organizational, aggregate student and teacher characteristics, separately. This makes the results of prior studies difficult to interpret. For example, alternative and traditional schools have different social environments, but these differences may be due to architectural characteristics (alternative schools are more likely to have open plan classes), organizational characteristics such as class size (open school classes are often smaller than traditional classes), aggregate student characteristics (students in open schools may be more oriented toward internal control and may need less structure), or teacher characteristics (teachers in open schools tend to be younger, more enthusiastic, and more innovative). In order to deepen our understanding of the factors that affect program implementation and generalization, we must understand to what extent a new educational program has unique effects on classroom environments and to what extent its effects are shared with other sets of indexes.

We have developed a conceptual model to focus on the interrelationships among five sets of classroom characteristics and on their relationship to classroom social climate (see Figure 16). The model suggests that the overall context (this includes type of school, educational program, and class subject matter) can affect social climate directly (alternative schools have different classroom social environments than traditional or vocational schools), or indirectly through its effect on architectural characteristics (the open plan classes in alternative schools facilitate innovative social environments), organizational characteristics (alternative schools tend to have smaller classes that are more cohesive), teacher characteristics (vocational schools have more men teachers who establish more structured classes), and aggregate student factors (artistic classes have more interpersonally oriented students who develop more cohesive classes).

Architectural characteristics can affect social climate directly (classes with movable walls facilitate innovation), or indirectly through their effect on organizational characteristics (open plan classes facilitate team teaching, which may lead to higher teacher support), teacher characteristics (interpersonally oriented teachers are more likely to select open plan classes and

Figure 16. A Model of the Determinants of Classroom Climate

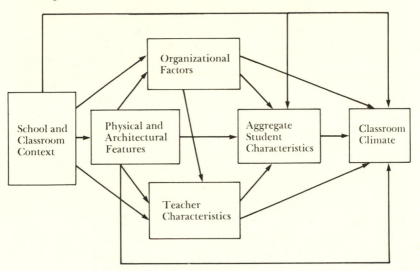

to establish supportive climates), and student characteristics (students who need less personal space and a less structured physical milieu may select open plan classes and facilitate the creation of innovative learning environments).

Organizational characteristics can affect social climate directly (small classes tend to be more cohesive), and indirectly through their effect on teacher and student characteristics (classes at higher grade levels may have more exploration oriented students who are less likely to develop control oriented classes). Teacher characteristics can affect the class social climate directly (women teachers tend to establish more cohesive environments), and indirectly through their influence on aggregate student characteristics (women teachers are more likely to be selected by female students, who tend to establish relationship oriented classes). Aggregate student variables can also influence social climate directly. For example, female students tend to develop somewhat more cohesive and less structured social environments than male students do.

This framework presents a simplified model of the interrelationships among these five sets of classroom characteristics and of their relationship to the overall institutional context. The model is simplified because a unidirectional causal flow is depicted, even though the sets of factors influence each other. For example, the social climate of a class can affect the type of students who select the setting (parents may wish their children to attend structured rather than innovative classes), the physical characteristics (students in innovative settings may decide to remodel their classrooms), the organizational structure (cohesive social climates may influence teachers to develop smaller classes), teacher characteristics (experiencing a control oriented setting may change a teacher's attitude or philosophy of teaching), and the overall context (students and teachers in innovation oriented classes may initiate new teaching programs). In the following sections we develop this model by focusing on how the type of school and subject matter affect social climate and by presenting an analysis of how four of the five sets of factors just described can influence the social climate of a class.

Five Types of Public Schools

Different social environments seem to emerge in schools with contrasting demographic and ecological characteristics. For example, the nostalgic recall of the intimacy of the one-room schoolhouse and the blooming, buzzing urban confusion of *Up the Down Staircase* (Kaufman, 1964) are two evocative portraits of how student life can differ. Coleman (1961) found normative differences in "value climate" among eleven Illinois high schools. From this finding Coleman inferred that it takes different personal qualities to emerge as a leader in different schools, because students value different qualities in their peers. Such ecological variables as size (Anderson and Walberg, 1972; Barker and Gump, 1964), socioeconomic and ethnic composition (Brookover and others, 1978; McDill and Rigsby, 1973), and turnover rate (Kelly and others, 1978) can also influence student experience.

These studies provide some direction and a rationale for regarding the school as an important socialization setting, but they do not address the issue of normative differences in contrasting types of schools. We focus on this issue here by comparing classes from five types of public schools: urban, suburban, rural, vocational, and alternative. While the average classroom of a school does not capture the rich environmental press of the school as a whole, it does reflect the broader culture of the school itself.

The analysis is based on data obtained from a representative sample of high schools in Connecticut. The sample is composed of 409 classes with over 6,000 students in 30 public high schools. Of these classes, 123 were in urban, 46 in suburban, 99 in rural, 99 in vocational, and 42 in alternative high schools. The alternative schools were "schools without walls" serving urban populations. An urban area had a population of at least 100,000; a suburban area consisted of a town directly adjacent to cities of 100,000 or more or a part of a string of communities extending from a metropolitan area; and a rural area was a small autonomous town far from any urban center.

Multivariate analysis of variance of the nine CES dimensions by the five types of schools was conducted with the school as the unit of analysis. The pattern of scores among the nine CES dimensions differed according to type of school. To understand the differences more precisely, classrooms were grouped by type of school, and nine one-way analyses of variance were conducted (one for each of the nine CES dimensions), all of which differentiated among the five types of schools (see Trickett, 1978, for methodological details and CES profiles of the five types of schools).

The most distinct types of classes were located in the alternative schools. True to their underlying ideologies, alternative school classes were highest on involvement, affiliation, and teacher support, indicating that they stress interpersonal relationships. These schools concentrate on the socialization of interpersonal values and the qualitative aspects of relationships. Contrary to popular stereotypes, alternative school classes were generally well organized (they were the highest on order and organization and were above the mean of the normative sample on clarity) and task oriented, although they reflected an anti-authoritarian (they were lowest on teacher control) and anticompetitive quality consistent with the emphasis on personal rather than role-related relationships. Alternative school classes also were the highest on innovation in teaching practices, which may relate to the increased participation of students in governance and in shaping their own educational experiences. These classes were like the innovation oriented type described earlier (see Figure 13 in Chapter Seven), although they were somewhat higher in task orientation, organization, and clarity.

These results are consistent with previous studies of alternative and open schools (see, for example, Ellison and Trickett, 1978; Walberg and Thomas, 1972). Epstein and McPartland (1975) showed that openness of instructional program had a positive impact on students' perceptions of the quality of student-teacher relationships. They noted that open schools involve a basic change in the school authority structure, in that students assume new responsibilities in monitoring their classroom behavior and academic progress, in selecting their assignments, and so forth. However, students in open and traditional schools were about equally committed to school, which the authors attribute to the fact that open schools do not change the formal rewards for performance in classwork.

Vocational schools presented a quite different picture. They were the lowest in teacher support and innovation and the highest in competition, the clarity of rules, and the exercise of strict teacher authority. The vocational school classes have a rather businesslike, hierarchical, "teacher-as-expert" environment, consistent with the aim of imparting clearly defined skills to students. One surprising finding, not totally consistent with this portrait of the vocational school, was the slightly below average emphasis on task orientation. This suggests that while student-teacher relationships are constrained by role-related rules and regulations, the classes per se are not particularly effective in sticking to classwork. The vocational school classes most closely resembled the unstructured competition and control oriented classes described earlier (see Figure 15 in Chapter Seven).

Alternative and vocational schools have distinct institutional missions. Alternative schools have arisen in reaction to perceived inadequacies in public schools, including the emphasis on rules and discipline, competition in academic matters, and the impersonality of the larger school. The results confirm that alternative schools reflect this ideological difference from regular public schools. Furthermore, alternative and vocational schools are the only ones that students choose to attend. The differences in institutional mission cause different kinds of students and teachers to select the two types of schools, who in turn influence the classroom social environments.

Rural, suburban, and urban school classes differed from each other, but not as sharply as the alternative and vocational schools. Suburban school classes, consistent with popular images, emphasized supportive teacher-student relationships, though not as much as alternative school classes did. They also stressed order and organization, but fell below the norm on competition and were far below the level of competition reported in vocational schools. Urban schools provided the most blatant conflict with popular wisdom, scoring highest on task orientation and higher than all except alternative schools on classroom involvement. Rural schools scored close to the mean of the normative sample on all nine dimensions. Young adolescents in urban, suburban, and rural schools create and need to cope with varying challenges in their classroom settings, but the overall contrasts among these three types of schools may be less salient than the differences between classes within each type.

Women's and Coed Private Schools

While public high schools serve the largest and most heterogeneous group of youth, private schools play a significant role in American education. Little systematic research has been done on these schools, but one recent study investigated how young women experienced and were affected by attending single-sex and coed private schools. The sample of fifteen schools (seven women's and eight coed) was chosen to be representative of American independent boarding schools. Students in seventy-eight classrooms (thirty-five from women's and forty-three from coed schools) selected from these fifteen schools completed the CES. These classes were representatively drawn from the subject areas of English, math, science, social studies, and history (see Trickett, Pendry, and Trickett, 1976, for information on sampling). Figure 17 compares the classes in the women's and coed schools with each other and with the normative sample of public school classes.

Figure 17. Mean CES Form R Profiles for Women's Single-Sex and Coed Classes

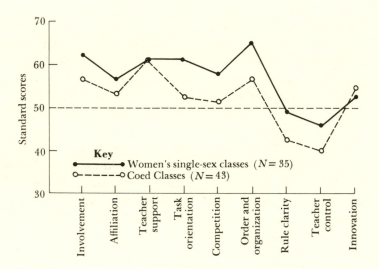

Private school students perceived higher involvement, greater affiliation with fellow students, more support from their teachers, and more order and organization in their classes. Private school classes were also seen as more task oriented and competitive, but they were lower than public school classes in rule clarity and teacher control. Compared with public school classes, private school classes place more emphasis on interpersonal relationships and less on rules and regulations governing classroom life.

Young women in single-sex schools reported more involvement in their classes, greater affiliation among students, and more emphasis on task orientation, competition, and organization. Rule clarity and teacher control were also higher in the young women's classes, but both sets of private school classes were below the mean of the normative sample on these two dimensions. Classes in the two types of schools were similar in innovative teaching practices and the degree of personal support given students by teachers. Other data showed young women in single-sex schools to be oriented more toward academic values and more involved in school activities (for example, they were more likely to select math or science as their favorite subject and reported spending more time on homework). The idea that single-sex schools may provide young women with richer opportunities for both academic and social development is consistent with our finding that college women in women's living groups show higher aspirations and less evidence of stress than women in coed units (see Chapter Five).

The results produce different portraits of single-sex and coed schools. Young women's single-sex classes are more academic than coed classes, which are more easygoing and unstructured. These differences should be viewed in the context of the broader picture provided by the public schools. That is, while single-sex classes are higher in clarity and strictness of rules than coed classes, they are still lower than public schools in this area. Likewise, while coed school classes show less affiliation among students than single-sex school classes, they are still above the public school norms. Comparisons of the classroom environments of the two types of private schools take on added contextual meaning when contrasted with the public school norms.

A Social-Ecological Conception of Adolescent Socialization

Portraits of classes found in different types of schools are relevant to theoretical issues in adolescent development, since they allow the reasonable inference that adolescents undergoing these various "treatments" have different socialization experiences and consequently different socialization outcomes. Multidimensional perspectives of environments make it possible to assess how specific aspects of a class relate to such outcomes as achievement, self-esteem, and interpersonal values. For example, Clinchy, Lief, and Young (1977) concluded that the social environments of progressive schools facilitated students' moral development by providing them with opportunities for cognitive conflict, taking other people's perspectives into account, and actively participating in a democratic community (see also Tjosvold, 1978).

One way to conceive of adolescence from a social-ecological perspective is to map out the normative properties of socialization settings. These include such pressures as those to dress, act, and think in certain ways, expectations about the nature of interpersonal relationships, and the valued and nonvalued goals of various groups. The norms of classroom environments in different types of schools mediate the socialization experience of students. Their specification is a step toward understanding how schools affect individual development. We have used the type of school as an organizing concept, but two or more schools of the same type can be studied in the same way.

Creating normative portraits of schools helps to focus on such issues as how teachers cope with individual differences in students, given the larger environmental context in which both must function. In a school with strict discipline and high surveillance by the principal, teachers may feel constrained to respond harshly to students who are misbehaving in class. They may be less likely to view student behavior as motivated by unique personal characteristics than are teachers whose school setting promotes an understanding and individualized handling of classroom disruptions. The importance of reference groups, such as teachers and students, can also be mediated by differences in normative structures of contrasting types of schools.

For example, perceived similarity to various reference groups is related to satisfaction with them. Students who see themselves as similar to their peers are more satisfied with them, whereas students who see themselves as more similar to teachers are more satisfied with their teachers. Ellison and Trickett (1978) speculated that this relationship might be mediated by the salience of the particular reference group involved. Where reference groups are influential, perceived similarity should be related to satisfaction with the group; where reference groups are not influential, the relationship between perceived similarity and satisfaction should be reduced in magnitude. Alternative and traditional schools provide a natural laboratory for assessing perceived self-environment similarity and satisfaction, because the relevant reference groups—other students, teachers, and the administration—play quite different roles.

Traditional schools emphasize the leadership of administrators and teachers. Students are usually not involved in decision making and select their educational curriculum from a prescribed set of courses. In alternative schools, students have more freedom to create their own education, to influence policy, and to promote student influence. In terms of the mediating concept of salience, students in alternative schools are more likely to determine each other's experiences than are students in traditional schools, since, for example, affiliation is higher in alternative school classes. Similarly, teachers and administrators in alternative schools are less salient than their counterparts in traditional schools.

Consistent with these expectations, Ellison and Trickett (1978) found that perceived similarity between self and other students was a better predictor of satisfaction in alternative schools, whereas perceived similarity between self and teachers or administrators was a better predictor in traditional schools. These findings underscore the importance of the formal structure of school settings as mediators of the relationship between individuals and reference groups, and they illustrate that the social-ecological context of high schools enriches our understanding of adolescent socialization.

Subject Matter and Classroom Climate

Many studies have related classroom subject matter to classroom climate (Anderson, 1971; Randhawa and Michayluk, 1975; Yamamoto, Thomas, and Karns, 1969), but because the research lacks a conceptual model, it has been limited to a descriptive focus. At present we do not know why classroom differences emerge as they do: Why, for example, do French classes have climates more similar to English and history than to mathematics classes? Proposing and testing conceptual models for subject-based variations in classroom climates can increase understanding of the empirically observed patterns of association.

One basis for such inquiry is Holland's (1973) conceptualization of personalities and environments. While the Holland scheme has been used in occupational contexts, educational settings such as student living groups, and academic departments (Smart, 1976), it must be extended substantively to apply it to high school classes. Holland proposes that people's vocational choices are expressions of their personalities and that occupations can be categorized into six groups, each group representing a different personality type. He describes six types of environments corresponding to the six personality types. For example, realistic environments encourage people to engage in manual activities, reward people for valuing such things as power and material possessions, and reinforce such personality traits as thriftiness and conformity (see Chapter Four for more detail on the six Holland types).

Class subject matter and vocational choice are only loosely analogous, but Holland's paradigm may nevertheless be applicable to high school classes. First, the subject matter itself may be related to climate. For example, mechanics classes may involve and encourage a fondness for dealing with material things and an absence of personal involvement with others. Second, according to Holland's research on personalities in various occupations, secondary school teachers are primarily oriented vocationally to their subjects, not to the general role of teacher. In this respect, we would expect a chemistry teacher to be primarily an investigative type, to use the leadership style of the investigative personality, and to set an appropriately investigative press and climate in the class, while a music teacher would primarily be an artistic type who creates an artistic classroom environment. Third, the students might tend in the aggregate toward the expected Holland orientation for the class, since they have some choice in the classes they take, and they may be malleable enough in their vocational and personality orientations to adopt the expected social style for the subject matter.

Characterizing Different Holland-Type Classes. To address these issues, we conducted an analysis involving students in 241 classes from twenty-three urban and suburban high schools included in the normative sample. Eight of the schools were vocational-technical and fifteen were general. The average class size was twenty-one students. Most classes included male and female students, although there were a few all-male and all-female classes. The classes were assigned to five of the six Holland types (realistic, investigative, artistic, social, and conventional) on the basis of agreement between two judges, who were informed by practice in previous inquiry at the college level (Smart and McLaughlin, 1974). No classes at the high school level were considered enterprising, since this ambitious orientation is manifested more in the college and occupational world. High school political science courses are considered social due to their informational social science slant.

Each of the 241 classes received a score indexing how closely it matched the model social environment of each of the six types of classes identified earlier (see Figures 13, 14, and 15 in Chapter Seven). We used a profile correlation (N = 9 CES subscales) to measure the similarity between the student-perceived social environment of each class and the modal social environment of each of the six types. This analysis, which followed the procedures used with student living groups, resulted in six climate-type scores indexing how close each of the classes was to the six types: innovation oriented, structured relationship oriented, supportive task oriented, supportive competition oriented, unstructured competition oriented, and control oriented. In subsequent analyses, we used these six climate-type scores to discriminate among the five Holland-type classes.

We found that investigative (mathematics and physical sciences) and conventional (business and typing) classes were more structured and relationship oriented than social (social science) and artistic (music, literature, and art) classes. The former two sets of classes provide a supportive climate with clear coherent rules and regulations but low teacher-dictated innovation (see the structured relationship oriented profile in Figure 13 in Chapter Seven). This emphasis on rule clarity in investigative and conventional classes is consistent with Holland's theory, but the relatively high student relationship emphasis in these classes seems to contradict the model. However, the lack of emphasis on rule orientation in social and artistic classes was as expected (see Hearn and Moos, 1978, for CES subscale means of each of the five Holland-type classes).

Realistic classes (electronics and mechanics) had a high emphasis on teacher control, which fits Holland's model, but they also had a moderately high relationship orientation, which was not forecast. One explanation might be that these realistic classes are run by especially committed teachers who "are what they teach." For example, auto mechanics teachers might be considered by themselves and by others as primarily mechanics, but English teachers might be more strongly identified as teachers. Thus, more than other teachers, the realistics may transmit to their students the attractions and challenges of their field, which may help them to create a warm and clear social climate that is high in structure but high in cohesion as well. This interpretation is supported by the fact that most of the realistic classes were in vocational schools, since teachers in these schools are more likely to be practitioners in their fields than are teachers of realistic classes in academically oriented high schools.

The social classes also presented some surprises from the perspective of Holland's theory. While predictably high on innovation and low on competition and teacher control, these classes were unexpectedly low on involvement and affiliation. The subject matter of these classes, which is largely history, economics, and government-related areas, may be dry and uninvolving to most students. Social studies often emphasize facts, dates, legal structure, and so forth, and thus may involve limited interaction. Also, perhaps the teachers themselves do not encourage or are not capable of promoting involvement of the students with each other, with their instructors, or with the subject. These speculations are supported by work on middle school-age children (Yamamoto, Thomas, and Karns, 1969) and on college social science classes, which are low in teacher-student involvement, have frequent teacher-student arguments, and often are seen as dull (Astin, 1965).

Some of the differences between our results and expectations from Holland's theory may reflect the fact that the subject matter or occupational task determines the climate more directly than Holland suggests. He sees the relationship as being mediated through personalities who choose a setting and play an important role in the type of climate that develops. For example, artists do not like to work the way engineers and bankers do. However, people can adapt their work and social types to different work situations. This might explain why conventional and realistic classes are not particularly nonsocial: lack of fraternizing is a characteristic related only to the occupational tasks involved (one cannot talk while typing) but not to the people themselves or to the social setting of the high school classroom.

Using Holland-based characterizations, educational administrators may be able to understand the diversity of their teaching staff better (Smart and McLaughlin, 1974). For example, Holland's model would propose that the realistic type is more likely to employ pragmatic and nonsocial influences, while the social type is more likely to be sensitive to social, interpersonal, and humanitarian influences. Using the typology in high school settings may clarify some of the conflicts between students, teachers, and administrators, and may assist those who fit into different Holland-type orientations to adapt to each other's personal styles.

Determinants of Classroom Climate

We follow our conceptual framework here by focusing on three additional sets of class-related characteristics: organizational variables, aggregate student characteristics, and teacher characteristics (see Figure 16). We first present simple correlations between indexes of these three domains and class social environments. We then employ multiple-regression analyses to identify the proportion of unique and shared variance in student perceptions of learning environments accounted for by these three sets of variables, as well as by school type and class subject matter. The sample was composed of the same 241 classes used in the class subject matter analysis.

The additional sets of class-related characteristics consisted of the following variables. There were two organizational characteristics: (1) *Class Size* (mean = 20.5). The class size was somewhat lower than average because vocational and alternative school classes were included. (2) *Grade Level* (mean = 10.5). The classes were approximately evenly distributed from the ninth through the twelfth grades.

A set of three aggregate student characteristics was used: (1) *Percent Female* (mean = 34.5). The average proportion of girls was low because the vocational school classes were composed primarily of boys. (2) *Internal Control.* This is a score derived from the Rotter Internal-External (IE) Control Scale (Lefcourt, 1976). In essence, the IE control scale measures the extent to which students feel they have personal control over what happens to them (internal control) versus the extent to which they think that external factors, such as luck and chance, determine their fate (external control). (3) *Social Exploration.* This is a score derived from the Edwards-Kelly Social Exploration Scale (Kelly and others, 1978), which measures the degree to which students are willing to explore, to take part in a variety of activities, and to be change agents in their environment.

Data were obtained on a set of nine teacher characteristics: (1) *Sex.* The proportion of women was low (29.7 percent) because the vocational school classes were taught primarily by men. (2) *Years of Teaching Experience* (mean = 9.1 years). (3) *Teacher Task Orientation.* This is a score derived from the Bass Orientation Inventory. According to Bass (1962), task-oriented people attempt to do the best job possible on a task and to complete it. Task orientation is associated with hard work, concern for group productivity, and assertiveness. A set of six philosophy-of-teaching items, rated on five-point scales, was used to evaluate teachers' goals. These items covered the extent to which teachers felt it was important to: (4) *Inculcate love of learning*; (5) *Prepare students for college*; (6) *Prepare students for work*; (7) *Be a friend to students*; (8) *Be seen as competent by students*; and (9) *Be considered competent by administrators.*

We expected larger classes and those in the lower grades to be less relationship and more control oriented. Classes taught by women teachers and those with a larger proportion of female students were expected to be more relationship and goal oriented but less structure oriented. Classes with students high on internal control and social exploration were expected to be high on innovation and low on control. Classes of task oriented teachers, who wanted to be seen as competent and to prepare students for work, were expected to be oriented more toward goals and structure and less toward relationships and innovation than classes of teachers who wanted to inculcate a love of learning and be a friend to students.

Organizational Characteristics. Although the relationships are not substantial, small classes are more likely to be innovation oriented, whereas large classes are more likely to be supportive task or unstructured competition oriented (see Table 12). The results are consistent with the idea that relationship dimensions are emphasized more in small classes, but it is surprising that larger classes are not more control oriented, particularly since many teachers feel that they institute greater structure when they have more students in a class.

Classes in the higher grades are more likely to be innovation and supportive task oriented and less likely to be structured relationship and control oriented (see Table 12). Not surprisingly, teachers feel the need to establish more orderly and controlled classes at lower grade levels (ninth and tenth grades) but are more able to emphasize variety and innovation at older grade levels (eleventh and twelfth grades).

Aggregate Student Characteristics. One of our most intriguing findings is that classes with a higher proportion of girls are more likely to be oriented toward innovation and support and less likely to be oriented toward structure and control. The basic difference is in the degree of structure: Teachers who have a higher proportion of boys in their classes develop more control oriented milieus.

Table 12. Correlations of Organizational, Aggregate Student, and Teacher Characteristics with Student-Perceived Class Milieu

Characteristic	Innovation Oriented	Structured Relationship Oriented	Supportive Task Oriented	Supportive Competition Oriented	Unstructured Competition Oriented	Control Oriented
Organizational						
Class size	-0.19^b	-0.03	0.14^a	-0.02	0.11^a	0.04
Grade level	0.18^b	-0.13^a	0.21^b	0.03	0.01	-0.22^b
Aggregate Student						
Percent female	0.15^b	-0.19^b	0.33^b	0.11^a	0.14^b	-0.26^b
Internal control	-0.04	0.14^a	0.00	0.17^b	0.01	0.02
Social exploration	0.26^b	-0.03	0.21^b	0.06	-0.14^a	-0.39^b
Teacher						
Sex (Female)	0.23^b	-0.23^b	0.22^b	0.01	-0.17^b	-0.20^b
Years of teaching experience	-0.09	0.11^a	0.02	0.10	-0.03	0.01
Task orientation	-0.13^a	0.18^b	-0.01	0.19^b	0.04	0.09
Inculcating love of learning	0.16^b	-0.13^a	0.16^b	0.07	0.02	-0.18^b
Preparing for college entrance	-0.16^b	-0.03	0.08	0.18^b	0.16^b	0.10
Preparing for work	-0.03	0.23^b	-0.33^b	-0.08	-0.19^b	0.17^b
Wishing to be students' friend	0.15^b	-0.12^a	0.15^b	-0.02	0.06	-0.13^a
Wishing to be seen as competent by students	0.11^a	-0.09	0.04	0.15^a	-0.08	-0.13^a
Wishing to be seen as competent by administrators	-0.10	0.16^b	-0.10	-0.15^a	0.05	0.16^b

Note: N = 241 classes.

[a] $p < 0.05$.

[b] $p < 0.01$.

Students who are high on social exploration facilitate innovation and supportive task oriented classroom environments but inhibit unstructured competition and control oriented classes. Since students who are high in personal exploration prefer environments that emphasize innovation and independence, these results indicate that teachers (and their students) tend to establish classroom environments congruent with students' personal orientations. Conversely, there is surprisingly little relationship between students' aggregate internal control orientation and the class environment. Classes composed of students high in average levels of internal control are more likely to be supportive competition and structured relationship oriented, but there is no relationship between students' personal control orientation and the control orientation of the class.

Teacher Characteristics. Female teachers facilitate the same kinds of social environments that female students do. That is, women teachers are more likely to establish innovation, supportive task, and unstructured competition oriented classes and less likely to establish structured relationship or control oriented classes. Men teachers may create more controlling and organized settings because they have a higher proportion of boys in their classes (as in vocational schools) and because they feel that boys need more structure than girls. The fact that men and women teachers are attracted to different subjects is also relevant. For example, carpentry, woodshop, and science classes, which are more likely to be taught by men, are generally perceived as having—indeed, necessitating—more emphasis on order than, for example, social studies or English classes.

There is essentially no relationship between years of teaching experience and type of class environment. This is contrary to previous findings that show more experienced teachers to create classes that are lower on democracy and intimacy and higher on clique formation, favoritism, and friction. Anderson, Walberg, and Welch (1969) posited that in classes with inexperienced teachers, students feel they are learning and contributing with the teacher. This "unity in a common task" leads to more positive classroom environments. The teachers in our sample may have had too much teaching experience (mean = 9.1 years) for this effect to occur.

As expected, task-oriented teachers were more likely to have supportive competition oriented and structured relationship oriented classes but less likely to have innovation oriented classes. This suggests that teachers' personal tendencies toward task orientation can be manifested in either the goal orientation or the system maintenance areas. We originally predicted that the degree of task orientation would be related to the subject matter taught (for example, a math teacher should be more task oriented than an art teacher). This prediction was not upheld, indicating that the relationship between task orientation and class social environment is not mediated by class subject matter.

The six philosophy of teaching indexes were predictably related to the type of class environment. Teachers who want to inculcate a love of learning and to be considered a friend of students are more likely to create innovation and supportive task oriented classes and less likely to create structured relationship and control oriented classes. Teachers who want to prepare students for college entrance are more likely to establish unstructured competition oriented classes and less likely to establish innovation oriented classes. Teachers who feel they are preparing students for work after high school and who want to be seen as competent by administrators are more likely to develop structured relationship and control oriented classes and less likely to develop supportive task or supportive competition oriented classes.

Commonality Analysis of Determinants of Learning Environments. To identify the unique and shared contributions of the four sets of variables in determining class learning environments, we conducted multiple-regression analyses in which the order of entry of each set of variables was varied systematically. In general, we expected the set of teacher characteristics to account for more of the unique variance than the set of aggregate student characteristics, since we thought teachers were more likely to influence classroom social environments. In light of our earlier findings, we also expected that the type of school and class subject matter would account for an important portion of the variance in each type of social environment. Furthermore, we expected that a reasonable portion of the predictable variance of each type would be shared among two or more of the four sets of classroom characteristics.

Taken together, the four sets of variables accounted for a significant proportion of the variance in student-perceived classroom climates. As shown in Table 13, the total variance explained ranges from a high of 34.8 percent for control oriented classes to a low of 19.5 for unstructured competition oriented classes. Each of the four sets of variables uniquely account for some of the predictable variance of one or more of the six climate-type indexes. There is also considerable variation from one index to another in the amount of variance accounted for by particular sets of variables.

Innovation and supportive competition oriented classes were most heavily influenced by school and subject matter and by teacher characteristics. Organizational characteristics explained a fair proportion of the predictable variance of innovation oriented climates, but they predicted none of the variance of supportive competition oriented climates. Essentially the reverse is true for aggregate student characteristics. The majority of the shared variance in these two classroom climates (and of the other four types as well) is related to interactions between the type of school and classroom subject matter blocks and between the aggregate student and teacher characteristics blocks. For example, regular public schools are more likely to have female students who are high in social exploration and female teachers who are low in task orientation, wish to inculcate a love of learning, and be seen as a friend to students. These characteristics in combination make it even more likely for innovation oriented classes to develop.

All four sets of predictive variables uniquely account for an important proportion of the variance in supportive task oriented and structured relationship oriented classes. Class and student characteristics are somewhat more important in determining supportive task oriented climates, whereas school and subject matter and various sources of shared variance account for more of the variance in structured relationship oriented climates. The results for unstructured competition oriented classes, however, are quite different, since the teacher character-

Table 13. Determinants of Student-Perceived Class Milieu

			Type of Social Environment			
Effect	Innovation Oriented	Structured Relationship Oriented	Supportive Task Oriented	Supportive Competition Oriented	Unstructured Competition Oriented	Control Oriented
Unique to school and subject matter	9.8	6.8	5.9	10.1	1.9	4.3
Unique to organizational characteristics	6.5	2.5	7.8	0.0	0.2	9.0
Unique to aggregate student characteristics	1.9	2.2	4.3	4.6	3.9	11.5
Unique to teacher characteristics	9.9	5.6	6.9	13.3	8.5	6.0
Shared variance	6.4	7.5	8.8	2.4	5.0	4.0
Total variance accounted for	34.5	24.6	33.7	30.4	19.5	34.8

Note: Percentage of variance explained in classroom climate; $N = 241$ classes.

istics block accounts for almost half of the explainable variance. As the simple correlations show (see Table 12), this type of class is more likely to be established by women teachers and by teachers who wish to prepare their students for college entrance.

The determinants of control orientation are different from those of the other five types. Control oriented climates are mainly determined by organizational characteristics (primarily grade level) and aggregate student characteristics (primarily a higher proportion of males and a lower social exploration orientation), although teacher characteristics (primarily male teachers, an orientation to prepare students for work, and a wish to be seen as competent by administrators) also are important. Aggregate student characteristics are much more influential in determining the control orientation of a class than in determining its innovation or structured relationship orientation.

Only between one-fifth and one-third of the variance of classroom social environments was accounted for by our four sets of determinants, which is much less than the 40 to 70 percent we accounted for in the social environments of student living groups (see Chapter Four). This is probably because we did not have as comprehensive a set of variables in the classroom analysis. A set of physical and architectural variables should be included, since indexes such as the amount of open space, the arrangement of desks and chairs, and the flexibility of the physical setting can affect the classroom environment independently of the other sets of factors. More importantly, we did not measure such characteristics as the composite ability level and socioeconomic status of the students in our classes, which are thought to influence and exert their effects through the type of social environment they help to create (see, for example, Alwin and Otto, 1977; Brookover and others, 1978). Including other contextual (such as the overall school organizational or social climate) and teacher characteristics also may have allowed us to explain more of the social environment of these classes. For example, Pond (1973) found that students saw classes that were taught by teachers who worked in open and responsive school settings as focusing more on personal growth and system maintenance.

Although the specific correlations and exact proportions of unique and shared variance related to the four sets of factors will vary from one sample of classes to another, the conceptual model provides a useful framework for guiding and interpreting future studies. Different types of schools and school programs affect classroom environments, but the extent to which these effects represent unique influences of the programs themselves is not clear. The foregoing model should help to determine how much school type and learning programs uniquely determine classroom social environments. It should also help to develop a more coherent understanding of the other sets of factors that affect the social environments of junior high and high school classes.

The results are useful in focusing on some of the major determinants of learning environments and in identifying which types of classes are most likely to change. Control oriented classes may be relatively resistant to change since they are "elicited" by certain classroom and student characteristics. Teachers may "know" that it is difficult or impossible to establish relationship oriented classes with certain types of students. Conversely, it should be quite possible to develop a more relationship oriented environment in a public school social or artistic class taught by a woman teacher interested in inculcating a love of learning in students. The findings indicate which types of classes may be most amenable to change and help to identify what kind of change is likely to occur.

9

Effects
of Classroom Settings
on Student Attitudes
and Learning

There is considerable controversy about the best types of learning environments to provide in schools and classrooms, and about their differential effects. On the one hand, lower achievement test scores and an increase in the number of secondary school students who lack reading, writing, and arithmetic skills have fueled a rapidly growing "back-to-basics" movement. On the other hand, advocates of open and other innovative educational programs argue that structured classes stifle creativity, lead to poor self-concepts among all but the most highly talented, and sacrifice students' intrinsic interest and continuing motivation to learn for such short-term gains as improved test scores.

I address these issues here by providing a model of the determinants of the outcomes of learning environments. I focus primarily on students' subjective reactions to classroom settings, but I also emphasize absenteeism, since a high rate of cutting classes is a major signal that a student has serious problems and may foreshadow dropping out of school. I also review work on the effects of classroom learning environments and discuss some underlying issues to illustrate the complexity of this area.

Students' Reactions to Learning Environments

In the last chapter some of the determinants of different types of learning climates were identified. I concentrate here on how the four sets of variables that help to determine classroom climate, in conjunction with classroom climate itself, affect student satisfaction and morale. After many years of dependence on achievement test scores as outcome criteria, a few investigators have begun to focus on other indexes, such as a sense of self-control and self-responsibility for learning (Wang and Stiles, 1976), cognitive preferences (Tamir, 1975), continuing motivation to learn (Maehr, 1976), and student satisfaction with the school and class setting.

Averch and others (1974) noted that socialization and the development of creativity and self-reliance are among the most important functions of schooling. They expressed the need for more noncognitive outcome indexes, since recent evidence shows low relationships between cognitive achievement (as measured by grades and standardized tests) and later success. Teacher grades and essay examinations are relatively poor measures, because they are influenced greatly by student characteristics not associated with cognitive performance, such as docility and social class. Furthermore, such indexes as cognitive preferences and students' general reactions to schools and classes can be more important than traditional achievement measures, since these characteristics may remain long after specific facts and even general principles are forgotten.

Such school innovations as open education have made teachers more aware of students' reactions to school and class settings. For example, students in open classrooms are expected to be happier, more involved, and have a more positive attitude toward learning. Epstein and McPartland (1976) noted that positive reactions to school increase the likelihood that students will stay in school, develop a lasting commitment to learning, and use the institution to advantage. They added that "higher satisfaction with school, greater commitment and more positive student-teacher relationships mean more enjoyable and stimulating hours spent in the compulsory school setting. In many respects, school satisfaction for youngsters is analogous to job satisfaction for adults. The school, like the job, provides the single out-of-family environment where a major proportion of time is spent" (pp. 27-28).

Following this logic, information was obtained on five indexes of student reactions: (1) *Friendship Formation* (How much do you like the other students in this class?). (2) *Sense of Well-Being* (How secure do you feel in this class?). (3) *Satisfaction with Learning* (How much actual material do you feel you are learning in this class?). (4) *Satisfaction with Teacher* (How satisfied are you with the teacher in this class?). (5) *Alienation* (How angry do you feel in this class?). These questions were answered by students on five-point scales, ranging from very low (1) to very high (5). Each of the five indexes discriminated among the six types of classes previously described (Moos, 1978b).

The analysis, which was conducted on the same sample of 241 classes described in Chapter Eight in the evaluation of Holland-type classes, proceeded as follows: Each of the five sets of environmental variables (type of school and class subject matter, organizational characteristics, aggregate student characteristics, teacher characteristics, and indexes of the six types of learning environments) were related to each of the five measures of student reactions. Multiple-regression analyses, systematically varying the order of entry of the five sets of environmental variables, were then performed to estimate the proportion of unique and shared variance they accounted for in the dependent variables.

The six types of learning environments were hypothesized to relate differentially to student reactions. Innovation
oriented classes were expected to facilitate student friendship
formation, well-being, and satisfaction with the teacher; structured relationship classes were expected to facilitate satisfaction
with learning, due to their emphasis on goal orientation. Supportive task and supportive competition oriented classes were
expected to facilitate positive reactions to both affective
(friendship formation and well-being) and cognitive (satisfaction
with learning) areas, and students in unstructured competition
oriented and control oriented classes were expected to be more
alienated and dissatisfied with the teacher. These expectations
follow from the belief that friendship, well-being, and satisfaction with the teacher are influenced most heavily by the social
and authority structures of the setting, whereas satisfaction
with learning is related closely to the task structure.

*Organizational, Aggregate Student, and Teacher Charac-
teristics.* Students in smaller classes were higher on friendship
formation, but none of the other four outcome indexes were
related to class size. Surprisingly, classes at upper grade levels
were lower on all five indexes (see Table 14). This suggests that
classes are less important overall to more advanced high school
students, particularly in light of the fact that these classes
would be expected to result in higher satisfaction and morale,
since they are more likely to be innovation and supportive task
oriented and less likely to be control oriented. With respect to
aggregate characteristics, students reacted more positively in
classes with a high proportion of females and in classes high on
aggregate social exploration. The latter variable alone predicted
between 14 and 30 percent of the variance in the five criteria.
Students who are innovative and who participate in a variety of
activities are likely to create friendly, satisfying classes.

There were relatively few relationships between the nine
teacher characteristics and the five indexes of student reactions.
Students with men teachers were likely to feel more alienated,
whereas those with teachers who had more teaching experience,
who were more task oriented, and who wanted to be seen as
competent by administrators tended to feel more satisfied with

Table 14. Correlations of Class Contextual Characteristics and Students' Reactions to Classes

Characteristic	Friendship Formation	Sense of Well-Being	Satisfaction with Learning	Satisfaction with Teacher	Alienation
Organizational					
Class size	-0.20[b]	-0.10	-0.10	-0.04	-0.09
Grade level	-0.18[b]	-0.27[b]	-0.30[b]	-0.25[b]	-0.34[b]
Aggregate student					
Percent female	0.30[b]	0.10	0.06	0.09	-0.11[a]
Internal control	0.08	0.09[b]	0.17[b]	0.04	0.01
Social exploration	0.55[b]	0.46[b]	0.37[b]	0.37[b]	0.03
Teacher					
Sex (female)	0.04	0.01	-0.01	-0.04	-0.19[b]
Years of teaching experience	0.05	0.06	0.11[a]	0.08	0.02
Task orientation	0.06	0.08	0.19[b]	0.10	-0.01
Inculcating love of learning	-0.05	0.08	0.06	0.15[b]	-0.13[a]
Preparing for college entrance	0.15[b]	-0.17[b]	-0.08	-0.19[b]	0.03
Preparing for work	-0.08	0.02	0.06	0.04	0.12[a]
Wishing to be students' friend	-0.08	0.05	0.01	0.10	0.01
Wishing to be seen as competent by students	-0.01	0.02	0.00	-0.01	0.06
Wishing to be seen as competent by administrators	0.03	0.02	0.12[a]	0.00	0.04
Student-perceived class climate					
Innovation oriented	0.05	0.22[b]	0.03	0.26[b]	-0.20[b]
Structured relationship oriented	0.04	0.10	0.22[b]	0.08	-0.08
Supportive task oriented	0.15[b]	0.20[b]	0.25[b]	0.38[b]	-0.35[b]
Supportive competition oriented	0.19[b]	0.10	0.30[b]	0.17[b]	-0.18[b]
Unstructured competition oriented	0.01	-0.13[a]	-0.02	-0.06	0.10
Control oriented	-0.15[b]	-0.33[b]	-0.19[b]	-0.41[b]	0.39[b]

Note: $N = 241$ classes.

[a] $p < 0.05$.
[b] $p < 0.01$.

learning. Teachers who wanted to prepare students for college entrance affected their students in unanticipated ways, since the students were higher on friendship formation but less satisfied with the teacher and felt less comfortable in class. In contrast, teachers who wanted to inculcate a love of learning had students who were satisfied with them and who felt less alienated.

Classroom Learning Environment. The relationships between the classroom learning environment and students' reactions were generally as predicted (see Table 14). Students were more satisfied with the teacher, higher on well-being, and less alienated in less structured classes emphasizing teacher-student and student-student support. Students in supportive task and competition oriented classes were also more satisfied with their learning experience and higher on friendship formation, whereas neither of these indexes was related to innovation orientation. Students in structured relationship oriented classes were more satisfied with learning; those in unstructured competition oriented classes were lower on well-being. As expected, students in control oriented classes felt more alienated and less secure, liked each other less, and were less satisfied with the teacher and their learning experience.

Unique and Shared Effects of Class Environmental Characteristics. To what extent are the relationships between the sets of classroom environmental descriptors and student reactions independent of each other? We know that aggregate student characteristics influence the social environment of a class, but do these characteristics also uniquely determine student reactions? How much of the connection between class climate and student reactions is related to the associations between classroom climate and the other sets of environmental characteristics? How much of the variance in student reactions is predictable from all five sets of classroom characteristics taken together?

To answer these questions, we conducted multiple-regression analyses in which the order of entry of the five blocks of classroom characteristics was varied systematically. The five blocks of variables accounted for a considerable proportion of the variance in students' reactions (see Table 15). The classroom

Table 15. Determinants of Students' Reactions to Classes

Effect	Friendship Formation	Well-Being	Satisfaction with Learning	Satisfaction with Teacher	Alienation
Unique to school and subject matter	0.8	2.3	3.2	0.2	8.8
Unique to organizational characteristics	3.3	7.3	8.9	9.7	3.7
Unique to aggregate student characteristics	17.8	10.3	8.6	3.8	6.8
Unique to teacher characteristics	8.1	2.7	3.6	6.4	3.0
Unique to student-perceived climate type	1.4	9.7	12.7	28.0	25.1
Shared between climate and other sets of variables	9.2	7.7	8.3	4.1	−0.8
All other shared effects	5.5	8.8	9.6	6.8	3.8
Total variance accounted for	46.1	48.8	54.9	59.0	50.4

Note: Percentage of variance explained in classroom climate; $N = 241$ classes.

climate and aggregate student characteristics each explained large portions of the unique variance (that is, the variance unique to one set of environmental characteristics). The classroom climate block uniquely explained about half the predictable variance in students' satisfaction with the teacher and feelings of alienation, and 20 to 25 percent of the predictable variance in their sense of well-being and satisfaction with learning. However, it uniquely explained only about 3 percent of the predictable variance in friendship formation. Aggregate student characteristics uniquely accounted for the largest portion (about 40 percent) of the predictable variance in this criterion. This is due primarily to the fact that friendship formation was higher in classes with a higher proportion of females and with students high in aggregate social exploration.

With respect to the other sets of variables, the school and subject matter block uniquely explained 17 percent of the predictable variance in student alienation but only relatively small portions of the variance in the other four indexes. The unique variance related to school and subject matter is accounted for by the following findings: Students in vocational schools were more alienated, students in investigative classes were lower in well-being, students in realistic and conventional classes were more satisfied with learning, and students in investigative classes were less satisfied with learning.

The unique variance attributable to class organizational characteristics is considerable, resulting primarily because students in upper grade levels scored lower on each of the five outcome indexes. The unique variance accounted for by the teacher characteristics block in satisfaction with the teacher is due mainly to the fact that this index was higher in classes of teachers who wanted to inculcate a love of learning and lower in classes of teachers who wanted to prepare students for college entrance. Friendship formation was higher, whereas student well-being was lower, in the latter classes. All five sets of environmental descriptors thus uniquely account for an important proportion of the explainable variance in one or more of the criterion indexes.

A moderate portion of the explainable variance in four of

the five indexes (all but alienation) was shared among two or more sets of environmental variables. The shared variance between the class social environment and the other four sets of variables is due primarily to the interrelation between social climate and aggregate student characteristics. Specifically, the proportion of females, the aggregate level of social exploration, and innovation and supportively oriented (both task and competition) climates shared positive relationships with friendship formation, commitment to learning, and well-being.

The other shared effects (second-, third-, and fourth-order combinations of sets of environmental variables other than social climate) are attributable primarily to the interrelation between aggregate student characteristics and the other three sets (other than social climate) of environmental indexes, particularly classroom organizational characteristics. For example, students in large classes at upper grade levels, composed primarily of males low in aggregate social exploration orientation, were low in well-being and friendship formation, were less committed to learning, and felt more dissatisfied with the teacher. The results show that each of the five sets of environmental characteristics need to be included in a conceptual framework to explain the determinants of students' reactions to their classes.

Although the substantive findings are of interest, the specific relationships and the relative portions of variance accounted for by these sets of classroom characteristics will vary depending on the indexes used in each set, the variability of each index, and the range and diversity of classes sampled. The proportion of variance attributable to student characteristics might have been higher had measures of the students' ability levels and of the socioeconomic and ethnic composition of the classes been included. Furthermore, a set of physical design characteristics might have accounted for some unique (thus increasing the total variance explained) and shared variance. For instance, high social exploration students in open plan classes, which tend to be innovation oriented, are probably higher on friendship formation and lower on alienation.

The relatively large portion of shared variance in the de-

termination of student reactions emphasizes the mutual interrelationships among different sets of classroom characteristics.
Leinhardt (1977) demonstrated the importance of shared variance by finding that students' initial performance levels (input)
were the primary predictors of their end-of-year performance
(output), though classroom processes contributed a small but
consistent amount. Student input alone explained 83 percent of
the variance in student output, 47 percent of which was unique
to input, while 36 percent was shared with classroom process
variables. Student abilities and educational practices in classrooms are highly interdependent. The majority of classroom
practices that relate positively to outcome occur more frequently in classes composed of students with higher entering
performance levels.

Classroom social environments affected student reactions
independently of the other four sets of class-related environmental characteristics. Students in supportive task and supportive competition oriented classes showed the most positive
reactions on the outcome criteria, including satisfaction with
learning. These classes combine an affective concern with students as people with an emphasis on students working hard for
academic rewards in a coherent, organized context. Contrary to
expectations, students in these classes did not have a lower
sense of well-being; in fact, they were higher on friendship
formation and lower on alienation. However, when competition
was emphasized in a relatively unstructured setting lacking
cohesion and support, students were more alienated and less
comfortable.

The relative emphasis on structure and support is important in mediating student reactions to the learning environment.
A moderate amount of structure (particularly clarity of expectations) in a class that emphasizes student-student interaction
and/or teacher support relates positively to commitment and
satisfaction. But the stress on task or maintenance orientation
can become too rigid and nonsupportive. These problems are
not related to teacher control per se, which was fairly high in
the supportive competition oriented classes, but to the context
in which the control occurs. The supportive competition oriented classes place much more weight on student affiliation,

teacher support, and innovation than the unstructured competition or control oriented classes. The same "objective" level of teacher control apparently is seen as more restrictive in settings that lack emphasis on the relationship dimensions.

Classroom Climate and Student Absences and Grades

Bernice Moos and I (Moos and Moos, 1978) studied two other variables related to the learning environment: the student absenteeism rate and the average class grade. We chose these variables because of their practical importance, because they are relatively objective (or at least readily ascertainable) measures of actual behavior, and because we thought they would be affected by classroom climate. In addition, each variable may mediate such classroom outcomes as achievement, satisfaction, dropping out, and the like. Students who are absent cannot avail themselves of relevant learning opportunities, lose the continuity of course content, tend to earn lower grades, and may show less-than-expected learning gains (Karweit, 1973).

We obtained a representative sample of nineteen classes from a high school in which almost all students were enrolled in a college preparatory curriculum. Attendance records were kept in each class, and final grades were obtained at the end of the semester. The nine CES student subscale means for each of these nineteen classes were correlated with the median number of absences and the mean grades of the students in each class. The rank-order correlation between absenteeism and grades was −0.45, indicating a tendency for student absences to be higher in classes with more stringent grading.

Students perceived classes with higher average final grades to be higher on all three of the relationship dimensions and on rule clarity but lower on teacher control. These classes tended to be structured relationship, supportive task, or supportive competition oriented. Classes that students saw as high in competition and teacher control and that teachers saw as low in teacher support had higher student absenteeism rates. These relationships held for both medically excused absences and other types of absences, such as cutting class.

We conducted further analyses to determine the specific

aspects of the classroom milieu that were most closely related to the absenteeism rate. We correlated the median class absenteeism rate with the proportion of students who answered each of the CES items in the true direction. Fourteen CES items were related significantly to the student absenteeism rate. Students in classes with high absenteeism rates felt they were often clock watching, that they had to be careful about what they said, that there were clear and set rules, and that getting into trouble in the class was relatively easy. These students also felt dissatisfied with the class, that they could not discuss outside activities in class, that passing the class was relatively difficult, and that the teacher was fairly strict (see Appendix B for the specific items, and Moos and Moos, 1978, for more details on the methods and results).

No causal implications can be drawn from these data, since class climate, student absenteeism, and grading practices are mutually interrelated in a complex manner. Teachers may establish their authority early in the development of a class, in which case students quickly learn the implicit and explicit rules governing classroom life. Teachers in this type of class can be more supportive, since they have relatively little need to justify their authority or to criticize students for their behavior. Students in these classes are more satisfied, have higher morale, and expect higher grades. Students are also more likely to earn—and teachers more likely to give—higher grades. Conversely, teachers may describe their grading policies initially, which may affect the development of the classroom environment. In turn, this can affect student motivation, absenteeism, achievement, and final grades. The grades students obtain—or expect to obtain— may also influence their evaluation of the classroom learning environment (Powell, 1977).

Although neither grades nor absenteeism rates differed among classes of different subjects, classroom climate, grading policy, and absenteeism can be affected by course content, as well as by grade level, student and teacher characteristics, and type of school. For example, students in one class may have higher average ability levels, be easier to get along with, be easier to control, or be more highly motivated and involved than students in another. Students who are more oriented toward social exploration facilitate the development of innovative and open classes, which they attend more regularly. Such students are also more satisfied and productive and earn higher grades in those classes. A conceptual framework such as the one proposed here should help to explore the relative importance of student background and school and classroom setting characteristics to absenteeism, grades, and other related outcome indexes.

Current Findings on Classroom Effects

Researchers have obtained surprisingly consistent findings in recent studies on the effects of learning environments. For example, students in more difficult and competitive (goal orientation dimensions) high school science classes gain more on measures of achievement, critical thinking, and understanding of science, whereas those in classes with less friction and apathy (relationship dimensions) gain more on measures of science interest and activities (Fraser, 1978; Walberg, 1969). Achievement in high school mathematics classes has been related to relationship (high cohesion and low favoritism, friction, apathy, and clique formation), goal orientation (high difficulty), and system maintenance and change (high organization and democracy) dimensions (O'Reilly, 1975). Comparisons of open and traditional programs indicate that students in open programs are more satisfied and self-reliant (Epstein and McPartland, 1975) and show more positive interpersonal relationships, but students in traditional classes usually score higher on measures of vocabulary, reading, and mathematics achievement. In addition, students in open and traditional classes do not seem to differ on tests of creativity (Forman and McKinney, 1978), even after they have been enrolled in open schools for three years or more (Wright, 1975).

Primary grade students make the greatest gains in reading and mathematics in classes that are warm, task oriented, and systematic and orderly, that is, classes that emphasize all three learning environment domains. Students in these classes do as well on such outcome criteria as creativity and positive self-concept as do students in classes that are warm and flexible but less task oriented and structured. However, children show higher scores on nonverbal reasoning, have lower absence rates, and display greater willingness to work independently when in flexible classroom settings that provide more exploratory materials and allow more individual freedom. Furthermore, students in classes that emphasize task orientation and structure but that are relatively low in warmth do well on standard achievement test measures but less well on indexes of creativity and self-esteem (see Bennett, 1976; Kennedy, 1978; Solomon and Kendall, in press; Stallings, 1975).

Relevant work has also been done on classroom reward structures, that is, on the rules by which students are rewarded for academic performance. The three major reward structures are competitive (grading on a curve), independent or individualistic (fixed performance criteria that all students can attain), and cooperative (such as in team sports or a class play). Cooperative reward structures increase interpersonal attraction, friendliness (especially interracial friendliness), positive group evaluation helpfulness, and other aspects of "social connectedness," that is, the degree to which an individual is attracted to others and feels and acts a part of a valued group (Slavin, 1977). But competitive or independent reward structures are more effective in strengthening students' task performance and in increasing such traditional outcome measures as achievement test scores (Michaels, 1977).

This extensive body of research suggests four major conclusions. First, relationship and innovation oriented classes can create student satisfaction and interest in the subject matter. These classes enhance social growth (friendliness and helpfulness) and personal growth (independence, self-esteem, and creativity) but do less well in facilitating traditional achievement scores. Second, high achievement gains can occur in classes that emphasize goal (task and competition) and maintenance (organization and clarity) areas and that are lower in warmth, but these classes do less well in facilitating student interest, morale, or creativity. Third, control oriented classes lead to dissatisfaction and alienation and do not facilitate personal, social, or academic growth.

Fourth, gains on traditional achievement measures are most likely to occur when there is a combination of warm and supportive relationships, an emphasis on specific academic tasks and accomplishments, and a reasonably clear, orderly, and well-structured milieu. These types of classroom settings, which have a high expectation and demand for performance, can also enhance creativity and personal growth. The results suggest that basic skills programs would have more positive effects if they emphasized relationship areas (that is, the classes should be supportive as well as task oriented), whereas open program classes should benefit from an emphasis on task orientation, though not at the expense of affiliation and support.

These conclusions are tentative because only a few studies have measured all three domains of classroom learning environments. For example, open school programs presumably are high on relationship and system change and low on teacher control, but the degree to which they emphasize task orientation, competition, organization, and clarity is much less clear. The work on reward structures focuses primarily on task orientation and competition but provides little or no information about the relative emphasis on relationship and maintenance areas. Future work needs to consider all three domains of classroom learning environments, since the effects of each domain depend on its emphasis relative to the other domains.

Rosenshine (1978) attempted to identify the mechanisms underlying these findings. He suggested that students in formal classes obtain better achievement test results because teachers use instructional techniques that require more time devoted to academics and greater coverage of content. Students in formal classes where academics are not emphasized (such as control oriented classes) should not do particularly well on achievement indexes, whereas students in informal classes with much academically engaged time and content covered (such as supportive task oriented classes) should show high performance gains. These ideas are supported by recent work showing that children in open program classes with enthusiastic teachers and a high press for achievement do better in mathematics (Eshel and Klein, 1978), and by studies noting the importance of signal input continuity by other students and the teacher and of fewer "call outs" (interruptions) during academic discussions (see, for example, Crawford and others, 1977; Kounin and Doyle, 1975).

Other possible mechanisms include the fact that students in more formal classes understand more clearly what is expected of them and that these classes have fewer disciplinary problems and waste less time. Greater day-to-day consistency in teacher behavior in formal classes should contribute to continuity, clarity of expectations, and learning and achievement gains. Teachers in formal classes may also persuade students that tests are important and give them more practice with formal tests. Furthermore, informal and innovative teaching methods are harder to implement (Kennedy, 1978) and tend to place much heavier demands on teachers, making teacher "burn out" and disorganization in class more likely.

Issues in Classroom Impact Research

I have drawn some tentative conclusions about the impacts of learning environments, but several important issues affecting these conclusions remain to be explored. Four such issues are discussed here: unintended or negative effects of classroom settings, student-environment congruence, the need for process studies, and the influence of the broader school and nonschool environment on the long-term effects of classroom settings.

Unintended or Negative Effects. Some emphasis on each of the three domains (relationship, growth, and maintenance) facilitates positive social and academic outcomes, but too much focus on any one area can have negative or unintended effects. Cohesion and affiliation facilitate learning in task oriented classes but can inhibit learning when there is little or no task orientation, since students who wish to become involved in academic pursuits may not feel free to do so. Cohesion can restrict students' freedom to pursue goals not shared by others in the class. Teacher support and a relaxed sociable class setting can exist alongside low expectations and standards of performance, resulting in too little challenge and poor social and academic functioning. In addition, too much mutual dependence (rela-

tionship orientation) among students for rewards may be ineffective, since students can receive rewards when they have
done little to earn them and may fail to receive rewards when
they are deserved (Slavin, 1977).

With respect to goal orientation, students learn more in
classes that emphasize difficulty and competition, but these
classes also have high absenteeism rates. Task orientation and
competition encourage cognitive growth for some students, but
for others they can result in absenteeism, poor grades, and an
increased chance of dropping out. Furthermore, attention to
academic tasks and extrinsic rewards (such as grades) can have
the opposite of the intended effect; that is, it may decrease interest in the material outside of class and inhibit intrinsic motivation to learn, particularly for achievement oriented students
(Maehr, 1976).

Individual competition, at least as typically implemented
in classrooms, can be ineffective for many students. Low-ability
students who need to try hardest are given the least incentive to
do so. Less able students experience more failure in competitive
reward structures and therefore are more anxious, less self-
assured, and less likely to benefit from mistakes, because they
often hide them to avoid ridicule. Johnson and Johnson (1974)
argued that these students will become oriented toward avoiding failure, will perform more poorly in subsequent competition, will try to obstruct other students' academic accomplishments, and eventually will become less achievement oriented.

Too much emphasis on personal growth areas can also
lead to anxiety and stress in noncompetitive alternative school
programs. The emphasis on responsibility and self-reliance (personal growth) in open school settings may result in greater
school anxiety and more stress, perhaps reflecting a lack of clarity about the events of the school day (Epstein and McPartland,
1975; Wright, 1975). Finally, an overemphasis on classroom
structure can make students dependent on the particular program. These students may rapidly lose their achievement gains
when they return to a regular "sink or swim" school setting in
which they get little individual attention (Averch and others,
1974).

A balanced emphasis on all three learning environment domains, either in each class or in different classes throughout the school day, may counteract these unintended effects. Various combinations of cooperative and competitive reward structures, such as competition between teams, hold promise for producing positive effects on both social connectedness and academic achievement (Slavin, 1977). Employing formal instruction in the morning and less structure in the afternoon to encourage exploration and independent inquiry might be useful in this regard. However, since students' interest and positive attitudes toward school are primarily a function of how well they perform academically (Bloom, 1976), teachers need to maintain a focus on basic skills and achievement.

Student-Environment Congruence. A major reason for measuring classroom social environments is to determine which type of learning environment is most beneficial for a particular student. Hunt (1975) developed a conceptual-level matching model that provides a framework for much of the extensive research in this area (see Cronbach and Snow, 1977). He noted that a person at a higher conceptual level is structurally more complex, more capable of responsible actions, and better able to adapt to a changing environment than someone at a lower conceptual level. The idea is that lower conceptual-level students (dependent on external standards and less capable of generating their own concepts) should profit more from a structured approach. High conceptual-level learners may profit from low structure or be less affected by variation in structure. Bloom (1976) noted that students who have developed effective learning and study skills should be less affected by variations in the quality of instruction than students whose academic skills are not as well developed.

Studies focusing on these hypotheses have found that structured classes are better for students with less prior achievement in a subject area, for students from disadvantaged socioeconomic backgrounds, and for students who have a high need for structure (Averch and others, 1974; Tobias, 1976). Students high in internal control (Daniels and Stevens, 1976) and in exploration orientation (Nielsen and Moos, 1978) and students who exhibit a need for achievement via independence (as opposed to a need for achievement via conformity) adjust better to and profit more from less structured learning environments.

These studies are consistent with expectations derived from Hunt's model, but some recent work indicates that students with less prior ability and achievement (such as some disadvantaged ethnic minority students) do worse in more structured classes, whereas students of high ability and achievement levels do better in these classes. For example, Ward and Barcher (1975), comparing reading achievement and creativity in traditional and open classes, found no differences among low IQ groups. Among high IQ groups, however, children in traditional classes obtained higher reading and figural creativity scores. Blaney and others (1977) found that ethnic minority students (blacks and Mexican-Americans) performed as well as white students in interdependent classes but less well in traditional classes. These studies suggest that self-confident, academically able students achieve better in relatively structured, task oriented, and orderly classes (see also Bennett, 1976; Rosenshine, 1978).

The essential characteristic of these classes is probably the emphasis on task orientation and mastering the basic skills necessary to help bright, well-motivated students to progress, rather than the structure of the traditional approach. The tendency of open classes to concentrate on the enjoyment and usefulness of the subject matter and to deemphasize the amount of content covered may mask the performance deficiencies of low-ability students and prevent bright students from reaching their optimum achievement levels. Students of high ability and achievement levels seem to perform best when the teacher exhibits a "critical demandingness," whereas they are less motivated by high rates of teacher evaluation and verbal praise (Crawford and others, 1977). Conversely, students who are less proficient in academic skills seem to be especially responsive to teachers who focus on interpersonal and communication skills, and may achieve optimally when the teacher is more supportive and makes appropriate use of verbal praise (Bloom, 1976; Crawford and others, 1977; Pascarella, 1978).

These findings can help determine the type of learning environment most likely to facilitate student achievement at different stages of conceptual and social maturity. Emphasis on the relationship domain is particularly important in the early phases of learning. Thus, it is of great value to students of low ability or low achievement, including many low socioeconomic status and ethnic minority students. These students need to be taught within a reasonably task-oriented and structured environment, as Hunt (1975) suggested, but they also need peer and teacher support and a high amount of praise and positive verbal reinforcement. As students develop more conceptual and personal maturity, an emphasis on relationship areas, especially immediate rewards or praise, becomes less important and may actually inhibit intrinsic motivation and the development of high internal standards of excellence. Bright, well-motivated students learn best under conditions of high expectation and demand, which often occur in conjunction with organization and control, but these latter characteristics are not critical in facilitating their achievement levels.

The Need for Process Studies. Greater understanding of within-classroom processes and the reciprocal influences between students and teachers is needed in studying the individual differences in achievement and morale among students attending the same classes. For example, Jackson and Cosca (1974) assessed the behavior of teachers toward students of different ethnic groups in schools in the southwestern United States. Observers used the Flanders system to code teacher verbal behaviors with reference to the ethnicity of the students. Six of twelve measures of interaction showed considerable differences between Chicano and Anglo students. Specifically, Chicanos were less likely to receive praise or encouragement, questioning, positive feedback, and noncriticizing teacher talk or to have their ideas accepted or used.

Although it is tempting to conclude that the teachers involved were biased, the unidirectional model of teacher-to-student influence implied in this research—and in most research on classrooms—is inadequate to explain these patterns of interaction. Fiedler (1975) studied reciprocally contingent interactions between teacher and students using the Hit-Steer Observational System, in which an observer assesses the number of times a teacher or pupil attempts to influence (hits) the other, and whether the other subsequently modifies his or her behavior (is steered). Results showed both teachers and students to be influenced, since students complied with 87 percent of all teacher hits and teachers complied with 89 percent of all pupil hits. Teachers made hits about twice as often as students, but both teachers and students complied with most attempts to influence them. Fiedler concluded that the behavior of "subordinates" (students) affects the behavior of "superiors" (teachers) and that interpersonal influence in the classroom is bidirectional.

Teachers need to be sensitized to these mutual influence processes and to the effects that their students have on them. Individual differences in how students interpret conditions in the classroom can provide important clues in this regard, since, for example, students who do not receive the amount of teacher encouragement and praise they need are likely to see the classroom environment as low in teacher support. Students' perceptions of the learning environment, which are less expensive and easier to obtain than observational data, can help to inform teachers about variations in their interactions with students.

The Broader Environmental Context. Studies of the effects of classroom settings must be broadened to consider overall school and nonschool influences. In traditional educational programs and evaluations, the notion of the environment has typically been bounded by the classroom, in which the key factors are either methods (lecture versus discussion) or climate-type variables (teacher leadership style and grading reward system). Classroom experience is but a fraction of the total education experience, which involves many classes and external factors that can play a key role in changing students' expectations, attitudes, and behavior. In this respect, Shea (1976) concluded that the influence of significant others on student aspirations and achievement is important, and that parents and peers are about equally influential and twice as influential as teachers.

Nonschool settings can influence school and classroom

settings by inhibiting their effects (as when the family or peer group does not reinforce an achievement oriented school environment), by potentiating their effects (as when home and family influences strongly reinforce an achievement oriented school setting), by compensating for their lack of effects (families can teach skills at home that children do not learn in school), or simply by teaching them useful social or academic skills. For example, Gallimore, Tharp, and Speidel (1978) found that boys from families who assigned child-care tasks to male siblings were more likely to be attentive in the classroom and in a dyadic peer tutoring situation. A child who is used to being cared for by older siblings may be more accustomed to learning from other children and thus be more responsive to a peer tutor. Conversely, some parents have high demands for academic achievement, which presumably are supportive of the school setting, but they do not give their children adequate instruction or support in implementing these demands.

The connections among different settings are important in relation to the long-term stability of the effects of learning environments. Averch and others (1974) noted that most of the short-run gains from intervention programs fade away after two or three years if they are not reinforced. This "fade-out" effect is greater for gains on achievement tests than for gains on intelligence tests, and is more evident for those highly structured programs that are most unlike regular public school classes. However, there is also some evidence of "diffusion" effects, in that younger siblings may benefit from an older brother or sister attending an enriched learning program. In this case, the school learning environment has a positive effect on the home environment, which influences children who did not themselves participate in the enrichment program.

The types of educational settings needed depend in part on the type of students and on the desired outcomes, but the above considerations clarify some of the issues involved. At the minimum, we need to focus on relationship, personal growth, and system maintenance and change dimensions in comparing, evaluating, and changing educational settings. A more differentiated conceptualization of the social environments of such settings may prevent sterile debates about the relative merits of open versus traditional schools and allow us to design more sophisticated studies that consider the full complexity of the educational process. We also need to focus on the extent to which these effects may be facilitated or inhibited by other important life settings, such as those of the family (Marjoribanks, in press) and the factory (Inkeles and Smith, 1974).

——10——

Learning Environments in Developing Countries

The evaluation of educational settings is especially significant in developing countries because the expectations regarding education and the challenges confronting educational planners in these nations are quite different from those in developed societies. Some Western nations are experiencing declining enrollments and school closures, but most developing nations are faced with an increased demand for access to education. The

Note: This chapter is authored by R. Michael Paige.

developed societies have sufficient resources to maintain and expand their systems of education, but an acute scarcity of resources characterizes the developing societies. Formal education is not organized to promote basic economic goals in the industrialized societies, since they already have achieved a high level of economic development. But formal education in the developing nations is explicitly designed to promote a wide range of economic and other development objectives. Harbison and Myers' (1964, p. 181) claim that "education is the key that unlocks the door to modernization" is rearticulated in one form or another by educational planners throughout the developing world.

Because formal education is expected to help the developing countries realize their objectives, and because the human and material resources that can be allocated to education are limited, educational research in these nations has become prominent. In a developing country, the research enterprise is intricately tied to the planning and policy-making process both by necessity and design. A given theoretical perspective and its a‘tendant research methodology is appropriate in a developing nation to the degree that it identifies school-related variables that have an impact on how children learn, isolates school-related variables that are potentially responsive to intervention, and produces findings that have specific policy implications.

My purpose is to examine the applicability of the classroom learning environment perspective to the evaluation of educational settings in developing countries. To describe the context in which classroom learning environment research must be fitted, I discuss the relationship between education and development. I then review prior educational research in developing nations as a prelude to an examination of the classroom learning environment literature. The central focus is on recent studies conducted in Brazil, Jamaica, and India, as well as on my own research in Indonesia. I review these studies in terms of their principal findings, the information they provide regarding the cross-cultural reliability and validity of classroom learning environment instruments, and their policy implications in the respective countries. I conclude with a general assessment of the utility of the learning environment perspective for educational researchers in developing countries.

Formal Education and National Development

"To support all these development efforts, it is clear that an education system suited to nation building in a broad sense should be developed. . . . This will become the basis for the establishment of a strong Indonesian society" (Suharto, 1973, p. 49).

"The education provided by Tanzania for the students of Tanzania must serve the purposes of Tanzania. . . . It must encourage the development of a proud, independent, and free citizenry which relies upon itself for its own development." (Nyerere, 1968, p. 290).

These statements by the political leaders of two nations representing significantly different political ideologies, cultures, and socioeconomic systems are indicative of the aspirations of many developing countries toward their national education systems. Formal education has been identified as one of the keys to national development in the emerging nations, and the postcolonial era has witnessed significantly increased investments in the education sector and the related expansion of formal education. This movement toward mass education is occurring worldwide, regardless of political orientation, cultural background, economic system, social structure, or geographic location. The United Nations (UNESCO, 1976) documented this growth with statistics showing that from 1965 to 1973, total world enrollment at the three levels of education (primary, secondary, and tertiary) rose from 419 to 531 million. These figures correspond to an average annual increase of 3.0 percent, compared with an average annual increase of 1.9 percent in the world population during the same period. When these enrollment figures are broken down for the developing and developed nations, the annual average enrollment increase between 1960-61 and 1970-71 is almost three times higher in the developing nations. In short, the education sector has assumed a dominant position in the developing world due to its function as a primary agency of development.

Planners who favor increased investments in education believe that formal schooling ultimately promotes change at the national level by initially focusing on the personal growth of the individual student. When a critical mass of educated students enters the social, political, and economic life of the nation, national development will be stimulated. These planners think that the socialization process that occurs in the schools changes individual students in ways that will ultimately encourage national integration, social stability, economic development, psychosocial modernization, and the formation and mobilization of a citizenry. They expect that the opportunity that formal education represents for the individual will result in increased levels of socioeconomic mobility and equality at the national level.

Anthropologists such as Geertz (1963) refer to the role of the formal school in the "integrative revolution," wherein the parochial, potentially divisive loyalties of the students are replaced with a higher loyalty to the nation, thus promoting national integration and social stability. Schools are also expected to increase socioeconomic mobility and to promote greater equality of opportunity for individuals who previously would have been assigned their socioeconomic status on the basis of race, family position, and ethnicity. Parents in developing nations, who themselves were denied any possibility of improving their status, are willing to make sacrifices in order to invest in their children's education. Parents retain the hope that in return their children and ultimately the family as a whole will have a better life.

One of the most compelling arguments in favor of increased investments in formal education has been advanced by economists such as Harbison and Myers (1964), who articulated the manpower development, or human capital formation, hypothesis. This perspective views schooling in terms of teaching individuals the skills required by the occupational sector. By producing skilled manpower, formal education stimulates development and promotes self-reliance; that is, nationals are prepared to fill important positions, thus reducing the nation's dependency on outside assistance. Although contemporary economists (see Windham, 1975) have criticized this perspective, it remains a persuasive justification for educational investments in many developing countries.

The formation and mobilization of the new citizenry—prepared to participate in the political life of the nation with appropriate citizenship skills and orientations—have been examined by political scientists, such as Almond and Verba (1963) and Massialas (1972). In almost every country, schools are expected to function as agencies of political socialization to promote a national identity and interest in the nation's development objectives and to increase awareness of political institutions and processes and loyalty to the regime. Given the absence of alternative institutional mechanisms for the formation of an appropriately trained citizenry during the early years of independence, the concept of the public school, organized by the state for the purposes of the state, was very attractive. The political socialization function of formal education remains an important role of education in the national development process.

Sociologists and social psychologists, such as Inkeles and Smith (1974), have shown that education is related to significant changes in the individual, such as increased levels of modernity or achievement motivation, which ultimately promotes more rapid national development. Many developing nations perceive schools to have an important role in modernizing children, in promoting the work ethic, in inculcating achievement motivation, and generally in encouraging personal transformations congruent with the development objectives of the national leadership. In some settings, for example, schools are expected to change the traditional desire for large families to a willingness to limit family size, thus helping the nation to slow its population growth. In other settings, schools are expected to promote a respect for manual labor or agrarian occupations, as opposed to the traditional desire of educated youth to move directly into urban white-collar positions.

The empirical literature on education and development does not consistently confirm or refute hypotheses derived from these conceptualizations. In fact, critics of formal education, such as Carnoy (1974) and Illich (1970), have raised profound questions about these so-called benign interpretations of schooling. These criticisms notwithstanding, most educational researchers find that developing nations have lofty expectations about what formal education can and should accomplish. These expectations are reinforced both by an internal social demand for greater educational opportunities and by an external demand, since educational indicators are used to determine a country's level of development within the international community. Furthermore, formal education symbolizes the commitment of a nation's leaders to provide for the public welfare, and it indicates a national integrity and independence and a nation's progress toward modernization.

Educational Research in Developing Nations

Educational research in developing nations has been characterized either by descriptive studies or by school effects studies guided by the framework of the economists' production function (Alexander and Simmons, 1975; Averch and others, 1974). Production function studies have focused on quantitative school input variables (such as expenditure per pupil, years of teacher experience, pupil-teacher ratio, class size), which are related to such educational outcomes as academic achievement. Because these studies provide information relevant to the allocation of educational resources, they have appealed to policy makers. They have been criticized for failing to examine classroom processes, for examining only the more easily measured (but perhaps less important) material resource inputs, and for lacking a sound foundation in learning theory. The evidence suggests that learning involves factors that are not part of the typical production function model. For example, in their review of the relevant literature, Alexander and Simmons (1975) concluded that "schools in developing countries do promote learning, but the average rate of learning of primary and early secondary students is not markedly affected by educational policy changes along traditional lines, such as providing more and/or better teachers and facilities" (p. 52).

The shortcomings of the production function model have

led to a search for alternative approaches that focus on classroom processes and learning environments (Averch and others, 1974; Levin and Snow, 1972). In this vein, Alexander and Simmons (1975) asserted: "Learning occurs mainly through a student being removed from his home environment and *being exposed to a learning environment at school*. The exact mechanism of this transmission of knowledge is not clear" (p. 52, italics added). Although the production function approach to education has limitations, the question remains as to whether including classroom process and learning environment variables can provide more useful models for evaluating and changing educational settings in developing countries. I turn now to a review of relevant work on learning environments in order to arrive at some general conclusions about the applicability of this type of research to developing countries.

Learning Environment Research in Developing Countries

The major work on classroom learning environments in developing countries has been conducted in the past ten years, and there are indications that such studies will become more common in the years ahead. The cross-national surveys conducted by the International Institute for the Evaluation of Educational Achievement (IEA) included, among other school-related variables, measures of the classroom learning environment (for a review and critique of the IEA surveys, see Inkeles, 1977; Purves and Levine, 1975). Although the scope of these measures was limited, the surveys generated considerable interest in the concept of learning environments. A replication of the IEA survey conducted by the Indonesian Ministry of Education in 1975 incorporated some classroom climate variables (Elley, 1976). In addition, a recent study of the IEA data from Germany and the United States has established that the classroom learning environment and the tolerance of political dissent are related (Nielsen, 1977).

I selected the studies reviewed here because they address the following issues: (1) the cross-cultural reliability and validity of learning environment instruments, (2) the effects of classroom environments on learning, and (3) implications of such effects for educational policy. Two additional criteria were applied in selecting studies: the countries studied should represent different levels of development, sociocultural milieus, and geographic regions; and the studies should be comparable in terms of their conceptualization and instrumentation. Accordingly, I chose four representative studies that were recently conducted in Brazil (Holsinger, 1972, 1973), Jamaica (Persaud, 1976), India (Walberg, Rasher, and Singh, 1977; Walberg and Singh, 1974; Walberg, Singh, and Rasher, 1977), and Indonesia (Paige, 1978). These studies all used instruments based on the Classroom Environment Scale (CES) and the Learning Environment Inventory (LEI). The studies in Brazil and Jamaica related a summary measure of the learning environment to such outcomes as students' level of information, modernity, and social development. The studies in India and Indonesia used achievement and modernity measures as criteria, but the learning environment was conceptualized in a more differentiated way as representing the domains of relationship, goal orientation, and system maintenance and change dimensions.

Classroom Learning Environments in Brazil. One of the earliest studies of learning environments in a developing country was conducted by Holsinger (1972, 1973) in Brazil. Holsinger designed his study to test the effects of classroom climate and other variables on cognitive learning (information) and noncognitive learning (individual modernity) among elementary school children. He hypothesized that the elementary school was a modernizing setting that exercised its influence, in part, by means of the classroom climate. Holsinger's classroom climate scale, which was based on an early version of the LEI, the Classroom Climate Inventory (CCI; Walberg and Anderson, 1968), consisted of one item from each of eight CCI subscales: pupil participation, pupil cooperation, class intimacy, group work, teacher interest, egalitarianism, competitive emphasis, and disorganization. The sample was composed of 2,533 pupils in ninety classes, thirty for each grade level, selected at random from third, fourth, and fifth grade classrooms in the Federal District of Brasilia. Based on information provided by the pupils, Holsinger developed his classroom climate measure using an unweighted linear combination of the eight items taken from the CCI subscales. The measure produced an internal consistency reliability of 0.79.

The effects of classroom climate were examined in cross-sectional analyses in which individual modernity and information scores were regressed on nine independent variables: amount of schooling, age, socioeconomic status (SES), TV exposure, classroom climate, teacher negativism, physical environment, social structure (peer liking patterns), and teacher modernity. These nine variables accounted for a sizable portion of the variance in mean classroom modernity ($R^2 = 0.64$) and information ($R^2 = 0.52$), and for a modest amount of variance in individual modernity ($R^2 = 0.19$) and information ($R^2 = 0.09$). Classroom climate was the third most powerful predictor of classroom modernity and individual modernity, following amount of schooling and TV exposure, and the fourth most powerful predictor of classroom information and individual information, following amount of schooling, age, and SES. Students in classes that were higher on the composite index of climate had higher modernity and information scores. The items in the index measure aspects of all three learning environment domains, but Holsinger did not estimate the relative contribution of each domain to the outcome criteria.

Holsinger also studied the relative effects of school-environmental and pupil-background variables. Five environmental variables (teacher modernity, physical environment, teacher negativism, social structure, and classroom climate) and two background variables (SES and television exposure) were combined into summary indexes and entered into a regression analysis, with the pupil background index being entered first. The school environment was a much better predictor of both modernity and information than the pupil's background. School environment produced an R^2 change almost twice that of pupil background.

Holsinger's study is important because it was one of the first to show that reliable instruments could be fashioned for school children outside of the United States based on scales originally developed in the United States. It also showed that the classroom learning environment is a powerful predictor of both cognitive and noncognitive learning compared with other determinants both inside and outside the classroom. In general terms, the school is shown to be a modernizing setting in two ways: over time, amount of schooling is associated with gains in classroom and individual modernity, and, within grade levels, certain types of learning environments—those emphasizing pupil participation and cooperation, teacher interest, organization, and egalitarianism, among other factors—are associated with higher levels of individual and group modernity. With respect to practical implications, Holsinger noted that policy makers need to examine the cost effectiveness of keeping children in school for a longer period of time versus changing the school environment before committing themselves to a particular policy.

Classroom Learning Environments in Jamaica. Persaud (1976) recently extended this line of research in a project conducted on elementary school children in Jamaica. The study, which used a classroom climate instrument based on the CES, was designed to examine the effects of classroom and school climates on such noncognitive outcomes as social development and aspiration levels. The sample consisted of 1,277 third and sixth grade students in eighteen elementary schools. Classroom climate was a summary measure of "openness" based on a classroom's properties in eight areas. More open classes were defined as high on involvement, cooperation, teacher support, teacher evaluation, and innovation, as moderate on task orientation and work organization, and as low on teacher rigidity. Principals and teachers were also asked about the openness of the classroom and school on similar dimensions.

Four other sets of independent variables included teacher characteristics (teacher qualifications, recency of training, and experience), principal characteristics (qualifications and experience), measures of the student's social structure (such as the type of school attended and the student's socioeconomic status and ethnicity), and indexes of concurrent influences on students (parental and peer emphasis on occupational choice and the student's exposure to and use of mass media). Two measures of student personal and social development were used as dependent variables. A summary index of social development measured the student's level of interpersonal trust, tolerance, self-esteem, and personal efficacy. The second index, labeled extrinsic motivation, assessed the student's aspirations and educational and occupational expectations.

Using regression analysis, Persaud found that an open school authority pattern (an average principal, teacher, and student classroom climate measure) predicted a greater amount of the variance in social development than did the other sets of independent variables. Extrinsic motivation was higher in open schools, but this variable was strongly influenced by the type of school and the sociodemographic characteristics of the students, as well as by such concurrent influences as parental and peer expectations. The finding that more open classroom climates are associated with a higher level of student social development is consistent with the results obtained in the United States (see Chapter Nine).

This study is important because it suggests that such personal attributes as trust, tolerance, and self-esteem may be enhanced by a more open classroom learning environment. According to Persaud, many teachers in developing societies believe that strongly controlled and disciplined classes are needed to ensure students' social and academic development. Persaud recommends that principals and teachers consider more open school and classroom environments, which, by his criteria, include an emphasis on teacher evaluation, task orientation, and work organization (goal and maintenance areas), as well as an emphasis on support, cooperation, and innovation (relationship and change areas).

Classroom Learning Environments in India. Walberg and his associates (Walberg, Rasher, and Singh, 1977; Walberg and Singh, 1974; Walberg, Singh, and Rasher, 1977) recently conducted a study of classroom learning environments in the State of Rajasthan, India. They designed the study to assess the cross-cultural validity of the LEI and to test a three-factor conceptualization of the social-psychological properties of classes and other small group settings.

The fifteen LEI subscales were translated into Hindi and administered to tenth grade students in eighty-three general science and sixty-seven social studies classes located in secondary schools randomly sampled from the twenty-six districts in the State of Rajasthan. The internal consistency reliability coefficients for the fifteen subscales ranged from 0.53 to 0.85 (Walberg, Rasher, and Singh, 1977). The study focused on the incremental predictive validity (that is, increases in explained variance beyond that accounted for by control variables) of the learning environment measures by regressing end-of-course science and social studies achievement scores on beginning-of-course measures of IQ and midcourse perceptions of the classroom learning environment.

The learning environment measures showed a pattern of results similar to that shown in studies conducted previously in the United States and other Western nations. IQ was a powerful predictor of general science ($r = 0.63$) and social studies ($r = 0.61$) achievement, but the increment associated with the LEI scales was considerable. IQ plus the LEI scales produced a multiple correlation of 0.82 with science and 0.90 with social studies achievement (Walberg, Singh, and Rasher, 1977). With IQ controlled, the median partial correlations of the fifteen LEI scales and achievement were 0.43 for general science and 0.58 for social studies. LEI dimensions such as cohesion (relationship), difficulty, speed, goal direction, and competition (goal orientation), and formality, democratic organization, and diversity (system maintenance and change) showed positive partial correlations with achievement. Dimensions such as cliqueness, favoritism, friction, and apathy (relationship) and disorganization (system maintenance and change) showed negative partial correlations with achievement (see Table 2 in Chapter One for a categorization of the LEI subscales into the three conceptual domains).

The authors also generated several composite learning environment indexes from the LEI subscales, three of which—affect, task, and competitiveness—they selected to represent the relationship, goal orientation, and system maintenance and change domains (their categorization of the LEI subscales was somewhat different from that shown in Table 2; see Walberg, Rasher, and Singh, 1977, p. 509). The control variables used in this analysis included IQ, type of school (urban-rural and private-public), and such teacher characteristics as sex, age, marital status, training, and previous teaching experience. Among the control variables, IQ and teacher training had the largest standardized regression weights. The domains of affect (relationship) and task (goal orientation) were positively and independently related to the achievement measures.

The authors discuss several policy implications of their study. They noted that only a quarter of the teachers in India are trained and that greater investments must be made in training programs. With respect to the classroom learning environment, they concluded: "It now seems justifiable and practically feasible to obtain such perceptions for evaluative and diagnostic purposes in natural settings to ascertain the extent to which classes are optimizing those social relations which are associated with higher rates of cognitive . . . learning" (Walberg, Rasher, and Singh, 1977, p. 512). The findings show that the LEI is useful in cross-cultural research and that affect and task orientation are associated with higher achievement scores in the Indian setting.

Classroom Learning Environments in East Java

My study in Indonesia (Paige, 1978) was designed to accomplish several purposes. The main methodological objective was to determine if valid and reliable classroom learning environment scales could be generated from data based on the perceptions of Indonesian elementary school children using specially adapted forms of the CES and LEI subscales. The four principal theoretical objectives were the following: (1) to examine the three-domain model of learning environments in the Indonesian context, (2) to assess the relationship between the learning environment and cognitive (academic achievement) and noncognitive (individual modernity) learning outcomes, (3) to estimate the relative effects of the learning environment variables in the context of a model that included plausible rival determinants of learning located inside and outside the school, and (4) to identify the school- and classroom-related factors that act as modernizing influences. The major policy objective was to provide Indonesian educators with information on which to base decisions regarding future research, and to formulate the implications for teacher training programs of focusing more heavily on a program of research on learning environments.

The Sample and Measuring Instruments. The study was conducted in the province of East Java, Indonesia, the most heavily populated of Indonesia's twenty-six provinces (approximately 26 million inhabitants according to the 1971 census). A stratified random sample of 30 rural and 30 urban elementary schools was drawn from a total population of 49 rural and 217 urban elementary schools located in two subdistricts of the Malang rural regency and the three subdistricts of the Malang urban municipality. Questionnaires were administered to 1,621 sixth grade pupils in the 60 schools early in the third term of the academic year. Indonesian elementary schools rarely have more than one sixth grade class; the school and the classroom are synonymous as the sampling unit for all practical purposes.

Classroom learning environments were assessed using the nine CES and three of the LEI subscales, which were translated into Indonesian and revised to fit the East Javanese sociocultural milieu. The three LEI subscales, which were used to expand the conceptualization of the classroom learning environment, were difficulty, speed, and physical environment. Three composite indexes—relationship, goal orientation, and system maintenance—were generated from the relevant subscales corresponding to the three major domains of classroom settings.

Additional scales were developed for the following key areas: the home learning environment, the school and classroom physical environment, teacher pedagogy (instructional style), teacher quality (training and experience), and individual modernity. Modernity was measured using items from the Inkeles and Smith (1974) modernity (OM) scale. Preliminary analyses indicated that the classroom learning environment scales, especially the three composite indexes and the twenty-six-item pupil modernity scale, had satisfactory internal consistency reliabilities. The remaining scales had reliabilities ranging from 0.47 (teacher quality) to 0.87 (school physical environment). Various procedures were used to determine the face validity, construct validity, and predictive validity of the scales (see Paige, 1978, pp. 300-337, for more details). The evidence confirmed the cross-cultural validity of the classroom learning environment constructs using data gathered in a sociocultural context quite different from that in which the instruments originated and from those in which the instruments had been used previously.

The Classroom Learning Environments. East Javanese pupils see their classes as promoting the relationship domain, with a particular emphasis on involvement and affiliation, and somewhat less emphasis on teacher support. The goal orientation domain presents a mixed picture. Although the pupils see their classes as strong on task orientation and competition, the classes are not perceived as being high on difficulty or speed; that is, they are not as satisfactory in terms of meeting the pupils' needs for personal challenge or individualized pacing of instruction. With respect to system maintenance and change, the classes are strongly oriented toward discipline, order, and control, and, as found in earlier studies of teacher instructional styles in Indonesia, have little emphasis on innovation.

Multiple regression was used to examine the effects of the classroom learning environment on academic achievement and individual modernity, relative to five other blocks of independent variables. The learning outcomes thus were regressed on six sets of variables: pupil background characteristics, the home learning environment, school and classroom physical environment and organizational characteristics, teacher and teaching style characteristics, the classroom learning environment, and rural-urban school location. This ordering of the variables, although theoretically appropriate (see Paige, 1978, pp. 81-84 and 232-233, for the rationale), provides a stringent test for the classroom learning environment variables, since they followed four other sets of determinants in the model.

Four regressions were run with each of the dependent variables so that the effects of both the discrete learning environment subscales and the composites could be examined, and individual-level and consensual (classroom mean score) measures of the classroom learning environment could be compared. The total set of variables showed an average multiple correlation of 0.35 with achievement and 0.52 with individual modernity (an average R^2 of 0.12 and 0.27, respectively). These findings, similar to those obtained by Holsinger ($R^2 = 0.19$ with individual modernity), are gratifying given that the model did not include variations in grade level since only sixth grade pupils were studied in Indonesia. On the average, the classroom learning environment indexes accounted for an increment of 2.2 percent of the variance in achievement and 2.9 percent of the variance in modernity.

The goal orientation domain was the most powerful and consistent predictor of individual learning, exercising a positive influence on both achievement and modernity. Specifically, task orientation, competition, and difficulty were most closely associated with individual modernity, and speed was the strongest predictor of achievement. The relationship domain had a modest positive influence on modernity (involvement and teacher support were the strongest predictors in this area) but did not have an impact on achievement. Classes higher in order and organization had students who were lower in modernity and, to a lesser degree, achievement. Since the Indonesian classes sampled were generally very highly structured, this finding suggests that an excessive emphasis on discipline can discourage learning. However, teacher control showed a modest positive relationship to modernity, which suggests that a balanced structuring of the environment can be beneficial when it sets behavioral "ground rules" for pupils and identifies the authority figure in the classroom.

How do the learning environment variables compare in relative terms with other determinants of learning? With variance added used as the criterion, the set of classroom learning environment variables is second most important in predicting achievement (following background characteristics, of which age is the most important) and fourth most important in predicting modernity (following background characteristics, the home learning environment, and school and classroom physical environment and organizational features). The findings regarding the relative importance of pupil background and home environment variables are consistent with the results of most of the studies conducted in other countries (see Alexander and Simmons, 1975). Although other variables, such as age and home environment, have greater overall importance than the classroom environment, the classroom environment does influence the acquisition of knowledge and attitudes among East Javanese elementary school children. Classrooms emphasizing the goal orientation or personal growth domains promote higher levels of modernity and achievement.

This study has several policy implications. First, the classroom learning environment instruments proved easy to administer, leading to the conclusion that obtaining student perceptions for diagnostic and other purposes is practically feasible. By administering the questionnaires to whole classes of students using a guided group interview approach, I found that the test could be administered reasonably quickly; thus, data collection caused only minimum disruption in the classroom routine. Since the measures were reliable and valid, and since the results showed that the classroom environment affects learning, one policy outcome would be the continued use of such instruments in future research programs.

The Indonesia study, consistent with the other three studies, has implications for teacher training programs. Policy makers might consider introducing learning environment concepts and related research methods into preparatory and inservice programs. Teachers can be made aware of the significance of the learning environment, their role in promoting certain types of environments, and techniques for assessing the environment, and can be trained to evaluate their teaching effectiveness by using such techniques. Feedback gained from this type of diagnostic procedure can be used to alter teacher behavior, create a more effective learning milieu, and promote higher rates of desired learning. The findings also focus on the home environment as a dominant external (nonschool) determinant of learning. Teachers can be trained to assist parents in establishing a more satisfactory home learning environment, particularly in rural and poor urban areas. Parents may not be able to alter their socioeconomic circumstances, but they probably can change their home environment to encourage a high level of learning among their children.

An Assessment of Learning Environment Research in Developing Countries

Earlier in this chapter I raised the question "Is classroom learning environment research appropriate for developing countries?" Several criteria for assessing a given theoretical perspective and its attendant research methodology were initially identified. In this section, I use these criteria to assess the learning environment perspective as it applies to developing nations.

Cross-Culturally Reliable and Valid Instruments. For a theoretical perspective or conceptualization to be appropriate, the instruments derived from it must produce reliable and valid measures of the phenomenon under investigation. The problem is compounded when measures developed in one sociocultural setting are introduced into another. Researchers need to show that the instruments possess satisfactory psychometric characteristics in the new setting. The four studies show that perceptual measures of classroom learning environments based on the CES and the LEI can be used in non-Western societies. Furthermore, two of the studies (Walberg's and mine) support the utility of the conceptualization of three domains of learning environments. The consistency of these findings indicates that the learning environment perspective meets the first criterion.

Identification of School-Related Variables That Affect Learning. A theoretical perspective should lead to the identification and measurement of school-related variables that influence learning. The four studies confirm the significance of the relationship between the classroom learning environment and a range of learning outcomes in developing nations. Each of the authors examined the relative strength of learning environment variables compared with other factors located inside and outside the school. The findings show that the learning environment predicts cognitive and noncognitive learning independently of other important sets of variables. Walberg and I subjected the learning environment variables to the most stringent statistical tests. These variables still add to the explained variance in outcome above and beyond that accounted for by other school and background factors. On the basis of this evidence, the learning environment perspective effectively meets the second criterion.

Identification of Factors Responsive to Intervention. For policy makers to focus exclusively on uncontrollable factors is of little value, although the identification of such factors in the context of the total learning process may be important. The policy relevance of a theoretical perspective depends on the degree to which it can isolate learning determinants that educators can alter and improve. The evidence suggests that adequately trained teachers can act as change agents in the classroom (see DeYoung, 1977; Chapter Eleven), but more applied research is needed to confirm this point in developing countries.

Policy Implications. The need for findings to guide policy in developing countries is acute, and the relevance of a theoretical perspective is likely to be judged on the basis of its practical implications. In this respect, the learning environment approach is quite satisfactory. Learning environments affect criteria that are clearly relevant to national goals of economic development (through individual gains in information and achievement), social development (through individual growth in self-reliance, personal efficacy, and trust), and modernization (through the acquisition of modern orientations). Furthermore, some of the influence of learning environments is independent of such indexes as socioeconomic status, ethnicity, and the home milieu, suggesting that they also enhance socioeconomic mobility and the equality of opportunity. Conversely, the relevant work in developing countries has just begun, and much more research is needed to establish firm conclusions about the specific effects of the three domains. The results suggest that an emphasis on the relationship and goal orientation areas enhances learning, but the influence of the system maintenance and change dimensions is much less clear. As evidence accumulates on the effects of classroom learning environments on a variety of outcomes, policy implications may become more precise.

Cost Effectiveness. Because of scarce resources in developing nations, educational planners must search for cost-effective approaches to improve their national education systems. Conducting research using learning environment instruments is practical in developing countries; it is not difficult to train test administrators or to administer the instruments. Holsinger and I suggested that interventions in the social-psychological environment of the classroom may prove to be more cost-efficient for changing educational settings than more traditional interventions, such as investments in school physical plants. There is a need for well-designed research programs to explore the question of cost effectiveness.

Implications for Educational Research. A theoretical perspective is relevant to developing nations to the degree that it guides research, suggests an appropriate methodology, stimulates researchers to confirm previous findings and to address unanswered questions, and contributes a coherent body of knowledge. The learning environment perspective and its attendant methods and instruments generally meet these criteria, although there is a need to refine current measures, replicate existing studies in other developing countries, and expand our conceptual frameworks. Numerous studies using the CES and the LEI have been conducted in the United States and other Western societies, and there is increasing demand for research of this type in developing nations. One of the benefits of conducting learning environment research is that a body of knowledge exists that suggests promising new directions to explore.

The evidence from studies conducted around the world is consistent on one major point: The classroom learning environment mediates and interprets for the pupil a wide range of educational inputs and stimuli. The four studies reviewed show that specific aspects of the learning environment can promote or inhibit personal and academic growth in ways that are conceptually linked to national development goals. Studies that include an assessment of this environment, especially those that locate environmental variables in a broader conceptual paradigm and are sensitive to the challenges of cross-cultural research, can provide significant information to educational planners in developing nations. Such information can be related directly to policy decisions affecting the classroom and other school, home, and community resources.

—◆—11—◆—

Practical Applications for Changing Educational Settings

This chapter focuses on the practical applications of the foregoing material. I recently identified several related areas in which a social-ecological perspective may be useful for evaluating and changing educational settings (Moos, 1976a). Five such areas are discussed here: maximizing educational information, facilitating and evaluating environmental change, implementing educational consultation, formulating ecologically relevant case descriptions, and enhancing environmental competence.

226

Maximizing Educational Information

The Need for Information. The rapid growth of new educational programs has increased the need for more accurate and complete descriptions of these programs. For example, colleges know much more about the characteristics of entering students than students know about the colleges they plan to enter. Students and staff might be prepared to make more effective use of new educational programs if they knew more about them. Since the social climate is a key element of an educational environment, program descriptions should include such information. Knowledge about a program's social milieu is important for prospective students, teachers, guidance counselors and university housing office administrators, and individuals interested in new developments in the field.

The program descriptions written to fill these needs have depended primarily on information about the physical setting, program emphasis, type of staffing, and student characteristics, which is sometimes supplemented by questionnaire or observational data. However, since most program descriptions are written by people involved in the programs, they usually omit information about the social environment as seen by program participants and fail to give an adequate picture of the program. For example, Speegle (1969) learned that the college environment, as described in eight college catalogues, was not congruent with students' perceptions as measured by the College Characteristics Index, and that none of the catalogues included descriptions of the informal social atmosphere of the colleges.

Methods like the CES and the URES can be used to specify the psychosocial or perceived climate characteristics of an educational setting. Students, teachers, and outside observers can fill out the scales on the basis of their experiences in the setting, and this information can help to provide an accurate picture of what the setting is like. For example, the CES has been used in a voucher program to provide information about classroom environments to help parents select a school for their child (Weiler and others, 1976). The voucher program offered a choice of ten educational programs, such as basic skills, individualized learning, open program, creative arts, and multicultural. Families were provided with a directory of "voucher choices" and a comprehensive evaluation report summarizing data on the characteristics and performance of each program during the previous school year. The report contained a section on "student feelings," which included student perceptions of four CES dimensions: involvement, affiliation (called friendship), teacher support, and teacher control. Although parents may have been overwhelmed by the amount of information they received, this project is a good example of the use of program descriptions to help parents make informed choices about their children's educational experiences.

A related application is the use of realistic job previews to give job candidates more accurate information. The usual job selection process almost always inflates the expectations of newcomers, leading to disappointment after they start work. Realistic job previews change people's expectations, but do not drive away prospective employees or make it more difficult for the organization to recruit the people it wants to hire. These previews may increase job tenure by helping prospective employees choose organizations more intelligently, by communicating an air of honesty to applicants who then feel freer to ask relevant questions, and by making individual expectations more congruent with the actual organizational climate, thus "inoculating" newcomers against the unpleasant aspects of a new environment (Wanous, 1977). This approach has been developed primarily in business settings, but it is applicable to selecting and recruiting teachers and other employees in educational settings.

One problem with these procedures is that organizations may not wish to reveal what their members think of them. For example, the Questionnaire on Student and College Characteristics (QSCC) provides information on the restrictiveness of rules, faculty-student interactions, student activism, the flexibility of the curriculum, the intellectual vigor of the college, and so on. Colleges and universities were provided free tests and scoring services and were encouraged to use the results to help describe themselves to prospective students. However, only about 25 percent of the 200 colleges involved actually made extensive use of the QSCC results (Baird, 1974). Not even a free voluntary program could get colleges to reveal what their students thought of them. Some of this resistance can be overcome by highlighting the beneficial uses of descriptions of educational settings and, in particular, by reminding administrators of the personal and institutional costs (such as high dropout and transfer rates) incurred when students select incongruent educational settings (but see Baird, 1974, for another perspective).

Giving and Taking Feedback. My colleagues and I began our work primarily from a research perspective. Our original intent in giving people feedback about the characteristics of their setting was to enhance their participation in and enthusiasm for our research. This was a good strategy, since we managed to obtain a high level of cooperation. It quickly turned out, however, that the process and dynamics of giving feedback became as interesting and as time consuming as the process of collecting and analyzing the data. In brief, we provided students and staff with information about how they perceived their social environment, how different groups compared (such as teachers and students, and students and resident assistants), how their setting compared with other similar settings, and, in some cases, how their setting compared with what they considered ideal.

In general, people want to learn more about their program and tend to find feedback useful, although the recipients of our feedback cope with it in a variety of ways. One major reaction is active interest and an indication of a desire to use the data to improve the setting.

This reaction is generally a good sign, but it sometimes takes a surprising turn. For example, in one case we gave feedback on the CES to several high school classes. Two students in one class printed a fake letterhead, composed a feedback letter ostensibly signed by our research assistant, and produced a highly authentic-looking computer printout of the CES results. All these materials were mailed to the hapless teacher and the school principal, with the return address of a recently rented post office box.

The letterhead read "Educational Environment Testing Service," and the "feedback" letter stated: "We are led to believe from students' answers on the surveys that your classroom is far from ideal. The students want an immediate change of classroom structure, whereas your answers indicate a very well organized and likable classroom atmosphere." Also included were such pithy remarks as "This teacher is still competing with rookie teachers, but is out of his league," "The teacher is obviously bored with the work and a definite change of atmosphere is needed," and "Although it will be hard to undo the damage that has been done, we are giving you a list of reforming methods that we urge you to use."

The ruse worked. Everyone thought it was authentic feedback from us. A considerable amount of anger, mistrust, and excitement was aroused, which threatened our relationships with all the schools in the area and necessitated several tense meetings to resolve (of course, the particular research assistant involved was away the day this story broke). I would not suggest this as a general strategy for implementing change, but, so far as I know, the learning environment of the classroom involved altered radically, although we did not attempt to reassess it!

Implementation of data-based feedback involves a number of complex issues such as: who should get the feedback (for example, only the administrator of the school, all the teaching staff, all the participants including students, or only those people designated by the administrator); whether the top administrators, such as the school district staff and superintendent, should also obtain feedback; and the extent to which classes or living groups should remain anonymous. If there are only a few settings in a facility, as is often the case in a small college or school, can feedback be given and anonymity maintained? Should one only give feedback to a high school principal, for example, after all the teachers have obtained individual feedback and have agreed to share the results? These complex issues need to be discussed before data collection and resolved before feedback when possible.

Contrary to first impressions, there is no single answer to

any of these questions. We have been in settings where an administrator would accept no feedback unless staff agreed that feedback should be given. We have also worked in a facility in which staff decided to have a joint meeting for giving feedback on each individual setting to the entire staff and administration. Of course, conflicts sometimes arise between administrators' desires for information about each of the settings under their jurisdiction (such as all the classes in one school or all the living groups in one university) and our usual procedures, which are to keep results confidential unless the setting participants wish to share them. Despite these and other problems, feedback generally is worthwhile, both to train the person giving it and to increase the understanding of the people receiving it.

Facilitating and Evaluating Environmental Change

Changing Social Climate. In some of the settings in which we gave feedback, interest developed in using the information to facilitate and evaluate environmental change. In a classroom, for example, a self-initiated analysis may result as discussion of the real CES profile leads to interest in the differences and similarities between teacher and student perceptions. As a natural consequence, teachers often explore their own and students' ideals, relating them to actual classroom performance. The CES guides the discussion, and teachers begin to formulate specific changes to improve their classes as a result of understanding their own and their students' goals more clearly. There are four steps involved in this process: (1) systematic assessment of the environment, (2) feedback to participating groups with particular stress on real-ideal setting differences, (3) planning and instituting specific changes, and (4) reassessment. Since there is no "end point" to the process, continual change and reassessment often occur (Moos, 1974a).

These procedures have been used to stimulate positive change in educational settings (Daher, Corazzini, and McKinnon, 1977; Holahan and Wilcox, 1977). For example, DeYoung (1977) used the CES in a college sociology class to obtain information regarding real-ideal class discrepancies. This information, which indicated that students wanted more involvement, greater stress on innovative teaching methods, and clearer organization and direction, led DeYoung to modify his approach in a subsequent class. Students indicated a desire to "get a group together for a project" (affiliation), to have the instructor "spend a little time just talking with students" (teacher support), and to "engage in unusual projects" and "do different things on different days" (innovation). Students also reported that they were confused about classroom policies and procedures. Therefore, students formed teams to report on specific topics, and DeYoung made efforts to see students individually, to discuss class subject matter and organization, and to clarify grading policies and appeal procedures. He also encouraged innovative projects and alternative classroom delivery and participation techniques.

Although the social climate desired by the students in the two classes was virtually identical, their actual learning environments differed substantially. Students in the second class perceived more emphasis on the relationship dimensions of involvement, affiliation, and teacher support and on rule clarity and innovation. They also showed greater interest and participation in class and attended class more regularly. These differences represent the specific areas the instructor attempted to influence; they indicate that one can change the learning environment along lines suggested by the CES.

One of the problems of having the participants in a setting determine change is illustrated by the fact that students wanted less emphasis on task orientation. Since the instructor decided that decreasing the emphasis on this dimension would jeopardize overall learning objectives, no attempt was made to alter the amount of attention given to course work. The effect of this disregard for students' wishes was demonstrated by the similarity of task orientation scores in the two classes, indicating that it is possible to restructure and improve a class without sacrificing attention to course content.

Some of the benefits of this process of planning and facilitating change include the following: (1) Participants can untangle and analyze the multiple dimensions of setting function-

ing. (2) Such important but often overlooked classroom characteristics as the clarity of expectations regarding class grading
policies are brought into awareness. (3) Student input is obtained in a manner that makes students feel comfortable and
competent. Although many junior high school and high school
students may not feel qualified to criticize a course, they do
feel able to act as reporters about its current functioning. (4) In
some behavioral science courses (sociology, social psychology,
and group dynamics) the issues raised by the use of the CES or
URES can provide relevant discussion topics, such as an analysis
of teacher versus student roles or of institutional sanctions and
sources of resistance to change. (5) Since participants can concentrate their attempts to change their setting on a few commonly defined areas, the possibility of confusion or conflicting
behavior is reduced and the likelihood that change will take
place in an orderly manner is enhanced. And (6) involvement
often is increased simply because people are engaged in the
common task of changing their own setting.

*Changing Architectural and Organizational Characteris-
tics.* These methods can be applied to changing the architectural
and organizational characteristics of educational settings, with
resulting effects on student behavior. Holahan (1977) consulted
with university administrators to evaluate the impact of design
changes in the dining area of a high-rise dormitory. The open
space communal dining room, which served 800 students, was
seen as an institutionalized, socially isolating setting that lacked
visual and auditory privacy. There were constant visual and behavioral intrusions from food lines entering through the dining
area and from students seeking seats and returning trays. The
design modification involved the construction of partitions sit-
uated to separate people who were eating from those involved
in distracting activities. The partitions were attractively designed, with a solid base and a partially open upper section so
that students could find seats. Self-reports and behavioral observations indicated that the changes improved the opportunity for
social contact, increased privacy, and diminished the institutional appearance of the setting (see also Conyne, 1975; Conyne
and Lamb, 1978).

Using a related approach, Schroeder (in press [b]) noted the importance of territoriality and suggested ways in which residence hall programs might facilitate the territorial behavior of students with respect to personalization of space, defensible space, social interaction and group stability, and privacy regulation. Personalization of space can be facilitated by actively encouraging students to paint and decorate their rooms, hallways, stairwells, and public areas. With respect to defensible space, residents could physically "mark" secondary territories, such as hallways and lounges, by painting and decorating them, by locking houses and corridors to restrict access to residents and their guests, and the like.

To promote social interaction and group stability, centrally located student rooms can be converted into group rooms, and residents can design, personalize, and control these areas according to their needs and desires. For example, in one residence hall a previously unused foyer was walled off to create a special lounge and homogeneous living unit for engineering students. Students can also enhance their privacy by redesigning the interiors of their rooms with partitions and lofts and creating natural boundaries through unique arrangements of bookcases, plants, and desks. This kind of active manipulation and personalization of the proximate physical environment supports territorial behavior and may be especially important to students who are searching for and attempting to develop new self-concepts (Becker, 1977).

Resistance to Change and Other Problems. The above procedures are no panaceas, and the evaluation and change process can encounter serious resistance. Resistance tends to arise when existing social relationships are ignored, when people feel that change may lead to an increase in disruptive or uncontrollable behavior (such as by students in classrooms), when change may cause staff to be uncertain of what is expected of them, or when the need for change is not adequately understood by setting participants (see Zaltman and Duncan, 1977, chap. 3, for an extended discussion).

Different concepts of ideal environments and resulting disagreement on the preferred direction of change can be a serious problem. Feedback and discussion of social climate information help to identify common values and to clarify differences in value orientations. Teachers, principals, parents, and school board administrators may disagree on the ideal emphasis on classroom competition, but they usually agree that involvement, affiliation, teacher support, and clarity are important. However, some people feel that classroom structure and organization are essential, whereas others are convinced that an emphasis on these dimensions retards the development of independence and intrinsic motivation to learn. To complicate matters further, people may not know what is best for them and may prefer to function in settings that maximize immediate satisfaction and comfort instead of basic learning skills and long-range social competence.

Another general issue involves temporary decreases in such areas as clarity and cohesion. New policies may initially be confusing, which indicates that the change process is incomplete. In these cases communication must be improved and the involvement of the setting participants must be increased. Since many changes are implemented by new policies or rules, efforts to increase task orientation or independence may be confounded by people's reactions to greater emphasis on system maintenance. For example, the initial changes in one of our studies led to greater structure and a concomitant decrease in the quality of interpersonal relationships, particularly spontaneity (Bliss, Moos, and Bromet, 1976). The continuing development process eventually brought about the desired changes, but a temporary decrease in cohesion and spontaneity can occur when attempts are made to increase program structure.

The fact that change may continue beyond the originally desired goals also presents a potential problem. Changes may take place within a consistent framework; that is, a program can retain its overall direction while a series of carefully thought out and graduated changes are made. But change may be difficult to control or stop once it has begun. In a follow-up to one of our studies, it was found that program modifications led to predictable changes in staff ideals, which in turn led to a desire for further change (Cooper, 1973). Feedback is a dynamic, ongoing process that may cause changes in values about an ideal environment as well as changes in the real environment.

A final issue is the maintenance of an innovation once it has been implemented successfully. The two most common problems involve a gradual decrease in the motivation of participants and changes in the overall setting (such as the college or school) that impinge on the particular subsetting (such as the living group or classroom) involved. Although there are no wholly satisfactory solutions to these problems, some recent work provides useful guidelines about factors that enhance the utility of feedback and the likelihood of implementing successful innovations.

The Utility of Feedback. McKeachie's (1976) analysis suggests that feedback works best when three basic conditions are met. First, the feedback must provide relevant information to the learner (consultee). McKeachie pointed out that studies of student ratings of college teachers and of videotaped feedback, based on the assumption that teaching will improve if teachers get feedback, often fail to show positive effects. One problem is that the feedback may not provide usable information. As McKeachie stated, "Anyone who has watched an English professor's eyes glaze over as she or he looks at a computer printout of means and standard deviations of student ratings on an 80-item form, is likely to have some doubts about the information communicated. . . . We can fail to understand because of *too much* information as well as too little" (p. 824).

Second, the recipients of feedback must be motivated to change. Competing motivations, such as reducing perceived threats to organizational control, maintaining traditional prerogatives and role status, and fear of external scrutiny, may frustrate well-intentioned change efforts. Initial feedback regarding "dysfunctional" behavior (such as high absenteeism, sick call, and dropout rates) is perceived to be relevant to program functioning and can enhance the relative strength of motivation toward constructive change. The characteristics of the social environment become more relevant once the connections between them and dysfunctional behaviors are clarified.

Third, respondents must realize that better alternatives

exist. Although participants may feel that the feedback is relevant and be motivated to change, they may feel that change is impossible because of the people in the setting, constricting bureaucratic policies, insufficient funding, and so forth. A recurring issue here is whether printed feedback or only one feedback session is sufficient to produce change. Printed feedback may be useful under certain conditions, but it generally is not very effective for implementing social system change (see McKeachie, 1976, for similar conclusions regarding the impact of printed versus personal feedback on teaching effectiveness). Outside motivational support and specific suggestions for implementing change are usually necessary to use feedback to foster long-term change.

In general, the methods we use are promising and work reasonably well, both because they are consonant with the above three principles and because of three additional ingredients: (1) They concentrate on relatively small social settings (classrooms instead of schools, student living groups instead of entire universities) that are very important to their members; (2) they focus on aspects of settings that tend to be under local control (that is, teachers and students *can* change the emphasis on involvement, affiliation, teacher support, task orientation, and rule clarity in their own classes); and (3) they address each individual's need for personal efficacy directly, including the need to mold his or her social environment.

Determinants of Successful Innovations. Fullan and Pomfret (1977) presented an overview of four sets of determinants of the success of innovations. First, the important aspects of innovation are the explicitness of the plans and the simplicity or ease of implementing them. Second, feedback mechanisms that stimulate interaction, problem identification, and participation in decision making are helpful when implementing the innovation. Continuous interaction between teachers and consultants is better than single workshops or preservice training. Change agents must also allow enough time for people in the setting to familiarize themselves with new materials and methods and to reflect and work on implementation problems. The time allotted for implementing innovations is often unrealistically short, primarily because the complexity of the change process is insufficiently understood or because of the immediacy of the perceived need for change.

Third, the characteristics of the adopting units (such as an adolescent residential center or a classroom) are important, particularly the organizational climate and degree of environmental support. High morale among teachers and the active support of principals and superintendents increase the chances of educational change and perceived program success. Such factors increase the effectiveness of the social climate scales, which, by increasing cohesion and morale, may facilitate the later introduction of a broader, more comprehensive innovation.

The fourth set of factors are macrosociopolitical, such as the degree to which the promotion of large-scale programs by political agencies increases the likelihood of adoption but decreases the likelihood of effective implementation. It is also possible that, due to the emphasis on rapid payoff and outcome, the political context may inhibit the identification of problems in implementation. Changing social settings is a complex process, and most successful innovations undergo gradual, continual change themselves during implementation, reflecting a process of mutual adaptation between the change advocate and the host setting (see also Berman and McLaughlin, 1976; Williams and Elmore, 1976).

Corwin (1972) noted that organizations can be changed more easily if they are staffed by young, flexible, supportive, and competent boundary personnel, or "gatekeepers," and if the organization's members have positions that are reasonably secure and protected from the status risks involved in change. He pointed out that liberal, creative, and unconventional outsiders with fresh perspectives are important, but that change agents with these characteristics may be a source of friction and arouse defensive reactions. The attempt to combine the change agent role with an apprenticeship system (for example, teacher interns who try to facilitate change in schools) precariously situates such interns between two powerful organizations. They are representatives of the outside organization that is attempting to facilitate change (the university), but can count on little direct support from remote university professors and are directly supervised by school personnel who may resist the change.

Finally, how to evaluate the success of an innovation must be determined. Hall and Loucks (1977) presented a developmental model to determine the extent to which an innovation has been implemented. They introduced the concept of levels of use of an innovation and described eight such levels. These range from level one, in which the user has little or no knowledge of the innovation, through orientation (level two), preparation (level three), and mechanical use (level four), in which the focus is on the short-term, day-to-day use of the innovation with little time for reflection. At this fourth level, changes are made primarily to meet user rather than client needs; the user is engaged in a step-by-step attempt to master the tasks required to implement the innovation, often resulting in disjointed and superficial operations. At level four, an innovation cannot be evaluated exclusively on the basis of behavioral changes, since such changes may represent only superficial or mechanical compliance.

Level five is routine use, in which the innovation is stabilized but little preparation or thought is given to improving it or its consequences. The next levels are refinement (level six), integration (level seven), and renewal (level eight), in which the user reevaluates the quality of the innovation, seeks major modifications or alternatives to it to achieve increased impacts on clients, examines new developments in the field, and explores new goals for the system. The logical end of an innovation is the development of another innovation; innovation is a continually changing, never ending process.

Implementing Educational Consultation

Information about various aspects of the organizational environment may help a consultant to gain a better understanding of an educational setting. Just as counselors build mental models of their clients to guide them in counseling, consultants create an image of the organization to assist them in their task. This image consists of observations and speculations about the structure, function, and dynamics of the organization. The CES and URES may provide a valuable contribution to this working image. A discrepancy between the CES and other information can be a source of new hypotheses for the consultant. For example, does an experimental classroom or student living unit program really deserve its reputation; that is, is its social environment different from more traditional settings? Furthermore, the measurement-feedback-planning sequence constitutes an assessment of variables relevant to the consultant's task, such as amount of resistance to change, resources for generating and maintaining innovations, and values and priorities of program staff.

The reactions of staff to data gathering and feedback are valuable clues to the functioning of an organization. How do administrators and teachers react to the idea of evaluating their environment? Is the initial resistance to evaluation understandable in terms of job security, or does it reflect a conflict among staff members about the worth of evaluation and classroom change? By judiciously interpreting reactions to each phase of the assessment-feedback-planning sequence and information that conflicts with the results of the social climate scales, an image of each classroom and of a school as a whole can be generated. This image can serve the consultant in the same way that a good personality assessment serves the counselor (see Moos, 1975, chap. 4, for an example of this process).

An incidental benefit of environmental assessment information is the exposure of staff to a differentiated framework for thinking about their programs and policies. For example, instead of locating their classes in a two-dimensional space defined by "traditional" and "open," staff are encouraged to use at least nine dimensions, the CES subscales. This cognitive shift facilitates change, since it precludes resistance in the name of traditionalism and eliminates categorizing teachers as either open or traditional. As teachers become more proficient in using the new vocabulary, program change discussions should generate less conflict. A final benefit in the consultant's use of environmental assessment procedures is the opportunity it gives staff members for redefining their roles. The discussion of feedback often shifts people's concern from individual students to the setting as a whole and its impact on all students. Suddenly, for example, residence hall staff, who are regarded as responsible for the policies and procedures of their living group, can expand their role to include program design and planning.

Schroeder (in press[a]) described a program of milieu management that can be used by organizational consultants. He used the Myers-Briggs Type Indicator (MBTI; Myers, 1962), derived from Jung's theory of psychological types, to provide data on housing office staff members' preferences for extraversion-introversion, sensing-intuiting, thinking-feeling, and judging-perception. Intuitive types prefer an open, independence-oriented social environment, while sensing types want their environment to emphasize formal structure and organization. Feeling types prefer environments to emphasize involvement, friendship, and supportive interaction, while thinking types want to be able to influence, control, and act on their setting. Schroeder used this information to develop a three-stage staff environmental design process.

During the initial stage, staff members discuss the goals associated with designing an ideal staff environment and complete the MBTI and the Ideal Form of the Group Environment Scale (GES; Moos and Humphrey, 1974). Stage two involves sharing the data obtained from the first stage with group participants. Each participant receives a profile describing each staff member's perception of the ideal environment, the leader's perception, and the average perceptions of the total group. Discussion of the characteristics of an ideal staff group environment ensues, leading to stage three, which involves the actual environmental design process and incorporates the substages of selecting environmental values, setting goals, translating goals into specific actions, developing social contracts, and implementing the resulting plans. Approximately one month after implementing the design plan, staff members complete the Real Form of the GES to assess their current perceptions of the group environment. The resulting data are given back to the group and become part of the ongoing social-environmental design process.

Formulating Ecologically Relevant Case Descriptions

Information about people's environments, such as their classroom, living group, and family settings, can be used in case descriptions and in overall planning for counseling and treatment. Consider the gain in information if one could describe the basic "ecological niche" in which an individual functions. Predictions of a student's behavior and mood would be greatly improved if we had information about the characteristics of the student's community settings (family, group, home, and social units). For example, Robert Fuhr and I (Fuhr and Moos, 1977) used the CES, the Family Environment Scale (FES), and the Work Environment Scale (WES), as well as a Health and Daily Living Questionnaire (HDL), to construct an ecologically relevant family case description. The family had applied for counseling because the fifteen-year-old Beth had dropped out of school. She was doing poorly in her classwork, was unable to concentrate on her lessons, was afraid of being ridiculed, and did not like the other students or her teachers. The counselor found it difficult to obtain specific information about school from Beth; the extent to which her problems were academic or social was unclear. The counselor wanted to know more about Beth's life outside the classroom. How did she actually spend her time? What type of family did she live in? Were her parents contributing to her problems in school?

To focus on Beth's reaction to school, we compared her description of her favorite class (history) to her concept of an ideal class. Beth had a sharply negative impression, feeling that students disliked the class and ignored the teacher, that students were unfriendly to each other, that the class was poorly organized, and that students had little say about how class time was spent. Additional information obtained from an activities profile indicated that Beth spent almost all of her time out of school either by herself (for example, she ate dinner and did housework alone) or in such passive, solitary pursuits as watching television.

In contrast to her parents, Beth rated her family very low on cohesion, feeling that there was a lack of togetherness and that family members got along poorly with each other. Beth gave the family the lowest possible score on active-recreational orientation, reporting that most weekends and evenings were spent at home, that nobody was active in sports, that friends did not come to visit often, and that the family rarely went camping, to the movies, or on other excursions. She also noted higher conflict in the family than her parents did. Her father felt that there were few disagreements and little expression of anger, but she felt that family members fought a lot, lost their tempers, and criticized each other often.

Information derived from the FES and WES indicated that Beth's parents viewed their relationship at home favorably and that they were highly committed to and satisfied with their jobs. Both worked hard, enjoyed a good deal of responsibility, and felt that their coworkers were friendly and supportive. The family status quo apparently was satisfactory for Beth's parents because of their demanding and rewarding work environments. However, this situation resulted in a lack of focus and energy on family activities and Beth's feeling that her parents did not care about her; for example, they did not even institute strict controls against which she could rebel.

These findings suggest that Beth's problems at school resulted from the family social environment. Considering that Beth greatly enjoyed reading for pleasure and desired more family intellectual and cultural activities, and noting that the major difference between her real and ideal class descriptions involved affiliation, we inferred that her school problems derived primarily from social rather than academic factors. Beth was suffering at school partly because her parents were deeply immersed in satisfying and time-consuming work settings and did not have enough time for her at home. In this way, a setting in which Beth was not directly involved (her parents' work milieu) affected her family environment and, in turn, her performance in school.

Educational counselors need to take nonschool settings into account to understand how students function. Furthermore, the usual student-centered focus in counseling may work well when family cohesion and support are relatively high, but it is less likely to be successful when they are low. In the latter instance, elements of cohesion may need to be developed before individual-focused counseling can be successful. In this connection, feedback of information derived from the FES and CES can be used productively in ongoing counseling and therapy (Fuhr, Moos, and Dishotsky, 1978).

Social-ecological assessment techniques should be useful to counselors because the information obtained can be used to organize the discussion of issues in counseling, to gain a heightened awareness of some of the powerful yet controllable influences of the physical and social environment, and to teach students to break down problems into clearly defined units that can be handled in an organized fashion. Counselors can also teach students to take an active part in shaping their own goals and to track their own progress. The semistructured, easily understandable format of the procedures enables a great deal of information to be collected very quickly. Also, the counselor need not be present for all phases of the assessment, although his or her presence may be preferable in some instances; a paraprofessional can be trained to obtain the information and to answer any questions.

Enhancing Environmental Competence

We are beginning to understand how environments actually function. We can assess some important dimensions that discriminate among environments and are related to human functioning. We can identify certain coping and adaptive mechanisms that are related to the successful handling of environmental pressure and stress. Given this information, we will soon be in a position to teach people how to create, select, and transcend environments, that is, to enhance environmental competence (Moos, 1976c, chap. 12).

Two examples illustrate the range of possibilities. First, the social climate approach can indicate what to look for in analyzing social settings. The three domains of dimensions provide a useful way of conceptualizing the confusing complexity of social settings. An understanding of these dimensions may help individuals to select a wide range of environments in which to participate in their everyday lives. In addition, those responsible for selecting the environments of others, such as parents who select school environments for their children, can do so with better awareness of the personal traits that different environments tend to foster.

Second, people could take advantage of progressive conformity and select environments that would favor the types of changes they wish to make in themselves. Using Schroeder's (in press[a]) environmental design process as an illustration, intuitive types, who prefer openness and independence, might participate in organized, structured environments, whereas sensing types, who prefer just such environments, might participate in open, independence-oriented settings. People might select environments not to maximize congruence but to maximize personal growth. Individual potential could be enhanced by selecting new environments that are optimally incongruent.

A final, more general idea involves the need for environmental educators, that is, people who can help individuals or organizations to use existing environments more effectively. Environmental educators could teach people about their environment, including how to conceptualize its component parts and their interrelationships and, most important, how to understand and control its potential impact on their everyday lives. These notions are consistent with current emphasis on competence building, self-control, and self-esteem, and the importance of perceived control over the environment. Cohen, Glass, and Phillips (1977) suggested that feelings of helplessness and an inability to control environmental stimuli may be more important than the actual characteristics of the environment itself. Langer and Saegert (1977) found that the consequences of stressful settings could be ameliorated by cognitive means. Providing information that explained and validated the experience of arousal reduced the emotional and behavioral consequences of stress.

We need experts who understand environments—the kinds of reactions they tend to elicit and the dimensions and psychological mediating mechanisms involved. The role of environmental educator can be implemented more fully when this knowledge is combined with information about how people cope with and adapt to social environments. While there are some examples of the use of social-environmental information to teach people about their settings (for example, the use of the FES in marriage and family living classes), the general utility of these ideas remains largely unexplored. Brownstein and I (Moos and Brownstein, 1977) pointed out that progress in this area may enhance our ability to cope with the social-ecological environment and thus help us to improve our social settings and to solve broader environmental problems.

12

Conclusions, Educational Implications, and Evaluation Issues

In this chapter I review and integrate the major findings, focusing on the concept of social climate, the basic types of living groups and classrooms, and the determinants and impacts of these types. I draw conclusions about the effects of social environments and discuss the processes by which environments exert their impacts. I also focus on some methodological and conceptual issues central to furthering our understanding of how educational settings function.

247

The Concept of Social Climate

Our work has been shaped by five broad principles: the importance of environmental assessment, the need for a flexible conceptual framework, the relevance of a focus on the perceived environment, the value of concentrating on the micro-settings in which people actually function, and the utility of developing practically useful procedures to monitor and change educational settings. These five principles and a considerable amount of empirical work resulted in the development of a University Residence Environment Scale (URES) and a Classroom Environment Scale (CES) to measure the social environments of student living groups and secondary school classrooms. The two scales have adequate psychometric characteristics. The subscales are reliable, measure different though somewhat interrelated dimensions, reflect change when it occurs, and are only minimally influenced by such response sets as acquiescence and social desirability. By using the three forms of each scale, the actual, preferred, and expected classroom and living group social environments can be compared.

From a conceptual perspective, varied settings can be characterized by three domains of social environment dimensions: relationship, personal growth or goal orientation, and system maintenance and change. Relationship dimensions measure the nature and intensity of personal interactions in the setting. The dimensions identified in living groups and classrooms are involvement, cohesion (affiliation), and support, but variables reflecting expressiveness (treatment programs) and conflict (families and sheltered-care programs) are identified separately in some settings. System maintenance and change dimensions assess the extent to which the environment is orderly, clear in its expectations, capable of maintaining control, and responsive to change. The dimensions are order and organization, clarity, control (student influence), and innovation.

Personal growth or goal orientation dimensions vary among settings, since the primary goals of people in different settings differ. College living groups vary in their focus on dating, going to parties, and other social activities, but these functions are not particularly germane to high school classrooms. Task orientation is relevant to classrooms but does not apply to student living groups, since they are basically social rather than task oriented. Although differences in the salience of personal growth dimensions limit the generalizability of results among different types of settings, the three domains of dimensions help in understanding existing research and in constructing new measures of educational environments.

For example, Nielsen (1977) used data from the International Institute for the Evaluation of Educational Achievement (IEA) studies to develop classroom learning environment indexes that are conceptually linked to the three domains. Indexes of classroom equality and peer group interaction measured the relationship domain, and teacher control and student power measured system maintenance and change. Personal growth dimensions included independence of thought, cognitive climate, political environment (items like "Students bring up current political events for discussion in class") and ritual climate (items like "We sing our national anthem in school"). Nielsen found that cognitive and ritual climate were related to civics knowledge and tolerance of dissent, but the relevant point here is his use of the three domains to organize existing data not originally collected with the domains in mind. The concepts have also been used to construct measures of open classrooms (Rentoul and Fraser, in press), academic departments (Hearn, 1978), and off-campus living groups (Moos and Lee, 1979).

Substantive Results: Student Living Groups

I turn now to a brief overview of the major results and conclusions. I present the information on student living groups and classrooms separately, focusing on the diversity of these settings and on the determinants and impacts of the basic types of social environments found in them.

The Diversity of Student Living Groups. Different types of living groups vary considerably. Compared with men's houses, for example, women's houses are much more organized and structured and place more emphasis on emotional support and social activities. Men's houses stress competitive and non-conformist qualities more heavily. Coed houses emphasize involvement, personal concern, and mutual support and value independence and intellectuality. The environments of coed groups are generally consonant with conventional wisdom and with the values underlying the development of coed living.

Compared with men's residence halls, fraternities emphasize involvement and support, are oriented toward social activities and competition (primarily around social status rather than grades), stress organization and student influence, and deemphasize independence and academic achievement. Although the social environments of living groups differ between types, they also vary considerably within types and overlap among types. Some men's residence halls are more cohesive than some fraternities, and some women's halls emphasize independence and intellectuality more than some men's or coed halls. I draw two conclusions from these results: (1) The type and sex composition of a living group are only two of many determinants of its social climate. (2) Scales such as the URES are useful because they obtain information that cannot be derived from existing categorizations of a living group, such as single sex or coed, or residence hall or student cooperative (see Chapter Two).

Much of the diversity among living groups is captured in six basic types of social environments. Two types focus on interpersonal relationships and social activities (relationship and traditionally socially oriented). Two types focus on academic concerns: one emphasizes academic achievement in a supportive context (supportive achievement), and the other stresses competition and achievement but lacks cohesion and a sense of community (competitive). Two types focus on intellectual and personal growth: one stresses independence and has moderate emphasis on support (independent), and the other places a high value on supportive interpersonal relationships and on intellectuality, student influence, and innovation (intellectual). These six clusters help to organize living group settings and to describe the major subcultures that students create within them (see Chapter Three).

Determinants of Living Group Climates. Why do varied

types of social environments develop in different living groups? Is the social milieu primarily a function of the types of students in the unit? To what extent do a unit's architectural characteristics influence the social milieu? To address these questions, I used a conceptual model of the relationships among four domains of environmental variables and of their influence on a living group's social environment. The model and the data indicated that architectural, organizational, and human aggregate variables, as well as the institutional context, can influence the social environment of a living unit. Aggregate student characteristics, such as sex composition and type of major, had the strongest independent influence on social climate. Architectural, organizational, and school context variables had some independent effects, but most of their influence on social climate was shared with the aggregate student indexes.

Certain combinations of characteristics were related to particular types of social environments. For example, supportive achievement oriented climates were more likely to develop in women's or coed living units with a high proportion of double rooms, better recreational facilities, and more scholarly and intellectual activities. These units had more students majoring in mathematics and the physical and biological sciences and fewer students majoring in history, economics, political science, and business. A high proportion of double rooms and the provision of recreational facilities also enhanced the emergence of both independent and intellectual climates, as did giving students more control over important house functions. Independence oriented settings tended to be composed of engineering, mathematics, and science majors, whereas intellectually oriented settings were more likely to be women's or coed units and to have more students majoring in education and the humanities. The conceptual framework and the findings help in understanding the social environment likely to emerge in a living unit. They can also help housing staff to select living groups that will foster a different type of climate than that which might otherwise develop (see Chapter Four).

The Impact of Living Group Climates. Living groups influence student stability and change in such areas as establishing autonomy and a sense of personal identity, developing more open interpersonal relationships, enhancing competence, and clarifying purposes and goals. In general, living groups exert an influence toward conformity; that is, they tend to stabilize or accentuate individual characteristics congruent with the dominant aspects of the setting. Relationship and socially oriented units maintain and facilitate the social and inhibit the academic aspects of student activities. Independence oriented settings maintain and facilitate academic growth and inhibit involvement in such conventional areas as religious concern, dating, and participation in student body activities. Intellectually oriented settings maintain and enhance aspiration and achievement levels. The press toward conformity also helps to explain an increase in alcohol consumption in high-drinking single-sex units and a decrease in aspiration levels in some coed units (see Chapters Five and Six).

The qualities students bring to a living group, especially qualities shared with other students, facilitate the creation of social environments that maintain and accentuate these shared qualities. In environments that are relatively homogeneous in certain respects (such as dating behavior or alcohol consumption), incongruent students tend to change in the direction of the majority, and those initially in the majority maintain or further accentuate their attitudes and behavior in these areas. A heterogeneous unit (such as one in which some students are abstainers, some are moderate drinkers, and some are heavy drinkers) has more conflicting influences and provides each student with a wider choice of friends. Students are more likely to find other students with similar attitudes and values and less likely to experience consistent pressure to change in such a setting.

Some living groups seem to induce stress. Students in competitive and intellectual units report more physical symptoms and show higher than expected health center utilization. Men and women in coed units use the student health center more often than their counterparts in single-sex units. Women in coed units are more likely to transfer into another living group or to drop out of college than women in single-sex units.

There are three related explanations for these effects: (1)

strong personal growth demands in the absence of cohesion, (2) conflicting expectations, and (3) an enveloping environment that is hard to resist. Environments emphasizing personal growth goals but lacking social support (such as competitive units) create stress, in contrast to those emphasizing growth that are cohesive (such as supportive achievement oriented units). This highlights the interrelationships among social-environmental dimensions. A setting oriented toward achievement or competition and support can have a different impact than one oriented toward achievement or competition but lacking in support.

The stress effects of coed units are probably due to a diversity of influences that is at odds with the broader institutional context. Coed units reward students for independent and intellectual pursuits, but other pressures, such as those from the student's family or major department, may demand social conformity and academic achievement. These divergent influences create internal conflicts, particularly for freshmen who have yet to develop stable self-concepts.

Cohesive, committed settings force students to take a stand with respect to the environment. It is usually not possible for a "deviant" student to adapt to these settings by "opting out" (that is, by a lack of involvement), since members tend to care about each other. Some students cope with the resulting environmental pressure by joining outside supportive groups that insulate them from the effects of the living unit. Some students conform, some resist, and some leave or drop out of the setting. Stress can accompany all three of these latter adaptations. Conformity can be stressful if it involves behavior that is inconsistent with a student's values (like the onset of drinking for a religious student of a fundamentalist sect). Resistance can be stressful since it runs counter to other students' values and often raises conflicts with peers. The decision to leave or drop out can be difficult and time consuming and is often accompanied by anxiety and ambivalent feelings.

Homogeneous settings can be stressful in still another way. For example, some low-ability students are negatively affected by living in intellectually oriented settings where most of their peers are highly academically talented. Social comparison processes in such cases work to the detriment of the less able students, many of whom are likely to feel alienated, depressed, and less efficacious. For all these reasons, relatively cohesive or homogeneous settings can create tension for a significant minority of students. It is important to note that most of these stress effects may be adaptive and foreshadow significant growth experiences. However, any setting that is powerful enough to influence students positively can probably affect them adversely as well. In this sense, Brothers and Hatch (1971) were correct in their concern that living groups may have negative influences, although the same caution also applies to every other type of social setting.

Substantive Results: Classroom Settings

The Diversity of Classroom Settings. Classroom learning environments vary considerably. A comparison of five types of public schools and of women's and coed private schools showed that some of this variability is due to the type of school. For example, alternative public school classes were highly innovative and oriented toward developing satisfying interpersonal relationships. These classes tended to be run democratically and had little emphasis on competition, but they were surprisingly well organized and task oriented. We also found that young women in women's schools reported more involvement in their classes, greater affiliation among students, and more emphasis on task orientation, competition, and organization than women in coed schools. In general, private school classes placed more emphasis on interpersonal relationships and less on rules and regulations than public school classes. These normative portraits of classroom social environments show that adolescents in different types of schools create and must adapt to different socialization experiences and, consequently, may have different socialization outcomes.

We conducted an empirical cluster analysis that identified six basic types of classroom learning environments. The first two types stress involvement and student-student and teacher-student relationships. One of these emphasizes openness and change (innovation oriented), whereas the other is more structured and focuses on clarity, organization, and teacher control (structured relationship oriented). The second two types (supportive task and supportive competition oriented) stress different aspects of goal orientation in a cohesive framework characterized by teacher support. The last two types both lack emphasis in the relationship areas. One type emphasizes goal orientation (primarily competition) in a framework lacking cohesion and structure, whereas the other (control oriented) stresses organization, teacher control, and strict rules for student behavior. These clusters help to comprehend the diversity of learning environments and indicate that the relative emphasis on personal relationships and system structure is important in characterizing secondary school classes (see Chapters Seven and Eight).

The Determinants of Classroom Climate. The basic conceptual model formulated for living groups was also applied to the relationships among five sets of environmental factors in classrooms (external context and architectural, organizational, aggregate student, and teacher characteristics) and on their connection to the learning environment. We implemented the model using four of the sets (all but architectural indexes) and found that each set influenced the development of each of the six types of classroom environments. For example, the following characteristics were related to the creation of innovative and supportive task oriented classes: higher grade level, higher aggregate student social exploration, larger proportion of female students, and a female teacher who wanted to instill a love of learning and be a friend to students. Innovative climates were also more likely to develop in alternative schools and in music, literature, and other humanities classes.

Control oriented classes were more likely to develop in vocational schools and at lower grade levels, to have male students and less exploration oriented students, and to be taught by men who wanted to prepare students for work and who wished to be seen as competent by school administrators. The results support the conclusion that teachers are somewhat more important in creating classroom learning environments than students are, although student characteristics uniquely affected each type of classroom milieu and were especially important in influencing the relative emphasis on teacher control.

The five sets of variables that affect classroom climate are usually considered separately; thus, the results of prior studies are difficult or impossible to interpret. For example, innovative school programs affect classroom environments, but it is not clear how much of this effect is a unique influence of the programs themselves and how much is due to the different types of students and teachers who select these programs. Although the influence of different sets of classroom characteristics on the learning environment will vary from one sample of classes to another, the conceptual model provides a useful framework to focus on such questions (see Chapter Eight).

The Impact of Classroom Climates. Following the model of determinants of learning environments, a framework was presented to focus on the impacts of classroom settings. The framework suggests that each of the sets of characteristics that influence the learning environment, as well as the learning environment itself, can affect student reactions and other classroom outcomes. Analyses implementing a part of this model showed that each set of environmental descriptors uniquely accounted for an important portion of the variance in such indexes as friendship formation, sense of well-being, and satisfaction with learning. The fact that much of the explainable variance in student reactions was shared by two or more sets of environmental indexes demonstrates the importance of the interrelationships among different sets of classroom characteristics.

Although there is controversy about the effects of learning environments, recent studies in the United States and in developing countries have yielded some consistent findings. An emphasis on the relationship and system change domains enhances satisfaction, interest in the subject matter, and social and personal growth but is less likely to facilitate academic achievement. Gains on standard achievement test measures are most likely to occur in a class with warm and supportive relationships, an emphasis on specific academic tasks and goals, and a clear, orderly, and well-structured milieu. These classroom settings, which have a high expectation and demand for performance, can also enhance creativity and personal growth. Large achievement gains may occur in classes that stress goal and maintenance (organization and clarity) areas and that are lower in warmth, but these classes are not as effective in facilitating student interest and morale, creativity, or personal growth. The results suggest that basic skills programs would have more positive effects if they were supportive as well as task oriented, and that open program classes should benefit from an emphasis on task orientation, though not if affiliation and support are deemphasized (see Chapter Nine).

Living Groups and Classrooms

Student living groups and secondary school classrooms serve different functions. There is some overlap, but living groups are directed primarily toward social and recreational goals, whereas classes are oriented mainly toward improving academic knowledge and learning skills. Given these differences, it is surprising that many of the basic issues and results in the two types of settings are similar. The following general conclusions apply to both settings: (1) They can be characterized by three social-environmental domains, although some of the specific dimensions within the domains differ; (2) a conceptual framework composed of roughly analogous sets of environmental variables is helpful in focusing on the determinants and impacts of their social environments; (3) the social environment in both settings mediates some of the effects of other sets of environmental variables (organizational and aggregate student) and has some unique effects of its own; and (4) there are similar practical applications of social climate assessments, such as maximizing accurate information, describing and comparing settings, monitoring and facilitating change, and measuring preferred and expected environments.

With respect to impact, both types of settings press toward conformity. An emphasis on the relationship domain enhances social and interpersonal growth, and an emphasis on learning goals (achievement and competition) facilitates academic development. Too much emphasis on the relationship or personal growth domain can have negative effects in either setting. Cohesion can restrict student growth by inhibiting involvement in academic interests or by enhancing change in potentially detrimental ways (such as influencing a student to drink excessively). In both types of settings, competition can be stressful in the absence of support, less able students may suffer in environments composed primarily of highly able peers, and strong emphasis on nonacademic goals (such as self-reliance in classes and intellectuality in living groups) can engender anxiety and tension.

These similarities in the findings and processes may make possible the development of general principles that apply to both living groups and classrooms. Furthermore, the differences between the two types of settings can help us to learn about the contrasting ways in which different settings operate. For example, too much emphasis on system structure may contribute to dependence in classrooms; however, this effect does not seem to occur in living groups, where the little structure that exists is largely created by the students themselves. The most important contrasts among settings may involve the degree of structure and how free people are to select them and to remain in them. In this respect, Newcomb (1978) found that institutional influences on youth were quite different in college and correctional settings and speculated that these differences were primarily due to the coercion and relative isolation involved in the prison setting. Comparisons of different types of settings should help investigators to develop a more inclusive framework to explain how varied environments function in relation to the people in them. Having provided a brief overview of the most important results, I turn now to a consideration of some of the methodological and conceptual issues involved in developing such a framework.

Methodological Issues

Several issues are involved in the process of constructing and validating procedures by which to assess environments and evaluate their impacts (see Moos, 1975; Moos, in press). Five such issues are reviewed here: the process of scale construction, the creation of typologies of settings, personal determinants of environmental perceptions, and the validity and cross-cultural applicability of perceived climate scales.

The Process of Scale Construction. The development of an environmental assessment technique is not simply a methodological exercise. My colleagues and I used a combination of conceptual, methodological, and practical criteria in our scale construction. When these sets of criteria conflict, it is often necessary to choose between alternative strategies. One typical problem relates to item format and wording. We used true-false items, even though most respondents would prefer to answer items on three- or four-point scales. Our pretest evidence indicated that a true-false format obtained as much information as other formats, while avoiding the problems related to personal styles, such as preferences for "middle of the road," undecided, extreme, or deviant responses. In this case we followed methodological rather than practical (respondent satisfaction) criteria, although in other situations we have been more concerned with item clarity than with the control of response sets (see Moos and others, in press).

Another issue involves the choice of items and subscales to include in a scale. We used both empirical and conceptual criteria to make these choices. Items and subscales must have face validity; that is, participants in the relevant setting must feel that they are reasonable indicators of the particular dimensions that they measure. However, although affiliation and involvement can be distinguished conceptually, their high intercorrelations in student living groups resulted in our combining them into one subscale in the URES. In a contrary example, factor analysis suggested the possibility of combining some support and competition items and some intellectuality and innovation items. Since the original subscales (that is, support, competition, intellectuality, and innovation) measured distinct dimensions, related to different impacts, and had varied practical implications, we kept them separate even though they were moderately interrelated.

Factor-analytic solutions are determined in part by rational conceptual considerations and in part by the specific statistical procedures and criteria employed. For example, although Trickett and Quinlan (in press) identified six CES factors using a sample of students from regular school classes, their analysis of a sample of vocational school classes resulted in a different factor solution—and factor analysis of teacher responses might result in still another solution. In this connection, factor analyses of the social climate scales and their derivatives have already resulted in two-factor (Kohn, Jeger, and Koretzky, in press), three-factor (Alden, 1978), four-factor (Mandersheid, Koenig, and Silbergeld, 1977), five-factor (Edelson and Paul, 1977), and six-factor (Trickett and Quinlan, in press) solutions. It is reasonable to try to identify a smaller number of dimensions by which social environments can be characterized. But the proliferation of factor dimensions may retard the development of dependable knowledge about the effects of consistently defined, conceptually meaningful environmental characteristics (see Buros, 1977, for a similar perspective on ability and aptitude testing).

The Creation of Typologies of Settings. Once satisfactory measures have been constructed, the issue of how to characterize settings arises. Settings can be characterized on one dimension at a time, such as cohesion, competition, or organization, but the meaning and impact of any one social-environmental dimension depends on the degree of emphasis on the other dimensions. For example, students' reactions to competition and control vary depending on whether they occur in a supportive framework. These interrelationships necessitate the development of a way to capture the overall "culture" of an educational setting.

This issue was addressed by constructing empirical typologies of living groups and classrooms. This is a useful procedure, and such typologies do reflect the interconnections among dimensions, but there are two problems that should be noted. First, even though statistical criteria, such as minimum levels of acceptable profile similarity, narrow the choices considerably, each clustering problem has a variety of possible empirical solutions. For example, our data on classrooms could be described as 200 clusters of one classroom each (this emphasizes the uniqueness of each class), as one cluster of 200 classes (this leaves no room for variability among classes), or, more logically, as a few conceptually and empirically meaningful clusters. Although there is some arbitrariness in this process, the final cluster solutions were selected according to criteria of meaningfulness and comprehensiveness.

Second, the social environments of the settings that fall into each type vary considerably, particularly if the investigator chooses (as I did) to identify a relatively small number of types. This within-type variability led me to develop climate-type scores to index the similarity of each living group or classroom to each of the six modal types of living groups and classrooms. These scores reflect the configuration of the social-environmental characteristics of a setting and are sensitive to both the within-type and between-type variability among settings. But the climate-type scores measure complex dimensions (that is, the overall similarity of a setting to a modal type of setting) and raise problems of interpretation, in that each living group or classroom is now characterized on six new dimensions: the six climate-type scores. It is also possible that these scores do not actually add much reliable information beyond that obtained by simply classifying a setting into one and only one type. However, I feel that the climate-type scores represent a conceptually and empirically useful approach, even though their potential weaknesses and problems should be kept in mind.

Personal Determinants of Environmental Perceptions. Perceived climate scales differentiate social settings, but individuals also differ in their perceptions of the "same" setting. This raises the issue that responses to these scales may reflect people's background and personality characteristics in addition to or instead of attributes of the environment. If personal attributes consistently influence environmental perceptions, then perceived climate scales could be regarded as personality scales that happen to have items pertaining to the social milieu.

Most of the evidence on this issue indicates that sociodemographic and other personal attributes are only minimally related to environmental perceptions (see Chapters Two and Seven; Moos, 1974a, chap. 3; Moos and Bromet, 1978; Pace,

1969). The characteristics people bring to an environment do not account for much of the variance in environmental perceptions, but how they function in the setting is related to their perceptions. In general, people who have more responsibility or control and who perform better view the environment more positively than those who have less responsibility or control and who perform poorly. For example, teachers see classrooms more favorably than students, and students who perform well tend to see them more favorably than those who perform poorly.

These differences are usually small (accounting for between 1 and 5 percent of the subscale variance), but they indicate that people with different role and performance characteristics function in varied subenvironments and face different demands within an overall setting. In this respect, Walberg (1976) suggested that a student's perception of an environment reflects the results of person-environment interaction, that is, that people who are congruent in a setting see the setting more positively and function better in it. Walberg noted that this may explain why students' perceptions of learning environments account for incremental predictive validity in outcome indexes of individual achievement (that is, for variance over and above that accounted for by initial achievement measures).

Other factors that can help to explain why different people have varied perceptions of the same setting include the degree of environmental uncertainty and heterogeneity. When uncertainty is high (such as in a large setting with unclear expectations), respondents have little dependable information about the environment and thus answer items in ways that are congruent with their need structure. Furthermore, people are more likely to try and create a congenial subenvironment in a heterogeneous setting. For example, a student interested in social activities may seek out other similarly oriented students, participate in more social activities with them, and thus perceive a living group as more socially oriented. The fact that there usually is more uncertainty and heterogeneity in larger settings may explain why personal functioning indexes are somewhat more closely related to environmental perceptions in living groups than in classrooms.

A fruitful way to pursue this issue would be to develop a model that focuses on the determinants of individual differences in perceptions of an environment. How an individual functions (role and performance) in a setting, the relevant characteristics of the setting (uncertainty and diversity), and certain item characteristics (the degree of clarity and specificity) need to be considered in such a model. This approach should help to specify the personal and environmental conditions under which personal attributes are related to responses on different types of measures of the perceived environment.

The Validity of Perceived Climate Scales. Typical examples of questions regarding validity are: Is there actually more teacher support in classes that students perceive to be high in teacher support? Is there actually more teacher control in classes that students perceive to be high in teacher control? Friendly teacher-student interaction was higher in classes that students perceived to be high in CES support, but CES teacher control was not related to the use of authority statements as rated from tape-recorded class sessions. However, authority-related teacher-student interactions were quite infrequent, suggesting that the intensity of these interactions may compensate for their relative lack of frequency. One occasion of sending a student to the principal's office for a minor rule infraction can be sufficient to cause students to perceive a high degree of teacher control.

Other problems involved in using behavioral observations to attempt to validate student perceptions are that teachers may convey personal interest in students outside of class, that different environmental dimensions may be most salient at different times (issues relating to organization and control are often dealt with quickly, whereas supportive relationships between teachers and students tend to evolve slowly), that teacher behavior is not consistent, and that perceptions of the classroom environment are a function of both verbal and nonverbal behaviors of teachers. These considerations raise serious questions about the extent to which observer-derived counts of specific behaviors can validate student perceptions.

Astin (1968) raised a related point by noting that the social climate of an environment does not constitute a stimulus (or a set of stimuli) and thus presumably cannot affect behavior. He illustrated his point by an example from the College Characteristics Index: "Many students drive sports cars." Astin pointed out that this item simply reflects the impression of the observer and that the observer's judgment is not a stimulus that can affect other students. He suggested another phrasing: "Did you drive a sports car at college during the past year?" The measure of the environment would then consist of the proportion of students at a college who respond positively. Driving a sports car represents a stimulus that can have an impact on the behavior and attitudes of other students.

Although this distinction may be important, Astin chose a favorable example to illustrate his point. Many items in his Inventory of College Activities (ICA) do not constitute stimuli for most students; examples are "Had psychotherapy or personal counseling," "Ate lunch or dinner alone," and "Violated college rules or regulations without getting caught." Another problem is that much of the relevant information about environments is judgmental. The ICA includes items asking students whether the instructors in their courses were "exceptionally well-grounded in the course subject matter," "were enthusiastic," "had a good sense of humor," "were often sarcastic," and "were often dull and uninteresting." Furthermore, the most important information about social environments may represent people's overall impressions of those environments.

It is necessary to include information about such potential stimuli (in my terms, these are aggregate student factors) in a differentiated analysis of educational settings. The extent to which these characteristics relate to perceived social climate, and the extent to which each characteristic relates to relevant outcomes can then be evaluated empirically. In fact, aggregate student characteristics are an important determinant of social climate and influence educational outcomes in conjunction with social climate and other sets of environmental factors. The development of general formulations regarding the determinants and impacts of varied sets of environmental indexes holds more promise than attempts to determine the validity of one set of environmental factors by obtaining information about another set.

Cross-Cultural Applicability. Evidence is growing that perceived climate scales can be useful in comparative cross-cultural studies (see Chapter Ten; Dauwalder, Chabloz, and Chappuis, 1978; Espvall and Astrom, 1974; Moos, 1974a, chaps. 3, 10; Schneewind and Lortz, 1978; Skalar, 1974), but investigators must use caution in applying these instruments and concepts in other countries. There are specific procedures to be followed in scale translations, including the important step of retranslation from the new language back to English. Other problems are that similar concepts may carry different meanings in different cultural milieus, easily comprehensible items may be difficult to develop, unique test administration biases may be introduced, and the items may not show equivalent psychometric properties in the new setting. For example, adequately translated learning environment items may not discriminate among Indonesian classrooms because these settings do not vary as much as American classes in certain characteristics. These problems are surmountable, but investigators cannot simply translate a scale and expect it to have adequate psychometric and conceptual validity in another cultural setting (see Hursh-Cesar and Prodipto, 1976; Paige, 1978, pp. 136-143, for further discussion).

Conceptual Issues

Four conceptual questions raised by the foregoing work are discussed here: the adequacy of the three domains, anabolic versus catabolic effects of environments, the extent to which environments have impacts, and processes of person-environment selection and creation.

The Adequacy of the Three Domains. The three domains of social-environmental dimensions are important, but are they either necessary or sufficient? Can one not identify other relevant domains? Can one not characterize environments adequately using only one or two domains?

Since relationship, personal growth, and system maintenance and change dimensions have been identified in all environments studied to date, they must be assessed if one wishes to have a reasonably complete picture of a social environment. The three domains help to conceptualize existing environments, to formulate and understand preferred and expected environments, and to develop more conceptually consistent research on environmental impact. But these dimensions are not the only ones by which social environments can be characterized. Additional dimensions and/or other conceptual frameworks need to be developed.

Some investigators have argued that a conceptualization of relationship and system maintenance domains is sufficient to understand social settings (Kohn, Jeger, and Koretzky, in press). These two sets of dimensions are the most consistent across different types of environments. However, personal growth or goal orientation dimensions measure the basic values and purposes of the setting, and can affect and be affected by the other two domains. Relationship dimensions may have different effects in a classroom depending on the degree of goal orientation. High cohesion can enhance achievement in a task-oriented class but may increase disorder and absenteeism in a non-task-oriented class. Every social setting is organized around a set of goals that must be assessed to obtain a complete picture of the environment. A two-domain conceptualization cannot capture the complexity of social settings or fully comprehend their effects.

Anabolic Versus Catabolic Effects of Environments. Some investigators have argued that certain dimensions of social environments are anabolic, or growth-producing, whereas others are catabolic, or growth-inhibiting (Stern, 1970). Is this accurate?

There is some evidence that relationship and goal orientation dimensions tend to be growth-producing (anabolic), since they help to maintain and enhance indexes of personal, social, and academic development. The system maintenance dimension of control tends to be growth-inhibiting (catabolic), since it is associated with dissatisfaction, anxiety, and alienation. However, some people react positively to control, and some social environments need high control to function adequately. Furthermore, a strong emphasis on any one of the three domains may inhibit growth, depending in part on the level of emphasis on the other two domains. Cohesion can create dependency and restrict change as well as lead to more open and intimate relationships. An emphasis on competition can increase dropout and absenteeism rates, and high stress on independence and autonomy may relate to maladaptive physiological arousal and/or physical and emotional symptoms (Moos, 1979).

A related point is that any given environmental characteristic may facilitate certain areas of development and inhibit others. An emphasis on independence in student living groups fosters aspiration and achievement levels but inhibits religious concern and student body involvement. An emphasis on intellectuality facilitates cultural orientation but inhibits academic achievement. Cohesion and support can help one student over a personal crisis, engender conformity to subgroup norms that restricts another student's independence, and cause a third student to feel isolated and left out. High expectations for task performance can facilitate achievement for one student but create debilitating anxiety for another. To make matters more complex, most changes can signal either an increase or a decrease in personal maturity (Feldman, 1972). Sociability may be related to warmer and more spontaneous relationships with a small circle of friends (an increase in maturity) or to dependency on a peer group and superficial interactions with a larger range of people (a decrease in maturity). Impulse expression can mean more openness to experiences and greater emotional freedom, or herald selfish, need-determined behavior that reflects poor ego control.

Powerful settings can have both growth-producing and growth-inhibiting effects. This is as true of families and work groups as it is of classrooms and student living groups. It is as true of cohesion and support as it is of organization and control. Therefore, specific settings or characteristics of settings cannot be regarded as either growth-producing or growth-inhibiting. Still, some environments are more likely (on the average) to contribute to maintaining and enhancing "desirable" personal qualities. We can use this information to create and change social settings, but we must be careful to obtain dependable empirical data regarding both the positive and negative effects of such settings on varied outcome criteria.

Do Environments Have an Impact? Most people feel that social settings are quite different and have important impacts. But the data indicate that the effects of social environments—and of various types of learning programs—are rather small. The research evidence is not consistent with common sense. Why is this so?

There are several related methodological and conceptual reasons for the confusing discrepancy between interpretations of the empirical data and the evidence of common sense. A central point is the common use of multivariate statistical procedures (primarily multiple regression) in estimating the impacts of social settings and new social programs. Environments are generally credited with the "variance added" after the "effects" of personal characteristics have been accounted for. This added or unique variance reflects only a part of the *differential* effects of environments, or, more specifically, it reflects the portion of an outcome criterion that can be predicted from environmental but not from personal characteristics.

The major problem with this procedure is that environments contribute to stability and to the predictable accentuation of initial characteristics. A high-drinking college student who enters and helps to create a living group in which other students drink heavily, and who maintains or accentuates his or her drinking, may be influenced by the living group milieu. The same logic applies to an abstaining student who lives in a low-drinking living group and who continues to abstain. This stability effect reflects both actual stability (no change in drinking habits) and predictable change (that is, changes in drinking habits that are predictable from initial personal characteristics). One portion of this stability effect is identified by the variance in outcome that is shared by personal and environmental characteristics. The point is that environmental factors can influence that portion of the variance in an outcome criterion that is predictable from personal characteristics.

Even when there is a strong press for conformity, people can relate to environments in a manner that stabilizes their personal characteristics. An abstaining student in a high-drinking living group can select a more congenial group of friends that helps to reinforce and maintain his or her abstinence. The student can also ignore the problem, selectively perceive the reality of the setting (by assuming that other students do not drink heavily), neutralize or eliminate the pressure by actively explaining his or her reasons for not drinking, try to change the other students, establish social activities that do not involve alcohol consumption, transfer to a more congruent living group, and so on. Environments can influence the selection and success of these varied coping styles, but they are usually credited with having effects only when students conform or resist in a manner that is not predictable from their personal characteristics.

Several other methodological and conceptual points also bear on this issue. Students who are dissatisfied with the settings they have chosen often leave these settings (25 percent of the students in our study of living groups either dropped out of college or transferred to another unit) and are not included in environmental impact studies. This lowers the estimate of the influence of environmental factors.

The proportion of variance in most outcome criteria due t˅ differences among settings is relatively small. This is important because this proportion represents the maximum amount of variance that can be accounted for by environmental factors. Given the logic of using overall characteristics of settings as predictors (for example, aggregate social climate indexes rather than each individual student's perceptions of social climate), the amount of variance among environments—and therefore the amount potentially attributable to environmental impact—is severely limited. Some investigators have concluded that educational environments do not differ very much (Bachman, O'Malley, and Johnston, 1978), but it is also likely that existing measures do not reflect the variations that do exist.

This raises the point that current measures of both environments and people are imperfect. Although variations among living groups accounted for an average of over 10 percent of the variance in different outcome criteria, our environmental measures explained only about half this amount. More importantly, measures of educational settings do not adequately reflect the unique environments experienced by individual students. Investigators have assessed the "average expected environment" of educational settings, but, by and large, they have not assessed the much more varied environments that individual students actually encounter. With respect to person-oriented measures, changes on such intangible criteria as self-confidence and emotional maturity are probably not adequately measured by questionnaire procedures. There may also be more consistency over time (and thus greater predictability and less environmental influence) in responses to questionnaires than in actual feelings or behavior. In addition, studies have usually focused on average changes in one outcome criterion at a time rather than on all the changes in one individual. This probably underestimates the degree of environmental influence, since many people may show small but related changes on several outcome criteria (Bowen, 1977).

The different environments in which students function may press for divergent outcomes. When two environments press toward congruent goals (such as an achievement oriented home and a task oriented school), they should facilitate each other's effects, and their combined impact should be measurable. But when two environments press toward incongruent or conflicting goals (such as a socially oriented living group and an academically oriented major department), their effects can cancel each other out, and their respective impacts may be unmeasurable. The fact that people are constantly experiencing varied environments also makes it difficult to adequately evaluate the influences that any one environment can have.

I derive two conclusions from these considerations. First, environments have much stronger impacts than the results of previous multivariate studies would suggest (see also Bryk, 1978). This conclusion is supported by the methodological points raised, but one additional point is even more basic. To adapt an overworked phrase: Prediction is not causation. Explained variance, be it unique or shared, does not necessarily reflect the relative importance of personal or environmental factors in affecting student stability and change.

Second, environments contribute to stability and predictable change more than they do to differential change. This is probably because the reciprocal interactions between people and environments tend to promote stability. In this respect, Barker (1968) identified mechanisms such as deviation-countering circuits (a teacher telling a student how to behave in class) and vetoing circuits (a teacher expelling a student from class) that help to produce a stable, patterned interaction between people and settings. These and other modes of adaptation, such as resistance to change, dropping out, selecting a different setting, or finding an alternate way to satisfy an unfulfilled need, tend to maintain the stability of both people and environments.

Person-Environment Selection and Creation. Environments have impacts on people, but is this not mainly because people select and create environments that are likely to have certain impacts? This issue has been raised by Wachtel (1973, p. 330):

> The understanding of any one person's behavior in an interpersonal situation solely in terms of the stimuli presented *to* him, gives only a partial and misleading picture, for to a very large extent these stimuli are *created* by him. They are responses to his own behaviors, events he has played a role in bringing about, rather than occurrences independent of who he is and over which he has no control. The seductive hysterical woman who is annoyed at having to face the aggressive, amorous advances of numbers of men, has much to learn about the origin of the stimuli she complains she must cope with. So, too, does the man who complains about the problems in dealing with his wife's nagging, but fails to understand how this situation, which presents itself to him, derives in turn from his own procrastinating, unresponsible behavior.

Much of a person's social environment is created by his or her own behavior. People create certain social environments that then "reciprocate" by fostering certain behaviors and attitudes. But, even in Wachtel's examples, a man's aggressive, amorous advances are *reactions* to his environment, that is, to being confronted with a seductive hysterical woman, and the wife's constant nagging is a *response* to her environment, that is, to her henpecked husband's irresponsible behavior. These examples show that the processes involved in the selection and creation of social environments are sometimes closely interwoven with those involved in environmental impact.

People are not passively molded by their environments, but neither are their environments passively molded by them. For example, people often cannot select the environment they desire or change the environmental conditions others have created. This is particularly true for young children and for the aged, but it is also generally the case in any environment where there is an imbalance of power. Students in most universities have only limited power to select or change their environment. This is true of students in most junior and senior high school classrooms and of employees in most work situations. Environments have powerful impacts that are quite independent of the processes of environmental selection and creation. There is mutual interaction between people and their environments, but, in general, individual students are influenced more by educational settings than those settings are influenced by them.

Implementing a Social-Ecological Perspective

Considerable work remains to be done before we will understand how educational and other settings function. In my view, research in the following three areas should receive the highest priority. First, we need to develop assessment procedures to evaluate each of the major domains of environmental variables more adequately. In this connection, my colleagues and I are constructing a Multiphasic Environmental Assessment Procedure (MEAP) to evaluate the architectural, organizational, human, and social-environmental resources of sheltered-care settings (such as nursing and residential care homes). The work completed so far indicates that it is possible to develop dimensions in each of these areas, that these dimensions have adequate conceptual and psychometric properties, and that the information derived can be useful to staff and residents in such settings (Moos and Lemke, 1979). This approach is applicable to educational and other types of social settings.

Second, we need to develop better ways to conceptualize and measure coping strategies and skills. Investigators have described how people adapt to stressful conditions and have identified some preliminary dimensions of coping behavior (see, for example, Haan, 1977; Moos, 1977), but much less is known about how people handle everyday demands and pressures. A better understanding of varied modes of adaptation is needed to clarify the conditions under which environments exert impacts.

Third, we should focus on the processes by which environments and people exert their influence on each other. Personal, environmental, and behavioral factors all operate as interlocking determinants of each other, and, in this sense, we may never be able to isolate an ultimate personal or environmental cause of behavior (Bandura, 1978). In fact, one of the major problems in this area is the use of conceptual frameworks and statistical procedures to sort out the "independent" influences of personal and environmental factors, even though these sets of factors are inextricably interwoven. We need to know more about the processes that relate to accentuation, conformity, and the stability and maintenance of behavior, and to design studies for dealing with the complex interrelationships among different settings as they affect these processes.

Although our current knowledge is limited, the policy implications of the findings and conceptual analyses I have presented are clear: Educational settings can and do make a difference in students' lives. This difference can be for better or for worse. Students, teachers, parents, and principals are correct in assuming that their choices and policies matter and that the educational settings they select and create have varied impacts. We need to pursue the search for viable conceptual frameworks to help us comprehend these basic realities.

Appendix A

University Residence Environment Scale Scoring Key

This appendix contains the scoring key for the subscales of the different forms of the University Residence Environment Scale (URES). The real form (Form R), ideal form (Form I), and expectations form (Form E) are directly parallel. All items are scored in the same direction on all three forms. An item listed as true (T) is scored 1 point if marked true by the individual taking the scale, and an item listed as false (F) is scored 1 point if marked false. The total subscale score is simply the number of items answered in the scored direction. Four items (numbers 94, 95, 96, and 97) are unscored and were added to make the URES an even 100 items and to facilitate hand scoring.

The University Residence Environment Scale and Manual have been published and are available for interested users (Moos and Gerst, 1974).

Involvement

Real, Ideal, and Expectations Form Item Number	Scoring Direction	
1	T	There is a feeling of unity and cohesion here.
11	F	Very few things around here arouse much excitement or interest.
21	T	In this house there is a strong feeling of belongingness.
31	T	Most people here have a strong sense of loyalty toward the house.
41	T	Most of the people in this house know each other very well.
51	F	This is a rather apathetic house.
61	T	People in the house often do something together on weekends.
71	T	There are a lot of spontaneous social activities here.
81	F	Very few people here participate in house activities.
91	F	People around here don't often go out of their way to be with one another.

Support

Real, Ideal, and Expectations Form Item Number	Scoring Direction	
2	T	People here are concerned with helping and supporting one another.
12	F	Around here people tend to hide their feelings from one another.
22	T	Trying to understand the feelings of others is considered important by most people in the house.
32	T	People here try to make others feel secure.
42	F	The people here are often critical of others in the house.
52	F	People around here are not very considerate of the feelings of others.
62	T	People here tell others about their feelings of self-doubt.
72	F	In this house people rarely show affection for one another.
82	T	Most people here tell one another their personal problems.
92	F	It is sometimes difficult to approach the house staff with problems.

Independence

Real, Ideal, and Expectations Form Item Number	Scoring Direction	
3	F	People here tend to check on whether their behavior is acceptable to others in the house.
13	T	People here pretty much act and think freely without too much regard for social opinion.
23	T	Around here people are not interested in upholding social conventions.
33	T	Behaving correctly in public is pretty unimportant in this house.
43	F	Most people here know and use the commonly accepted rules of social conduct.
53	T	Behaving properly in social situations is not considered important here.
63	F	Around here people try to act in ways that will gain the approval of others in the house.
73	F	People in the house tend to fit in with the way other people do things here.
83	T	People around here don't worry much about the way they dress.
93	T	People here tend to rely on themselves when a problem comes up.

Traditional Social Orientation

Real, Ideal, and Expectations Form Item Number	Scoring Direction	
4	T	Dating is a recurring topic of conversation around here.
14	T	Some people here spend a lot of time preparing for dates.
24	F	People here consider other types of social activities to be more important than dating.
34	F	In this house dating is not important.
44	T	Nearly everyone here tries to have a date on weekends.
54	F	Few people in this house go on dates.
64	T	Having exchanges and parties is a high priority activity in this house.
74	T	In this house people would rather go on a date than do something with others in the residence.
84	F	Being popular with the opposite sex is not very important here.
94	(filler item)	Around here very little of people's extracurricular lives is concerned with dating matters.

Competition

Real, Ideal, and Expectations Form Item Number	Scoring Direction	
5	T	Around here discussions frequently turn into verbal duels.
15	F	People don't try to impress each other here.
25	F	In this house people tend not to compete with each other.
35	T	People here are always trying to win an argument.
45	F	In this house people don't try to be more "cool" than others.
55	T	People here try to appear more intellectual than others in the house.
65	T	People who have lots of dates tend to let others in the house know.
75	F	Intellectual one-up-manship is frowned upon here.
85	T	People here always seem to be competing for the highest grades.
95	(filler item)	Academic competition is frowned upon here.

Academic Achievement

Real, Ideal, and Expectations Form Item Number	Scoring Direction	
6	F	People around here hardly ever seem to be studying.
16	F	Around here studies are secondary to most activities.
26	T	People here work hard to get top grades.
36	T	Most people here consider studies as very important in college.
46	T	People around here tend to study long hours at a stretch.
56	F	Most people plan activities other than studying for weekends.
66	F	Around here people don't let studies interfere with the rest of their lives.
76	F	Around here people who are "academic grinds" are looked on with amusement.
86	T	In the evening many people here begin to study right after dinner.
96	(filler item)	There are a lot of study groups around here.

Intellectuality

Real, Ideal, and Expectations Form Item Number	Scoring Direction	
7	T	People around here talk a lot about political and social issues.
17	T	There is a good deal of concern about intellectual awareness in the house.
27	F	People here very rarely discuss intellectual matters.
37	F	There is not much appreciation here for classical music, art, literature, and so on.
47	T	The people in this house generally read a good deal of intellectual material other than class assignments.
57	F	Around here people tend not to value ideas for their own sake.
67	T	The people here are generally pretty interested in cultural activities.
77	T	Discussions around here are generally quite intellectual.
87	F	The people in this house do not have a great deal of intellectual curiosity.
97	(filler item)	People here rarely read or talk about serious matters (for example, world affairs, philosophy, and so on).

Order and Organization

Real, Ideal, and Expectations Form Item Number	Scoring Direction	
8	F	The house officers function in a somewhat haphazard manner.
18	F	The jobs of house officers are not clearly defined.
28	T	House procedures here are well established.
38	T	House activities are pretty carefully planned here.
48	T	Meetings and activities follow a pretty regular schedule in the house.
58	T	Around here the staff usually sets an example of neatness and orderliness.
68	F	House finances are handled in a pretty loose fashion.
78	T	House officers are regularly elected in the house.
88	F	This is a pretty disorderly house.
98	F	There is a great deal of confusion during house meetings.

Student Influence

Real, Ideal, and Expectations Form Item Number	Scoring Direction	
9	F	The staff here decide whether and when the residents can have visitors of the opposite sex in their rooms.
19	T	The students formulate almost all the rules here.
29	F	The staff here have the last say about student discipline.
39	T	House finances are handled exclusively by students here.
49	T	Students enforce house rules here.
59	F	Around here the staff decide who gets the single rooms.
69	F	Rules about social conduct are sometimes enforced by the staff.
79	F	The students do not take part in staff selection.
89	T	The students here determine the times when meals will be served.
99	T	The students here determine who their roommates will be.

Innovation

Real, Ideal, and Expectations Form Item Number	Scoring Direction	
10	T	New approaches to things are often tried here.
20	F	Innovation is not considered important here.
30	T	In this house people often do unusual things.
40	T	Doing things in a different way is valued around here.
50	F	The people here seem to be doing routine things most of the time.
60	T	Around here there is a minimum of planning and a maximum of action.
70	F	There is a sense of predictability about this house.
80	T	Constantly developing new ways of approaching life is important here.
90	F	Things rarely "just happen" around here.
100	F	There is a methodical quality about this house.

Items and scoring key for the URES symptom risk subscale (see Chapter 5):

> Involvement: 1F, 31F, 71F, 81T
> Support: 92T
> Competition: 35T, 55T
> Intellectuality: 17T
> Student Influence: 19F, 29T, 39F, 49F

Items related to alcohol consumption in men's and women's residence halls (see Chapter 6):

> Traditional Social Orientation: 4T, 44T, 64T
> Order and Organization: 8F, 18F, 28T, 68F
> Student Influence: 9T, 19F, 29T, 39F, 69T
> Innovation: 10F, 70T

Items related to alcohol consumption in coed halls (see Chapter 6):

> Support: 22T, 62T, 72F
> Independence: 13T, 23T, 33T, 53T, 83T
> Academic Achievement: 26F, 86F
> Intellectuality: 37F, 47T, 87F
> Innovation: 40T

Appendix B

Classroom Environment Scale Scoring Key

This appendix contains the scoring key for the subscales of the different forms of the Classroom Environment Scale (CES). The real form (Form R), ideal form (Form I), and expectations form (Form E) are directly parallel. All items are scored in the same direction on all three forms. An item listed as true (T) is scored 1 point if marked true by the individual taking the scale, and an item listed as false (F) is scored 1 point if marked false. The total subscale score is simply the number of items answered in the scored direction.

The Classroom Environment Scale and Manual have been published and are available for interested users (Moos and Trickett, 1974).

Involvement

Real, Ideal, and Expectations Form Item Number	Scoring Direction	
1	T	Students put a lot of energy into what they do here.
10	F	Students daydream a lot in this class.
19	F	Students are often "clockwatching" in this class.
28	T	Most students in this class really pay attention to what the teacher is saying.
37	F	Very few students take part in class discussions or activities.
46	F	A lot of students "doodle" or pass notes.
55	T	Students sometimes present something they've worked on to the class.
64	F	A lot of students seem to be only half awake during this class.
73	T	Students sometimes do extra work on their own in the class.
82	T	Students really enjoy this class.

Affiliation

Real, Ideal, and Expectations Form Item Number	*Scoring Direction*	
2	T	Students in this class get to know each other really well.
11	F	Students in this class aren't very interested in getting to know other students.
20	T	A lot of friendships have been made in this class.
29	T	It's easy to get a group together for a project.
38	T	Students enjoy working together on projects in this class.
47	T	Students enjoy helping each other with homework.
56	F	Students don't have much of a chance to get to know each other in this class.
65	F	It takes a long time to get to know everybody by his first name in this class.
74	F	There are groups of students who don't get along in class.
83	F	Some students in this class don't like each other.

Teacher Support

Real, Ideal, and Expectations Form Item Number	Scoring Direction	
3	F	This teacher spends very little time just talking with students.
12	T	The teacher takes a personal interest in students.
21	T	The teacher is more like a friend than an authority.
30	T	The teacher goes out of his way to help students.
39	F	Sometimes the teacher embarrasses students for not knowing the right answer.
48	F	This teacher "talks down" to students.
57	T	If students want to talk about something this teacher will find time to do it.
66	T	This teacher wants to know what students themselves want to learn about.
75	F	This teacher does not trust students.
84	F	Students have to watch what they say in this class.

Task Orientation

Real, Ideal, and Expectations Form Item Number	Scoring Direction	
4	T	Almost all class time is spent on the lesson for the day.
13	T	Students are expected to stick to class-work in this class.
22	F	We often spend more time discussing outside student activities than class-related material.
31	T	Getting a certain amount of classwork done is very important in this class.
40	F	Students don't do much work in this class.
49	T	We usually do as much as we set out to do.
58	T	If a student misses class for a couple of days, it takes some effort to catch up.
67	F	This teacher often takes time out from the lesson plan to talk about other things.
76	F	This class is more a social hour than a place to learn something.
85	T	The teacher sticks to classwork and doesn't get sidetracked.

Competition

Real, Ideal, and Expectations Form Item Number	Scoring Direction	
5	F	Students don't feel pressured to compete here.
14	T	Students try hard to get the best grade.
23	T	Some students always try to see who can answer questions first.
32	F	Students don't compete with each other here.
41	T	A student's grade is lowered if he gets homework in late.
50	F	Grades are not very important in this class.
59	F	Students here don't care about what grades the other students are getting.
68	T	Students have to work for a good grade in this class.
77	T	Sometimes the class breaks up into groups to compete with each other.
86	F	Students usually pass even if they don't do much.

Order and Organization

Real, Ideal, and Expectations Form Item Number	*Scoring Direction*	
6	T	This is a well-organized class.
15	T	Students are almost always quiet in this class.
24	F	Students fool around a lot in this class.
33	F	This class is often in an uproar.
42	T	The teacher hardly ever has to tell students to get back in their seats.
51	F	The teacher often has to tell students to calm down.
60	T	Assignments are usually clear so everyone knows what to do.
69	F	This class hardly ever starts on time.
78	T	Activities in this class are clearly and carefully planned.
87	T	Students don't interrupt the teacher when he's talking.

Rule Clarity

Real, Ideal, and Expectations Form Item Number	Scoring Direction	
7	T	There is a clear set of rules for students to follow.
16	F	Rules in this class seem to change a lot.
25	T	The teacher explains what will happen if a student breaks a rule.
34	T	The teacher explains what the rules are.
43	T	The teacher makes a point of sticking to the rules he's made.
52	F	Whether or not students can get away with something depends on how the teacher is feeling that day.
61	T	There are set ways of working on things.
70	T	In the first few weeks the teacher explained the rules about what students could and could not do in this class.
79	F	Students aren't always sure if something is against the rules or not.
88	T	The teacher is consistent in dealing with students who break the rules.

Teacher Control

Real, Ideal, and Expectations Form Item Number	Scoring Direction	
8	F	There are very few rules to follow.
17	T	If a student breaks a rule in this class, he's sure to get in trouble.
26	F	The teacher is not very strict.
35	T	Students can get in trouble with the teacher for talking when they're not supposed to.
44	F	Students don't always have to stick to the rules in this class.
53	T	Students get in trouble if they're not in their seats when the class is supposed to start.
62	T	It's easier to get in trouble here than in a lot of other classes.
71	F	The teacher will put up with a good deal.
80	T	The teacher will kick a student out of class if he acts up.
89	T	When the teacher makes a rule, he means it.

Innovation

Real, Ideal, and Expectations Form Item Number	Scoring Direction	
9	T	New ideas are always being tried out here.
18	T	What students do in class is very different on different days.
27	F	New and different ways of teaching are not tried very often in this class.
36	T	The teacher likes students to try unusual projects.
45	F	Students have very little to say about how class time is spent.
54	T	The teacher thinks up unusual projects for students to do.
63	F	Students are expected to follow set rules in doing their work.
72	T	Students can choose where they sit.
81	F	Students do the same kind of homework almost every day.
90	T	In this class, students are allowed to make up their own projects.

Items related to classroom absenteeism (see Chapter 9):

> Involvement: 19T, 82F
> Teacher Support: 84T
> Task Orientation: 22F
> Competition: 86F
> Rule Clarity: 7T, 43T, 61T
> Teacher Control: 17T, 26F, 53T, 62T, 71F
> Innovation: 18F

References

Alden, L. "Factor Analysis of the Ward Atmosphere Scale." *Journal of Consulting and Clinical Psychology*, 1978, *46*, 175-176.

Alexander, C. N., Jr., and Campbell, E. Q. "Peer Influences on Adolescent Drinking." *Quarterly Journal of Studies on Alcohol*, 1967, *28*, 444-453.

Alexander, K., and Eckland, B. "Sex Differences in the Educational Attainment Process." *American Sociological Review*, 1974, *39*, 668-682.

Alexander, K., and McDill, E. "Selection and Allocation Within Schools: Some Causes and Consequences of Curriculum Placement." *American Sociological Review*, 1976, *41*, 963-980.

Alexander, L., and Simmons, J. "The Determinants of School Achievement in Developing Countries: The Educational Production Function." Staff Working Paper No. 201. Washington, D.C.: International Bank for Reconstruction and Development, 1975.

Almond, G. A., and Verba, S. *The Civic Culture: Political Attitudes and Democracy in Five Nations.* Princeton, N.J.: Princeton University Press, 1963.

Alwin, D. F., and Otto, L. B. "High School Context Effects on Aspirations." *Sociology of Education,* 1977, *50,* 259-273.

Anderson, G. J. "Effects of Course Content and Teacher Sex on the Social Climate of Learning." *American Educational Research Journal,* 1971, *8,* 649-663.

Anderson, G. J., and Walberg, H. J. "Class Size and the Social Environment of Learning: A Replication." *Alberta Journal of Educational Research,* 1972, *4,* 277-286.

Anderson, G. J., and Walberg, H. J. "Learning Environments." In H. J. Walberg (Ed.), *Evaluating Educational Performance.* Berkeley, Calif.: McCutchan, 1974.

Anderson, G. J., Walberg, H. J., and Welch, W. W. "Curriculum Effects on the Social Climate of Learning: A New Representation of Discriminant Functions." *American Educational Research Journal,* 1969, *6,* 315-328.

Armstrong, D. "Team Teaching and Academic Achievement." *Review of Educational Research,* 1977, *47,* 65-86.

Astin, A. W. "Classroom Environment in Different Fields of Study." *Journal of Educational Psychology,* 1965, *56,* 275-282.

Astin, A. W. *The College Environment.* Washington, D.C.: American Council on Education, 1968.

Astin, A. W. *Preventing Students from Dropping Out.* San Francisco: Jossey-Bass, 1975.

Astin, A. W. *Four Critical Years: Effects of College on Beliefs, Attitudes, and Knowledge.* San Francisco: Jossey-Bass, 1977.

Astin, A. W., and Panos, R. *The Educational and Vocational Development of College Students.* Washington, D.C.: American Council on Education, 1969.

Averch, H. A., and others. *How Effective Is Schooling? A Criti-*

cal Review of Research. Englewood Cliffs, N.J.: Educational Technology Publications, 1974.

Bachman, J. G., O'Malley, P. M., and Johnston, J. *Adolescence to Adulthood: Change and Stability in the Lives of Young Men.* Ann Arbor: Institute for Social Research, University of Michigan, 1978.

Bailey, K. "Cluster Analysis." In D. Heise (Ed.), *Sociological Methodology 1975.* San Francisco: Jossey-Bass, 1974.

Baird, L. "The Practical Utility of Measures of College Environments." *Review of Educational Research,* 1974, *44,* 307-329.

Bales, R. *Personality and Interpersonal Behavior.* New York: Holt, Rinehart and Winston, 1970.

Bandura, A. "The Self System in Reciprocal Determinism." *American Psychologist,* 1978, *33,* 344-358.

Barclay, J. "Needs Assessment." In H. J. Walberg (Ed.), *Evaluating Educational Performance.* Berkeley, Calif.: McCutchan, 1974.

Barker, R. G. *Ecological Psychology.* Stanford, Calif.: Stanford University Press, 1968.

Barker, R. G., and Gump, P. *Big School, Small School.* Stanford, Calif.: Stanford University Press, 1964.

Baron, R. M., and others. "Effects of Social Density in University Residential Environments." *Journal of Personality and Social Psychology,* 1976, *34,* 434-446.

Barrall, M. E., and Hill, D. A. "A Survey of College Students' Exposure to and Preference for Eight Instructional Options." *Research in Higher Education,* 1977, *7,* 315-328.

Bass, B. M. *The Orientation Inventory.* Palo Alto, Calif.: Consulting Psychologists Press, 1962.

Baum, A., and Valins, S. *Architecture and Social Behavior: Psychological Studies of Social Density.* Hillsdale, N.J.: Lawrence Erlbaum Associates, 1977.

Becker, F. D. *User Participation, Personalization, and Environmental Meaning: Three Field Studies.* Ithaca, N.Y.: Programs in Urban and Regional Studies, Cornell University, 1977.

Bennett, N. *Teaching Styles and Pupil Progress.* Cambridge, Mass.: Harvard University Press, 1976.

Berman, P., and McLaughlin, M. W. "Implementation of Educational Innovation." *Educational Forum,* 1976, *40,* 347-370.

Bickman, L., and others. "Dormitory Density and Helping Behavior." *Environment and Behavior,* 1973, *5,* 465-490.

Blaney, N. T., and others. "Interdependence in the Classroom: A Field Study." *Journal of Educational Psychology,* 1977, *69,* 121-128.

Blashfield, R. "Mixture Model Tests of Cluster Analysis: Accuracy of Four Agglomerative Hierarchical Methods." *Psychological Bulletin,* 1976, *83,* 377-388.

Bliss, F., Moos, R. H., and Bromet, E. "Monitoring Change in Community-Oriented Treatment Programs." *Journal of Community Psychology,* 1976, *4,* 315-326.

Bloom, B. S. *Human Characteristics and School Learning.* New York: McGraw-Hill, 1976.

Bowen, H. R. *Investment in Learning: The Individual and Social Value of American Higher Education.* San Francisco: Jossey-Bass, 1977.

Braucht, G. N., and others. "Deviant Drug Use in Adolescence: A Review of Psychological Correlates." *Psychological Bulletin,* 1973, *79,* 92-106.

Bromet, E., and Moos, R. H. "The Impact of Organizational Structure and Change." In R. H. Moos, *The Human Context: Environmental Determinants of Behavior.* New York: Wiley, 1976.

Bronfenbrenner, U. "Toward an Experimental Ecology of Human Development." *American Psychologist,* 1977, *32,* 513-531.

Brookover, W., and others. "Elementary School Social Climate and School Achievement." *American Educational Research Journal,* 1978, *15,* 301-318.

Brothers, J., and Hatch, S. *Residence and Student Life.* London: Tavistock Publications, 1971.

Brown, C. R. "The Relationship Between Psycho-Social Factors and the Scholastic Achievement of College Students." Unpublished doctoral dissertation, Montana State University, 1973.

Brown, R. D. "Manipulation of the Environmental Press in a

College Residence Hall." *Personnel and Guidance Journal,* 1968, *46,* 555-560.

Brown, R. D., Winkworth, J., and Braskamp, L. "Student Development in a Coed Residence Hall: Promiscuity, Prophylactic, or Panacea?" *Journal of College Student Personnel,* 1973, *12,* 98-104.

Bruch, M. A. "Psychological Screening Inventory as a Predictor of College Student Adjustment." *Journal of Consulting and Clinical Psychology,* 1977, *45,* 237-244.

Bryk, A. S. "Evaluating Program Impact: A Time to Cast Away Stones, A Time to Gather Stones Together." In S. B. Anderson (Ed.), *New Directions for Program Evaluation: Exploring Purposes and Dimensions,* no. 1. San Francisco: Jossey-Bass, 1978.

Burke, W. M. "Attitudes and Utilization of Health Services." *Journal. of the American College Health Association,* 1974, *22,* 320-324.

Buros, O. K. "Fifty Years in Testing: Some Reminiscences, Criticisms and Suggestions." *Educational Researcher,* 1977, *6,* 9-15.

Cahalan, D., Cisin, I., and Crossley, H. *American Drinking Practices: A National Study of Drinking Behavior and Attitudes.* Monograph 6. New Brunswick, N.J.: Rutgers Center of Alcohol Studies, 1969.

Carlson, K. A. "A Method for Identifying Homogeneous Classes." *Multivariate Behavioral Research,* 1972, *7,* 483-488.

Carnoy, M. *Education as Cultural Imperialism.* New York: McKay, 1974.

Centra, J. A. *The College Environment Revisited: Current Descriptions and a Comparison of Three Methods of Assessment.* Research Bulletin #70-44. Princeton, N.J.: Educational Testing Service, 1970.

Centra, J. A., Hartnett, R. T., and Peterson, R. E. "Faculty Views of Institutional Functioning: A New Measure of College Environments." *Educational and Psychological Measurement,* 1970, *30,* 405-416.

Chambers, T. "An Empirical Study of Leadership and Management Styles of Head Staffs in College/University Residence

Halls." Unpublished doctoral dissertation, University of Notre Dame, 1976.

Chickering, A. W. *Education and Identity*. San Francisco: Jossey-Bass, 1969.

Chickering, A. W. "Undergraduate Academic Experience." *Journal of Educational Psychology*, 1972, *63*, 134-143.

Chickering, A. W. *Commuting Versus Resident Students: Overcoming Educational Inequities of Living Off Campus*. San Francisco: Jossey-Bass, 1974.

Chickering, A. W., and McCormick, J. "Personality Development and the College Experience." *Research in Higher Education*, 1973, *1*, 43-70.

Clark, B., and Trow, M. "The Organizational Context." In T. Newcomb and E. Wilson (Eds.), *College Peer Groups: Problems and Prospects for Research*. Chicago: Aldine, 1966.

Clinchy, B., Lief, J., and Young, P. "Epistemological and Moral Development in Girls from a Traditional and a Progressive High School." *Journal of Educational Psychology*, 1977, *69*, 337-343.

Cohen, S., Glass, D., and Phillips, S. "Environment and Health." In H. Freeman, S. Levine, and L. Reeder (Eds.), *Handbook of Medical Sociology*. Englewood Cliffs, N.J.: Prentice-Hall, 1977.

Coleman, J. S. *The Adolescent Society*. Glencoe, Ill.: Free Press, 1961.

Coleman, J. S. "Methods and Results in the IEA Studies of Effects of School on Learning." *Review of Educational Research*, 1975, *45*, 335-386.

Comstock, L. K., and Slome, C. "A Health Survey of Students: I. Prevalence of Perceived Problems." *Journal of the American College Health Association*, 1973, *22*, 150-155.

Conyne, R. "Environmental Assessment: Mapping for Counselor Action." *Personnel and Guidance Journal*, 1975, *54*, 150-155.

Conyne, R., and Lamb, D. "A Role for the Professional Psychologist in Campus Environmental Change." *Professional Psychology*, 1978, *9*, 301-307.

Cooper, L. "Staff Attitudes About Ideal Wards Before and

After Program Change." *Journal of Community Psychology,* 1973, *1,* 82-83.

Copeland, W. D. "Processes Mediating the Relationship Between Cooperating-Teacher Behavior and Student-Teacher Classroom Performance." *Journal of Educational Psychology,* 1978, *70,* 95-100.

Corwin, R. "Strategies for Organizational Innovation: An Empirical Comparison." *American Sociological Review,* 1972, *37,* 441-454.

Crawford, J., and others. "Classroom Dyadic Interaction: Factor Structure of Process Variables and Achievement Correlates." *Journal of Educational Psychology,* 1977, *69,* 761-772.

Cronbach, L. J., and Snow, R. E. *Aptitudes and Instructional Methods.* New York: Irvington, 1977.

Crowne, D. P., and Marlowe, D. *The Approval Motive.* New York: Wiley, 1964.

Daher, D. M., Corazzini, J. D., and McKinnon, R. D. "An Environmental Redesign Program for Residence Halls." *Journal of College Student Personnel,* 1977, *18,* 11-15.

Daniels, R. L., and Stevens, J. P. "The Interaction Between the Internal-External Locus of Control and Two Methods of College Instruction." *American Educational Research Journal,* 1976, *13,* 103-113.

Dauwalder, J. P., Chabloz, D., and Chappuis, J. M. "L'Echelle de l'Atmosphere dans les Services Psychiatriques (EAS)." *Social Psychiatry,* 1978, *13,* 175-186.

Davies, J., and Stacey, B. *Teenagers and Alcohol: A Developmental Study in Glasgow.* Vol. 2. London: Her Majesty's Stationery Office, 1972.

DeCoster, D. A. "Housing Assignments for High Ability Students." *Journal of College Student Personnel,* 1966, *7,* 19-22.

DeCoster, D. A. "Effects of Homogeneous Housing Assignments for High Ability Students." *Journal of College Student Personnel,* 1968, *9,* 75-78.

DeShong, B. R. "Student Involvement in University Policy Groups and Resultant Attitude Change." *Research in Higher Education,* 1976, *4,* 185-192.

DeYoung, A. "The Social Ecology of University Student Living Units and Its Effect on Selected Behavioral, Subjective and Performance Variables." Unpublished doctoral dissertation, Stanford University, 1975.

DeYoung, A. "Classroom Climate and Class Success: A Case Study at the University Level." *Journal of Educational Research*, 1977, *70*, 252-257.

DeYoung, A., and others. "Expectations, Perceptions, and Change in University Student Resident Climate: Two Case Studies." *Journal of College and University Student Housing*, 1974, *4*, 4-11.

DiMarco, N. "Life Style, Learning Structure, Congruence, and Student Attitudes." *American Educational Research Journal*, 1974, *11*, 203-209.

Donovan, J. E., and Jessor, R. "Adolescent Problem Drinking: Psychosocial Correlates in a National Sample Study." *Journal of Studies on Alcohol*, 1978, *39*, 1506-1524.

Duncan, J. "Emphasis on Education in Coeducational Living." In D. DeCoster and P. Mable (Eds.), *Student Development and Education in College Residence Halls*. Washington, D.C.: American College Personnel Association, 1974.

Edelson, R., and Paul, G. "Staff 'Attitude' and 'Atmosphere' Scores as a Function of Ward Size and Patient Chronicity." *Journal of Consulting and Clinical Psychology*, 1977, *45*, 874-884.

Elley, W. B. *National Assessment of the Quality of Indonesian Education: Second Report on the Survey of Achievement in Grade Six*. Wellington, New Zealand: New Zealand Council for Educational Research, 1976.

Ellison, T. A., and Trickett, E. J. "Environmental Structure and the Perceived Similarity-Satisfaction Relationship in Traditional and Alternative Schools." *Journal of Personality*, 1978, *9*, 57-71.

Endler, N. S., and Magnusson, D. *Interactional Psychology and Personality*. Washington, D.C.: Hemisphere Publishing, 1976.

Engs, R. C. "Drinking Patterns and Drinking Problems of College Students." *Journal of Studies on Alcohol*, 1977, *38*, 2144-2156.

Epstein, J. L., and McPartland, J. M. *The Effects of Open School Organization on Student Outcomes.* Report No. 194. Baltimore: Center for Social Organization of Schools, Johns Hopkins University, 1975.

Epstein, J. L., and McPartland, J. M. "Classroom Organization and the Quality of School Life." Report No. 215. Baltimore: Center for Social Organization of Schools, Johns Hopkins University, 1976.

Eshel, Y., and Klein, Z. "The Effects of Integration and Open Education on Mathematics Achievement in the Early Primary Grades in Israel." *American Educational Research Journal,* 1978, *15,* 319-323.

Espvall, M., and Astrom, M. "A Study of the Ward Atmosphere in a Psychiatric Unit for Short-Term Treatment." *Acta Psychiatrica Scandinavica,* 1974, *255,* 309-317.

Feldman, K. A. "Measuring College Environments: Some Uses of Path Analysis." *American Educational Research Journal,* 1971, *8,* 51-70.

Feldman, K. A. "Some Theoretical Approaches to the Study of Change and Stability of College Students." *Review of Educational Research,* 1972, *42,* 1-26.

Feldman, K. A. "Grades and College Students' Evaluations of Their Courses and Teachers." *Research in Higher Education,* 1976, *4,* 69-111.

Feldman, K. A., and Newcomb, T. M. *The Impact of College on Students.* San Francisco: Jossey-Bass, 1969.

Fiedler, M. L. "Bidirectionality of Influence in Classroom Interaction." *Journal of Educational Psychology,* 1975, *67,* 735-744.

Flanders, N. "Interaction Analysis as a Feedback System." In E. Amidon and J. Hough (Eds.), *Interaction Analysis: Theory, Research, and Application.* Palo Alto, Calif.: Addison-Wesley, 1967.

Ford, M. "The Social Ecology of University of Northern Colorado Residence Halls." Unpublished doctoral dissertation, University of Northern Colorado, 1975.

Forman, S. G., and McKinney, J. D. "Creativity and Achievement of Second Graders in Open and Traditional Classrooms." *Journal of Educational Psychology,* 1978, *70,* 101-107.

Forslund, M. A., and Gustafson, T. J. "Influence of Peers and Parents and Sex Differences in Drinking by High School Students." *Quarterly Journal of Studies on Alcohol,* 1970, *31,* 868-875.

Fraser, B. "Curriculum Evaluation." In H. Walberg (Ed.), *Educational Environments and Effects: Evaluation and Policy.* Berkeley, Calif.: McCutchan, 1978.

Frichette, S. "Factors Associated with the Social Climate of Single-Sex and Coeducational Residence Halls, Cooperatives, Fraternities, and Sororities, on the Oregon State University Campus." Unpublished doctoral dissertation, Oregon State University, 1976.

Fuhr, R. A., and Moos, R. H. "The Clinical Use of Ecological Concepts: A Family Case Description." Paper presented at the 85th annual meeting of American Psychological Association, San Francisco, August 1977.

Fuhr, R. A., Moos, R. H., and Dishotsky, N. *The Clinical Utility of the Family Environment Scale in Ongoing Family Therapy.* Stanford, Calif.: Social Ecology Laboratory, Stanford University, 1978.

Fullan, M., and Pomfret, A. "Research on Curriculum and Instruction Implementation." *Review of Educational Research,* 1977, *47,* 335-397.

Gallimore, R., Tharp, R., and Speidel, G. "The Relationship of Sibling-Caretaker and Attentiveness to a Peer Tutor." *American Educational Research Journal,* 1978, *15,* 267-273.

Geertz, C. "The Integrative Revolution: Primordial Sentiments and Civil Politics in the New States." In C. Geertz (Ed.), *Old Societies and New States: The Quest for Modernity in Asia and Africa.* New York: Free Press, 1963.

Gerst, M., and Moos, R. "Social Ecology of University Student Residences." *Journal of Educational Psychology,* 1972, *63,* 513-525.

Gerst, M., and Sweetwood, H. "Correlates of Dormitory Social Climate." *Environment and Behavior,* 1973, *5,* 440-464.

Getzels, J. "Images of the Classroom and Visions of the Learner." *School Review,* 1974, *82,* 527-540.

Goebel, J. "Alienation in Dormitory Life." Unpublished doctoral dissertation, Texas Christian University, 1976.

Grant, G., and Riesman, D. *The Perceptual Dream*. Chicago: University of Chicago Press, 1978.

Greenley, J., and Mechanic, D. "Patterns of Seeking Care for Psychological Problems." In D. Mechanic (Ed.), *The Growth of Bureaucratic Medicine: An Inquiry into the Dynamics of Patient Behavior and the Organization of Medical Care*. New York: Wiley, 1976.

Grush, J. E., and Costin, F. "The Student as Consumer of the Teaching Process." *American Educational Research Journal*, 1975, *12*, 55-66.

Gusfield, J. R. "The Structural Context of College Drinking." *Quarterly Journal of Alcohol Studies*, 1961, *22*, 428-443.

Haan, N. *Coping and Defending: Processes of Self-Environment Organization*. New York: Academic Press, 1977.

Hall, G. E., and Loucks, S. F. "A Developmental Model for Determining Whether the Treatment Is Actually Implemented." *American Educational Research Journal*, 1977, *14*, 263-276.

Harbison, F., and Myers, C. A. *Education, Manpower and Economic Growth*. New York: McGraw-Hill, 1964.

Hartshorne, H., and May, M. A. *Studies in Deceit*. New York: Macmillan, 1928.

Hays, W. L. *Statistics for the Social Sciences*. New York: Holt, Rinehart and Winston, 1973.

Hearn, J. C. "Major Department and Other Vocation-Related Factors in the Lives of College Students: A Longitudinal Study." Unpublished doctoral dissertation, Stanford University, 1978.

Hearn, J. C., and Moos, R. H. "Social Climate and Major Choice: A Test of Holland's Theory in University Student Living Groups." *Journal of Vocational Behavior*, 1976, *8*, 293-305.

Hearn, J. C., and Moos, R. H. "Subject Matter and Classroom Climate: A Test of Holland's Environmental Propositions." *American Educational Research Journal*, 1978, *15*, 111-124.

Holahan, C. J. "Consultation in Environmental Psychology: A Case Study of a New Counseling Pole." *Journal of Counseling Psychology*, 1977, *24*, 251-254.

Holahan, C. J. *Environment and Behavior.* New York: Plenum Press, 1978.

Holahan, C. J., and Wilcox, B. "Ecological Strategies in Community Psychology: A Case Study." *American Journal of Community Psychology,* 1977, *5,* 425-433.

Holahan, C. J., and Wilcox, B. "Residential Satisfaction and Friendship Formation in High and Low Rise Student Housing: An Interactional Analysis." *Journal of Educational Psychology,* 1978, *70,* 237-241.

Holland, J. *Making Vocational Choices: A Theory of Careers.* Englewood Cliffs, N.J.: Prentice-Hall, 1973.

Holsinger, D. B. "The Elementary School as an Early Socializer of Modern Values: A Brazilian Study." Unpublished doctoral dissertation, Stanford University, 1972.

Holsinger, D. B. "The Elementary School as Modernizer: A Brazilian Study." *International Journal of Comparative Sociology,* 1973, *14,* 180-202.

Horner, M. "Toward an Understanding of Achievement-Related Conflicts in Women." *Journal of Social Issues,* 1972, *28,* 157-175.

Hunt, D. "Person-Environment Interaction: A Challenge Found Wanting Before It Was Tried." *Review of Educational Research,* 1975, *45,* 209-230.

Hursh-Cesar, G., and Prodipto, R. (Eds.). *Third World Surveys: Survey Research in Developing Nations.* New Delhi: Macmillan Company of India, 1976.

Igra, A., and Moos, R. H. "Drinking Among College Students: A Longitudinal Study." Stanford, Calif.: Social Ecology Laboratory, Stanford University, 1978.

Illich, I. *Deschooling Society.* New York: Harper & Row, 1970.

Inkeles, A. "The International Evaluation of Educational Achievement: A Review." *Proceedings of the National Academy of Education,* 1977, *4,* 139-200.

Inkeles, A., and Smith, D. H. *Becoming Modern: Individual Change in Six Developing Countries.* Cambridge, Mass.: Harvard University Press, 1974.

Jackson, G., and Cosca, C. "The Inequality of Educational Opportunity in the Southwest: An Observational Study of Ethnically Mixed Classrooms." *American Educational Research Journal,* 1974, *11,* 219-229.

Jackson, P. W. *Life in Classrooms.* New York: Holt, Rinehart and Winston, 1968.

Jessor, R., and Jessor, S. *Problem Behavior and Psychosocial Development: A Longitudinal Study of Youth.* New York: Academic Press, 1977.

Jessor, R., Jessor, S., and Finney, J. "A Social Psychology of Marijuana Use: Longitudinal Studies of High School and College Youth." *Journal of Personality and Social Psychology,* 1973, *26,* 1-15.

Johnson, D. W., and Ahlgren, A. "Relationship Between Student Attitudes About Cooperation and Competition and Attitudes Toward Schooling." *Journal of Educational Psychology,* 1976, *68,* 92-102.

Johnson, D. W., and Johnson, R. "Instructional Goal Structure: Cooperative, Competition or Individualistic." *Review of Educational Research,* 1974, *44,* 213-240.

Jones, M. "Personality Correlates and Antecedents of Drinking Patterns in Adult Males." *Journal of Consulting and Clinical Psychology,* 1968, *32,* 2-12.

Jones, M. "Personality Antecedents and Correlates of Drinking Patterns in Women." *Journal of Consulting and Clinical Psychology,* 1971, *36,* 61-69.

Kamens, D. "Legitimating Myths and Educational Organization: The Relationship Between Organizational Ideology and Formal Structure." *American Sociological Review,* 1977, *42,* 208-219.

Kandel, D. "Stages in Adolescent Involvement in Drug Use." *Science,* 1975, *190,* 912-914.

Kaplan, B., Cassel, J., and Gore, S. "Social Support and Health." *Medical Care,* 1977, *15,* 47-58.

Karweit, N. L. "Rainy Days and Mondays: An Analysis of Factors Related to Absence from School." Report No. 162. Baltimore: Center for Social Organization of Schools, Johns Hopkins University, 1973.

Katz, J., and Associates. *No Time for Youth: Growth and Constraint in College Students.* San Francisco: Jossey-Bass, 1968.

Kaufman, B. *Up the Down Staircase.* Englewood Cliffs, N.J.: Prentice-Hall, 1964.

Kaye, S., Trickett, E., and Quinlan, D. "Alternative Methods for Environmental Assessment: An Example." *American Journal of Community Psychology,* 1976, *4,* 367-377.

Kelly, J. G., and others. *The High School: Students and Social Contexts in Two Midwestern Communities.* Hillsdale, N.J.: Lawrence Erlbaum Associates, 1978.

Kennedy, M. "Findings for the Follow-Through Planned Variation Study." *Educational Researcher,* 1978, *7,* 3-11.

Kiritz, S., and Moos, R. H. "Physiological Effects of Social Environments." *Psychosomatic Medicine,* 1974, *36,* 96-114.

Kohn, M., Jeger, A., and Koretzky, M. "Social-Ecological Assessment of Environments: Toward a Two-Factor Model." *American Journal of Community Psychology,* in press.

Kolb, D. A., and Fry, R. "Toward an Applied Theory of Experiential Learning." In C. Cooper (Ed.), *Theories of Group Processes.* New York: Wiley, 1975.

Kounin, J. S., and Doyle, P. H. "Degree of Continuity of a Lesson's Signal System and the Task Involvement of Children." *Journal of Educational Psychology,* 1975, *67,* 159-164.

Kozol, J. *Death at an Early Age.* Boston: Houghton Mifflin, 1967.

Langer, E., and Saegert, S. "Crowding and Cognitive Control." *Journal of Personality and Social Psychology,* 1977, *35,* 175-182.

Lawton, P., and Nahemow, L. "Ecology and the Aging Process." In C. Eisdorfer and P. Lawton (Eds.), *The Psychology of Adult Development and Aging.* Washington, D.C.: American Psychological Association, 1973.

Lazarus, R. S., and Cohen, J. B. "Environmental Stress." In I. Altman and J. F. Wohlwill (Eds.), *Human Behavior and Environment: Advances in Theory and Research.* Vol. 2. New York: Plenum Press, 1977.

Lefcourt, H. *Locus of Control: Current Trends in Theory and Research.* Hillsdale, N.J.: Lawrence Erlbaum Associates, 1976.

Leinhardt, G. "Program Evaluation: An Empirical Study of Individualized Instruction." *American Educational Research Journal,* 1977, *14,* 277-293.

Levin, H., and Snow, R. E. "The Emerging Interaction of Economics and Psychology in Educational Research." In J. E. Bruno (Ed.), *Emerging Issues in Education.* Lexington, Mass.: Lexington Books, 1972.

Levinson, G. "The Ecology of Development: Environmental Forces in the Everyday Lives of the Same Children in Two Different Milieus." Unpublished doctoral dissertation, Stanford University, 1978.

Long, S. "Students' Orientations Toward the University: An Investigation of the Clark-Trow Typology." *Research in Higher Education,* 1977, *7,* 13-28.

Loper, R., Kammeier, M., and Hoffman, H. "MMPI Characteristics of College Freshman Males Who Later Became Alcoholics." *Journal of Abnormal Psychology,* 1973, *82,* 159-162.

McDill, E. L., and Rigsby, L. C. *Structure and Process in Secondary Schools: The Academic Impact of Educational Climate.* Baltimore: Johns Hopkins University Press, 1973.

McKeachie, W. "Psychology in America's Bicentennial Year." *American Psychologist,* 1976, *31,* 819-833.

McKinnon, R. "A Study of the Expected and Experimentally Perceived Environment of a Residence Hall at Michigan State University." Unpublished doctoral dissertation, Michigan State University, 1976.

McLaughlin, T. "Self-Control in the Classroom." *Review of Educational Research,* 1976, *46,* 631-663.

Maehr, M. "Continuing Motivation: An Analysis of a Seldom Considered Educational Outcome." *Review of Educational Research,* 1976, *46,* 443-462.

Mandersheid, R. W., Koenig, G. R., and Silbergeld, S. "Dimensions of Classroom Psychosocial Environment." *American Journal of Community Psychology,* 1977, *5,* 299-306.

Marjoribanks, K. *Family Environments and Children's School Outcomes.* London: Routledge & Kegan Paul, in press.

Massialas, B. G. (Ed.). *Political Youth, Traditional Schools.* Englewood Cliffs, N.J.: Prentice-Hall, 1972.

Mechanic, D., and Greenley, J. "The Prevalence of Psychological Distress and Help-Seeking in a College Student Population." *Social Psychiatry,* 1976, *11,* 1-14.

Michaels, J. "Classroom Reward Structure and Academic Performance." *Review of Educational Research,* 1977, *47,* 87-98.

Mood, A. M. "Partitioning Variance in Multiple Regression Analyses as a Tool for Developing Learning Models." *American Educational Research Journal,* 1971, *8,* 191-202.

Moos, R. H. *Evaluating Treatment Environments: A Social Ecological Approach.* New York: Wiley, 1974a.

Moos, R. H. *The Social Climate Scales: An Overview.* Palo Alto, Calif.: Consulting Psychologists Press, 1974b.

Moos, R. H. *Evaluating Correctional and Community Settings.* New York: Wiley, 1975.

Moos, R. H. "Evaluating and Changing Community Settings." *American Journal of Community Psychology,* 1976a, *4,* 313-326.

Moos, R. H. (Ed.). *Human Adaptation: Coping with Life Crises.* Lexington, Mass.: Heath, 1976b.

Moos, R. H. *The Human Context: Environmental Determinants of Behavior.* New York: Wiley, 1976c.

Moos, R. H. (Ed.). *Coping with Physical Illness.* New York: Plenum Press, 1977.

Moos, R. H. "Social Environments of University Student Living Groups: Architectural and Organizational Correlates." *Environment and Behavior,* 1978a, *10,* 109-126.

Moos, R. H. "A Typology of Junior High and High School Classrooms." *American Educational Research Journal,* 1978b, *15,* 53-66.

Moos, R. H. "Social-Ecological Perspectives on Health." In G. Stone, F. Cohen, and N. Adler (Eds.), *Health Psychology: Theories, Applications, and Challenges of a Psychological Approach to the Health Care System.* San Francisco: Jossey-Bass, 1979.

Moos, R. H. "Social Climate Feedback and the Development of Environment Competence." In R. Muñoz, L. Snowden, and J. Kelly (Eds.), *Research in Social Contexts: Bringing About Change.* San Francisco: Jossey-Bass, in press.

Moos, R. H., and Bromet, E. "Relation of Patient Attributes to Perceptions of the Treatment Environment." *Journal of Consulting and Clinical Psychology,* 1978, *46,* 350-351.

Moos, R. H., and Brownstein, R. *Environment and Utopia: A Synthesis.* New York: Plenum Press, 1977.

Moos, R. H., DeYoung, A., and Van Dort, B. "Differential Impact of University Student Living Groups." *Research in Higher Education,* 1976, *5,* 67-82.

Moos, R. H., and Gerst, M. *The University Residence Environment Scale Manual.* Palo Alto, Calif.: Consulting Psychologists Press, 1974.

Moos, R. H., and Humphrey, B. *The Group Environment Scale.* Palo Alto, Calif.: Consulting Psychologists Press, 1974.

Moos, R. H., and Lee, E. *Comparing Residence Hall and Independent Living Settings.* Stanford, Calif.: Social Ecology Laboratory, Stanford University, 1979.

Moos, R. H., and Lemke, S. *Multiphasic Environmental Assessment Procedure (MEAP): Preliminary Manual.* Stanford, Calif.: Social Ecology Laboratory, Stanford University, 1979.

Moos, R. H., and Moos, B. S. "Classroom Social Climate and Student Absences and Grades." *Journal of Educational Psychology,* 1978, *70,* 263-269.

Moos, R. H., Moos, B. S., and Kulik, J. A. "College-Student Abstainers, Moderate Drinkers, and Heavy Drinkers: A Comparative Analysis." *Journal of Youth and Adolescence,* 1976, *5,* 349-360.

Moos, R. H., Moos, B. S., and Kulik, J. A. "Behavioral and Self-Concept Antecedents and Correlates of College Student Drinking Patterns." *International Journal of the Addictions,* 1977, *12,* 603-615.

Moos, R. H., and Otto, J. "The Impact of Coed Living on Males and Females." *Journal of College Student Personnel,* 1975, *16,* 459-467.

Moos, R. H., and Trickett, E. J. *Classroom Environment Scale Manual.* Palo Alto, Calif.: Consulting Psychologists Press, 1974.

Moos, R. H., and Van Dort, B. "Physical and Emotional Symptoms and Campus Health Center Utilization." *Social Psychiatry,* 1977, *12,* 107-115.

Moos, R. H., and Van Dort, B. "Student Physical Symptoms and the Social Climate of College Living Groups." *American Journal of Community Psychology,* in press.

Moos, R. H., and others. "A Typology of University Student Living Groups." *Journal of Educational Psychology,* 1975, *67,* 359-367.

Moos, R. H., and others. "Assessing Social Environments in Sheltered Care Settings." *The Gerontologist,* in press.

Murray, H. *Explorations in Personality.* New York: Oxford University Press, 1938.

Myers, I. B. *Myers-Briggs Type Indicator: Manual.* Princeton, N.J.: Educational Testing Service, 1962.

Myrick, R. and Marx, B. S. *An Exploratory Study of the Relationship Between High School Building Design and Student Learning.* Washington, D.C.: Bureau of Research, Office of Education, U.S. Department of Health, Education and Welfare, 1968.

Nelson, E. A., and Uhl, N. P. "The Development of Attitudes and Social Characteristics of Students Attending Predominantly Black Colleges: A Longitudinal Study." *Research in Higher Education,* 1977, *7,* 299-314.

Newcomb, T. "Youth in College and in Corrections: Institutional Influences." *American Psychologist,* 1978, *33,* 114-124.

Newcomb, T., and others. *Persistence and Change: Bennington College and Its Students After Twenty-Five Years.* New York: Wiley, 1967.

Nielsen, H. D. *Tolerating Political Dissent: The Impact of High School Social Climates in the United States and West Germany.* Stockholm: Almqvist and Wiksell, 1977.

Nielsen, H. D., and Moos, R. H. "Student-Environment Interaction in the Development of Physical Symptoms." *Research in Higher Education,* 1977, *6,* 139-156.

Nielsen, H. D., and Moos, R. H. "Exploration and Adjustment in High School Classrooms: A Study of Person-Environment Fit." *Journal of Educational Research,* 1978, *72,* 52-57.

Nielsen, H. D., Moos, R. H., and Lee, E. A. "Response Bias in Follow-Up Studies of College Students." *Research in Higher Education,* 1978, *9,* 97-113.

Nyerere, J. K. "Education for Self-Reliance." In J. K. Nyerere, *Freedom and Socialism.* New York: Oxford University Press, 1968.

O'Reilly, R. "Classroom Climate and Achievement in Secondary School Mathematics Classes." *Alberta Journal of Educational Research,* 1975, *21,* 241-248.

Orford, J., Waller, S., and Peto, J. "Drinking Behavior and Attitudes and Their Correlates Among University Students in England." *Quarterly Journal of Alcohol Studies,* 1974, *35,* 1316-1374.

Pace, C. R. "Implications of Differences in Campus Atmosphere for Evaluation and Planning of College Programs." In R. L. Sutherland and others (Eds.), *Personality Factors on the College Campus.* Austin: University of Texas, 1962.

Pace, C. R. *College and University Environment Scale Technical Manual.* (2nd ed.) Princeton, N.J.: Educational Testing Service, 1969.

Paige, R. M. "The Impact of the Classroom Learning Environment on Academic Achievement and Individual Modernity in East Java, Indonesia." Unpublished doctoral dissertation, Stanford University, 1978.

Pascarella, E. "Interactive Effects of Prior Mathematics Preparation and Level of Instructional Support in College Calculus." *American Educational Research Journal,* 1978, *15,* 275-285.

Peng, S. S., Bailey, J. P., and Ekland, B. K. "Access to Higher Education: Results from the National Longitudinal Study of the High School Class of 1972." *Educational Researcher,* 1977, *6,* 3-7.

Persaud, G. "School Authority Pattern and Students' Social Development in Selected Primary Schools in Jamaica." Unpublished doctoral dissertation, Stanford University, 1976.

Peterson, R., and others. *Institutional Functioning Inventory: Preliminary Technical Manual.* Princeton, N.J.: Educational Service, 1970.

Pond, W. "Interrelationships Between the Organizational Climate of Secondary Classrooms as Perceived by Both the Teachers and Students of Those Classrooms." Unpublished doctoral dissertation, University of Maryland, 1973.

Powell, R. W. "Grades, Learning, and Student Evaluation of

Instruction." *Research in Higher Education,* 1977, *7,* 193-206.

Purves, A. C., and Levine, D. U. (Eds.). *Educational Policy and International Assessment, Implications of the IEA Surveys of Achievement.* Berkeley, Calif.: McCutchan, 1975.

Randhawa, B. S., and Michayluk, J. O. "Learning Environment in Rural and Urban Classrooms." *American Educational Research Journal,* 1975, *12,* 265-285.

Reid, E. A. "Effects of Coresidential Living on the Attitudes, Self-Image, and Role Expectations of College Women." *American Journal of Psychiatry,* 1974, *131,* 551-554.

Rentoul, A., and Fraser, B. "Conceptualization and Assessment of Inquiry Based on Open Classroom Learning Environments." *Journal of Curriculum Studies,* in press.

Richman, J. M. "The Effects of Homogeneous Housing Assignments upon the Adjustment of Transfer Students." Unpublished doctoral dissertation, Florida State University, 1977.

Rogers, E. M. "Reference Group Influences on Student Drinking Behavior." *Journal of Alcohol Studies,* 1958, *19,* 244-254.

Rosenshine, B. V. Book review of N. Bennett, *Teaching Styles and Pupil Progress.* In *American Educational Research Journal,* 1978, *15,* 163-169.

Salili, F., and others. "A Further Consideration of the Effects of Evaluation on Motivation." *American Educational Research Journal,* 1976, *13,* 85-102.

Sanford, N., and Singer, S. "Drinking and Personality." In J. Katz and Associates (Eds.), *No Time for Youth: Growth and Constraint in College Students.* San Francisco: Jossey-Bass, 1968.

Scarr, S., and Weinberg, R. A. "IQ Test Performance of Black Children Adopted by White Families." *American Psychologist,* 1976, *31,* 726-739.

Schneewind, K., and Lortz, E. "Familienklima und Elterliche Erziehungseinstellungen ["Family Climate and Parental Child-Rearing Attitudes"]. In K. Schneewind and H. Lukesch (Eds.), *Familiäre Sozialisation: Probleme, Ergebnisse, Perspektiven [Family Socialization: Problems, Findings, Perspec-*

tives]. Stuttgart, Federal Republic of Germany: Kleft-Cotta, 1978.

Schroeder, C. C. "Designing Ideal Staff Environments Through Milieu Management." *Journal of College Student Personnel,* in press (a).

Schroeder, C. C. "Territoriality: Conceptual and Methodological Issues for Residence Educators." *Journal of College and University Student Housing,* in press (b).

Schroeder, C. C., and Griffin, C. "A Novel Living-Learning Environment for Freshman Engineering Students." *Engineering Education,* 1976, *67,* 159-161.

Schroeder, C. C., and LeMay, M. L. "The Impact of Coed Residence Halls on Self-Actualization." *Journal of College Student Personnel,* 1973, *14,* 105-110.

Scott, M. "Some Parameters of Teacher Effectiveness as Assessed by an Ecological Approach." *Journal of Educational Psychology,* 1977, *69,* 217-226.

Scott, W. A. *Values and Organizations.* Chicago: Rand McNally, 1965.

Shavelson, R., and Dempsey-Atwood, M. "Generalizability of Measures of Teaching Behavior." *Review of Educational Research,* 1976, *46,* 553-611.

Shea, B. "Schooling and Its Antecedents: Substantive and Methodological Issues in the Status Attainment Process." *Review of Educational Research,* 1976, *46,* 463-526.

Shouval, R., and others. "Anomalous Reactions to Social Pressure of Israeli and Soviet Children Raised in Family Versus Collective Settings." *Journal of Personality and Social Psychology,* 1975, *32,* 477-489.

Skalar, V. "Social Climate in the Experimental and Control Institutions." In K. Vodopivec (Ed.), *Maladjusted Youth: An Experiment in Rehabilitation.* Hants, England: Saxon House, 1974.

Skeels, H. "Adult Status of Children with Contrasting Early Life Experiences: A Follow-Up Study." *Monographs of the Society for Research in Child Development,* 1966, *31.*

Slavin, R. "Classroom Reward Structure: An Analytical and

Practical Review." *Review of Educational Research,* 1977, *44,* 633-650.

Smail, M. M., DeYoung, A. J., and Moos, R. H. "The University Residence Environment Scale: A Method for Describing University Student Living Groups." *Journal of College Student Personnel,* 1974, *15,* 357-365.

Smart, J. C. "Duties Performed by Department Chairmen in Holland's Model Environments." *Journal of Educational Psychology,* 1976, *68,* 194-204.

Smart, J. C., and McLaughlin, G. W. "Variations in Goal Priorities of Academic Departments: A Test of Holland's Theory." *Research in Higher Education,* 1974, *2,* 377-390.

Solomon, D., and Kendall, A. J. "Individual Characteristics and Children's Performance in 'Open' and 'Traditional' Classroom Settings." *Journal of Educational Psychology,* 1976, *68,* 613-625.

Solomon, D., and Kendall, A. J. *Individual Characteristics and Children's Performance in Varied Educational Settings.* New York: Praeger, in press.

Speegle, J. "College Catalogs: An Investigation of the Congruence of Catalog Descriptions of College Environments with Student Perceptions of the Same Environments as Revealed by the College Characteristics Index." Unpublished doctoral dissertation, Syracuse University, 1969.

Stallings, J. "Implementation and Child Effects of Teaching Practices in Follow Through Classrooms." *Monographs of the Society for Research in Child Development,* 1975, *40.*

Stern, G. *People in Context: Measuring Person-Environment Congruence in Education and Industry.* New York: Wiley, 1970.

Straus, R., and Bacon, S. D. "The Problems of Drinking in College." In D. J. Pittman and C. R. Snyder (Eds.), *Society, Culture and Drinking Patterns.* New York: Wiley, 1962.

Stubbs, M., and Delamont, S. (Eds.). *Explorations in Classroom Observation.* New York: Wiley, 1976.

Suharto. Address of state by the President of the Republic of Indonesia before the House of People's Representatives on the eve of the 28th Independence Day, 1973. Jakarta, Indonesia: Department of Information.

Tamir, P. "The Relationship Among Cognitive Preference, School Environment, Teacher's Curricular Bias, Curriculum and Subject Matter." *American Educational Research Journal*, 1975, *12*, 235-264.

Tars, S. E., and Appleby, L. "The Same Child in Home and Institution: An Observational Study." *Environment and Behavior*, 1973, *5*, 3-28.

Terenzini, P. T., and Pascarella, E. T. "Voluntary Freshman Attrition and Patterns of Social and Academic Integration in a University: A Test of a Conceptual Model." *Research in Higher Education*, 1977, *6*, 25-43.

Tjosvold, D. "Alternative Organizations for Schools and Classrooms." In D. Bar-tal and L. Saxe (Eds.), *Social Psychology of Education: Theory and Research*, Washington, D.C.: Hemisphere Publishing, 1978.

Tobias, S. "Achievement-Treatment Interactions." *Review of Educational Research*, 1976, *46*, 61-74.

Trickett, E. J. "Towards a Social-Ecological Conception of Adolescent Socialization: Normative Data on Contrasting Types of Public School Classrooms." *Child Development*, 1978, *49*, 408-414.

Trickett, E. J., Kelly, J. G., and Todd, D. M. "The Social Environment of the High School: Guidelines for Individual Change and Organizational Redevelopment." In S. F. Golann and D. Eisendorfer (Eds.), *Community Psychology and Mental Health*, New York: Appleton-Century-Crofts, 1972.

Trickett, E. J., and Moos, R. H. "The Social Environment of Junior High and High School Classrooms." *Journal of Educational Psychology*, 1973, *65*, 93-102.

Trickett, E. J., and Quinlan, D. M. "Three Domains of Classroom Environment: An Alternative Analysis of the Classroom Environment Scale." *American Journal of Community Psychology*, in press.

Trickett, E. J., and Wilkinson, L. "Using Individual or Group Scores on Perceived Environment Scales: Classroom Environment Scale as Example." *American Journal of Community Psychology*, in press.

Trickett, P. K., Pendry, C., and Trickett, E. J. "A Study of Women's Secondary Education: The Experience and Effects of Attending Independent Secondary Schools." New Haven, Conn.: Department of Psychology, Yale University, 1976.

UNESCO. *Statistical Yearbook, 1975.* Paris: UNESCO, 1976.

Van Horn, R. "Effects of the Use of Four Types of Teaching Models on Student Self-Concept of Academic Ability and Attitude Toward the Teacher." *American Educational Research Journal,* 1976, *13,* 285-291.

Vreeland, R. S., and Bidwell, C. E. "Organizational Effects on Student Attitudes: A Study of the Harvard Houses." *Sociology of Education,* 1965, *38,* 233-250.

Wachtel, P. L. "Psychodynamics, Behavior Therapy, and the Implacable Experimenter: An Inquiry into the Consistency of Personality." *Journal of Abnormal Psychology,* 1973, *82,* 324-334.

Walberg, H. J. "The Social Environment as a Mediator of Classroom Learning." *Journal of Educational Psychology,* 1969, *60,* 443-448.

Walberg, H. J. "The Psychology of Learning Environments." In L. S. Shulman (Ed.), *Review of Research in Education.* Vol. 4. Itasca, Ill.: Peacock, 1976.

Walberg, H. J., and Anderson, G. "Classroom Climate and Individual Learning." *Journal of Educational Psychology,* 1968, *59,* 414-419.

Walberg, H. J., Rasher, S. P., and Singh, R. "An Operational Test of a Three-Factor Theory of Classroom Social Perception." *Psychology in the Schools,* 1977, *14,* 508-513.

Walberg, H. J., and Singh, R. "Teacher Quality Perceptions and Achievement in Rajasthan." *Alberta Journal of Educational Research,* 1974, *20,* 226-232.

Walberg, H. J., Singh, R., and Rasher, S. P. "Predictive Validity of Student Perception: A Cross-Cultural Replication." *American Educational Research Journal,* 1977, *14,* 45-49.

Walberg, H. J., and Thomas, S. "Open Education: An Operational Definition and Validation in Great Britain and the United States." *American Educational Research Journal,* 1972, *9,* 197-208.

Wang, M., and Stiles, B. "An Investigation of Children's Concept of Self-Responsibility for Their School Learning." *American Educational Research Journal,* 1976, *13,* 159-179.

Wanous, J. "Organizational Entry: Newcomers Moving from Outside to Inside." *Psychological Bulletin,* 1977, *84,* 601-618.

Ward, W. D., and Barcher, P. R. "Reading Achievement and Creativity as Related to Open Classroom Experience." *Journal of Educational Psychology,* 1975, *67,* 683-691.

Wechsler, H., and Thum, D. "Teenage Drinking, Drug Use, and Social Correlates." *Quarterly Journal of Alcohol Studies,* 1973, *34,* 1220-1227.

Weiler, D., and others. "A Public School Voucher Demonstration: The First Year of Alum Rock, Summary and Conclusions." In G. Glass (Ed.), *Evaluation Studies Review Annual.* Vol. 1. Beverly Hills, Calif.: Sage, 1976.

West, N. "The Effectiveness of Assignment to Living Units by Personality Types on the Satisfaction, Achievement, and Self-Development of Freshmen Males." Unpublished doctoral dissertation, Auburn University, 1976.

White, R. W. "Strategies of Adaptation: An Attempt at Systematic Description." In G. V. Coelho, D. A. Hamburg, and J. E. Adams (Eds.), *Coping and Adaptation.* New York: Basic Books, 1974.

Wilcox, B., and Holahan, C. J. "Social Ecology of the Megadorm in University Student Housing." *Journal of Educational Psychology,* 1976, *68,* 453-458.

Williams, A. "College Problem Drinkers: A Personality Profile." In G. L. Maddox (Ed.), *The Domesticated Drug: Drinking Among Collegians.* New Haven, Conn.: College and University Press, 1970.

Williams, A., and Elmore, R. F. (Eds.). *Social Program Implementation.* New York: Academic Press, 1976.

Wilson, J. A., Spelman, B. J., and Trew, K. J. "Experimental Validation of Two Observation Systems." *Journal of Educational Psychology,* 1976, *68,* 742-753.

Windham, D. M. "The Macro-Planning of Education: Why It Fails, Why It Survives, and the Alternatives." *Comparative Education Review,* 1975, *19,* 187-201.

Witkin, H., and others. "Field Dependent and Field Independent Cognitive Styles and Their Educational Implications." *Review of Educational Research,* 1977, *47,* 1-64.

Wolins, M. *Successful Group Care: Explorations in the Powerful Environment.* Chicago: Aldine, 1974.

Wright, R. J. "The Affective and Cognitive Consequences of an Open Education Elementary School." *American Educational Research Journal,* 1975, *12,* 449-468.

Yamamoto, K., Thomas, E. C., and Karns, E. A. "School-Related Attitudes in Middle-School Age Students." *American Educational Research Journal,* 1969, *6,* 191-206.

Zaltman, G., and Duncan, R. *Strategies for Planned Change.* New York: Wiley, 1977.

Index